First World War
and Army of Occupation
War Diary
France, Belgium and Germany

51 DIVISION
154 Infantry Brigade,
Brigade Trench Mortar Battery
14 January 1916 - 28 February 1918

WO95/2888/3

The Naval & Military Press Ltd
www.nmarchive.com
Published in association with The National Archives

Published by

The Naval & Military Press Ltd

Unit 10 Ridgewood Industrial Park,

Uckfield, East Sussex,

TN22 5QE England

Tel: +44 (0) 1825 749494

www.naval-military-press.com

www.nmarchive.com

This diary has been reprinted in facsimile from the original. Any imperfections are inevitably reproduced and the quality may fall short of modern type and cartographic standards.

© **Crown Copyright**
Images reproduced by permission of The National Archives, London, England, 2015.

Contents

Document type	Place/Title	Date From	Date To
Heading	WO95/2888-2 154th Brigade Machine Gun Company		
Heading	51st Division 154th Infy Bde 154th Machine Gun Coy. Jan 1916-Feb 1918		
Heading	War Diary of 154 Inf Bde M.G Coy From 14-1-16 to 31-3-16 Vol X I II & II		
War Diary	Cardonette	14/01/1916	06/02/1916
War Diary	La Neuville	07/02/1916	28/02/1916
War Diary	Mirvaux	29/02/1916	09/03/1916
War Diary	A. 22 B Sheet 51B. N W I Scale 1:20000	10/03/1916	12/03/1916
War Diary	A 22 B	13/03/1916	17/03/1916
War Diary	A. 23. A. 0.4 Sheet 51 B.N.W.I.	18/03/1916	18/03/1916
War Diary	A. 12 Sheet 51 B N.W. Scale 1:20000	19/03/1916	19/03/1916
War Diary	A 22 B Sheet 51 B N.W.I.	19/03/1916	19/03/1916
War Diary	B. 13. C. 44 Sheet 51 B. NW. 1	20/03/1916	20/03/1916
War Diary	A 23a. 66	21/03/1916	21/03/1916
War Diary	B 13d. 1.9.	21/03/1916	21/03/1916
War Diary	A 22 Sheet 51 B NW	22/03/1916	31/03/1916
Heading	War Diary of 154th Inf Bde M.G. Coy From 1st April 1916 to 30th April 1916 (Volume 4)		
War Diary	A 22 Sheet 51 B. N.W.	01/04/1916	01/04/1916
War Diary	B. 7.c.9.5	01/04/1916	01/04/1916
War Diary	B.7.d.5.2	01/04/1916	01/04/1916
War Diary	Boyau A	01/04/1916	01/04/1916
War Diary	A 22	02/04/1916	30/04/1916
Heading	War Diary of 154th Inf Bde M G Coy From 1st May 1916 to 31st May 1916 Vol 5		
War Diary	A 22 Roclincourt 51 B.N.W.I	01/05/1916	03/05/1916
War Diary	A 22	04/05/1916	31/05/1916
Heading	War Diary of 154th M.G. Coy From 1/6/16 To 30/6/16 Volume IV		
War Diary	A 22 51. BNWI	01/06/1916	02/06/1916
War Diary	A 22	03/06/1916	30/06/1916
Heading	51st Highland Division. 154th Brigade Machine Gun Company July 1916		
Heading	War Diary of 154th M.G. Coy From 1-7-16 To 31-7-16 (Vol. 5)		
War Diary	A 22 Sheet 51 B NWS	01/07/1916	02/07/1916
War Diary	A 22	03/07/1916	12/07/1916
War Diary	Etrun	13/07/1916	13/07/1916
War Diary	Etrun Herlin Le Vert	14/07/1916	14/07/1916
War Diary	Herlin Le Vert Brevillers	15/07/1916	15/07/1916
War Diary	Brevillers Bernaville	16/07/1916	16/07/1916
War Diary	Bernaville	17/07/1916	19/07/1916
War Diary	Meaulte	20/07/1916	20/07/1916
War Diary	S. 19 d Sheet 57c Trench	21/07/1916	23/07/1916
War Diary	S. 19. d (57c)	23/07/1916	25/07/1916
War Diary	S. 19. d.	25/07/1916	26/07/1916
War Diary	Meaulte	27/07/1916	31/07/1916
Heading	154th Brigade 51st Division. 154th Brigade Machine Gun Company August 1916		

War Diary	Meaulte	01/08/1916	01/08/1916
War Diary	Mametz Wood	02/08/1916	05/08/1916
War Diary	Dernacourt	06/08/1916	07/08/1916
War Diary	Poullanville	08/08/1916	08/08/1916
War Diary	Bellifontaine	09/08/1916	09/08/1916
War Diary	Lynde	10/08/1916	13/08/1916
War Diary	Lynde Armentieres	14/08/1916	14/08/1916
War Diary	Armentieres	15/08/1916	26/08/1916
War Diary	Armentieres Bailleul	27/08/1916	28/08/1916
War Diary	Bailleul	29/08/1916	31/08/1916
Heading	War Diary of 154th Coy M.G.C. From 1/9/16 To 30/9/16 Vol 9		
War Diary	Bailleul	01/09/1916	02/09/1916
War Diary	Armentieres	03/09/1916	21/09/1916
War Diary	Armentieres Erquinghem	22/09/1916	22/09/1916
War Diary	Erquinghem	23/09/1916	24/09/1916
War Diary	Erquinghem Estaires	25/09/1916	25/09/1916
War Diary	Estaires	26/09/1916	29/09/1916
War Diary	Estaires Fienvillers	30/09/1916	30/09/1916
Heading	War Diary of 154th Coy. M.G.C. From 1st Oct 1916 To 31st Oct 1916		
War Diary	Fienvillers	01/10/1916	02/10/1916
War Diary	Fienvillers Thievres	03/10/1916	03/10/1916
War Diary	Thievres Bus-Les-Artois	04/10/1916	04/10/1916
War Diary	Bus	05/10/1916	07/10/1916
War Diary	Bus Colincamps	08/10/1916	08/10/1916
War Diary	Colincamps	08/10/1916	08/10/1916
War Diary	Colincamps K 25c.7.3 Sheet 57D NE	09/10/1916	09/10/1916
War Diary	Colincamps K 25c 7.3	10/10/1916	11/10/1916
War Diary	Colincamps	12/10/1916	12/10/1916
War Diary	Louvencourt	13/10/1916	16/10/1916
War Diary	Louvencourt Forceville	17/10/1916	17/10/1916
War Diary	Forceville Lealvillers	18/10/1916	18/10/1916
War Diary	Lealvillers	19/10/1916	21/10/1916
War Diary	Mailly Matllet Wood	22/10/1916	22/10/1916
War Diary	Auchonvillers	23/10/1916	30/10/1916
War Diary	Raincheval	31/10/1916	31/10/1916
Heading	War Diary of 154th Coy. M.G.C. from 1/11/16 to 30/11/16		
War Diary	Raincheval	01/11/1916	03/11/1916
War Diary	Auchonvillers	04/11/1916	12/11/1916
War Diary	Auchonvillers Beaumont Hamel	13/11/1916	17/11/1916
War Diary	Beaumont-Hamel	13/11/1916	17/11/1916
War Diary	Beaumont Hamel	13/11/1916	18/11/1916
War Diary	Beaumont Hamel Mailly Wood	19/11/1916	19/11/1916
War Diary	Mailly Wood	20/11/1916	22/11/1916
War Diary	Varennes	23/11/1916	23/11/1916
War Diary	Pushevillers	24/11/1916	26/11/1916
War Diary	Sheet 57D W 17 b.0.8 Aveluy	27/11/1916	27/11/1916
War Diary	Sheet 57 D W.18	28/11/1916	30/11/1916
Miscellaneous	154 Coy. M.G.C. December 1916		
War Diary	W. 18 Ouvillers Huts	01/12/1916	03/12/1916
War Diary	R 29 Central	04/12/1916	09/12/1916
War Diary	Aveluy	10/12/1916	10/12/1916
War Diary	Wolseley Huts	10/12/1916	10/12/1916
War Diary	Bouzincourt	11/12/1916	15/12/1916

Type	Location	From	To
War Diary	Wolseley Huts Aveluy	16/12/1916	20/12/1916
War Diary	R 29 Central	20/12/1916	26/12/1916
War Diary	Wolseley Huts	27/12/1916	27/12/1916
War Diary	Bouzincourt	28/12/1916	31/12/1916
Miscellaneous	154th Machine Gun Company. January 1917		
Heading	War Diary of 154th Coy M.G.C. from 1/1/17 to 31/1/17 Vol I		
War Diary	Bouzincourt	01/01/1917	03/01/1917
War Diary	Ovillers	04/01/1917	07/01/1917
War Diary	R. 29 Central	08/01/1917	12/01/1917
War Diary	Rubempre	13/01/1917	13/01/1917
War Diary	Domesmont	14/01/1917	14/01/1917
War Diary	Neuf Moulin	15/01/1917	15/01/1917
War Diary	Nolette	16/01/1917	31/01/1917
Miscellaneous	154th Machine Gun Company February 1917		
Heading	War Diary of 154th Coy. M.G.C. from 1/2/17 to 28/2/17 Vol 2		
War Diary	Nolette	01/02/1917	05/02/1917
War Diary	Forest Dabbaye	06/02/1917	06/02/1917
War Diary	Acquet	07/02/1917	07/02/1917
War Diary	Boffles	08/02/1917	08/02/1917
War Diary	Nuncq	09/02/1917	09/02/1917
War Diary	Orlencourt	10/02/1917	11/02/1917
War Diary	Caucourt	12/02/1917	25/02/1917
War Diary	ACQ	26/02/1917	26/02/1917
War Diary	ACQ Sheet 51B. N.W. A.28.a	27/02/1917	27/02/1917
War Diary	A.28a.	28/02/1917	28/02/1917
Miscellaneous	154th Machine Gun Company March 1917		
Heading	War Diary of 154th Coy M.G.C. 1/3/17 to 31/3/17 Vol 16		
War Diary	A 28a (Sheet 51 BNW)	01/03/1917	01/03/1917
War Diary	A 28a	02/03/1917	16/03/1917
War Diary	Bray	17/03/1917	17/03/1917
War Diary	La Comte	18/03/1917	22/03/1917
War Diary	Maroeuil	23/03/1917	31/03/1917
Miscellaneous	154th Machine Gun Company April 1917		
Heading	War Diary of 154 Company M.G.C. From 1.4.17 to 30.4.17 Vol 16		
War Diary	Maroeuil	01/04/1917	08/04/1917
War Diary	Roclincourt (Chemin Creux)	09/04/1917	10/04/1917
War Diary	Roclincourt (Chemin Creux)	09/04/1917	11/04/1917
War Diary	Y Huts, "D" between Maroeuil and Duisans.	12/04/1917	15/04/1917
War Diary	St. Laurent Blangy	16/04/1917	22/04/1917
War Diary	Sunken Road H. 24.b.	23/04/1917	25/04/1917
War Diary	Penin	26/04/1917	30/04/1917
Miscellaneous	154th Machine Gun Company May 1917		
Heading	War Diary of 154th Company Machine Gun Corps From 1/5/17 to 31/5/17 Vol 17		
War Diary	Penin	01/05/1917	12/05/1917
War Diary	Y Huts Arras-St Pol Road	13/05/1917	14/05/1917
War Diary	Arras	15/05/1917	16/05/1917
War Diary	St Laurent Blangy	16/05/1917	16/05/1917
War Diary	Sunken. Rd H 23.b.	17/05/1917	29/05/1917
War Diary	Sunken Road	30/05/1917	30/05/1917
War Diary	Arras Houvelin	31/05/1917	31/05/1917
Map	Hostile Activity Map.		

Miscellaneous	154th Machine Gun Company June 1917		
Heading	War Diary of 154 Machine Gun Company for the month of June 1917		
War Diary			
War Diary	Houvelin, Pas-De-Calais	01/06/1917	01/06/1917
War Diary	Houvelin	01/06/1917	04/06/1917
War Diary	Monneville Pas-De-Calais	05/06/1917	05/06/1917
War Diary	Vincly Pas-De-Calais	06/06/1917	06/06/1917
War Diary	Vincly	07/06/1917	07/06/1917
War Diary	La Recousse	08/06/1917	22/06/1917
War Diary	Kinderbelck	23/06/1917	30/06/1917
Miscellaneous	154th Machine Gun Company June 1917		
Heading	War Diary of 154th Coy. M.G.C. From 1st July. 1917 to 31st July, 1917 Vol XIX		
War Diary	Kinderbelck	01/07/1917	09/07/1917
War Diary	D Camp A. 30 Central	10/07/1917	11/07/1917
War Diary	Coy. Hqrs. C. 25. A. 8.2.	12/07/1917	12/07/1917
War Diary	Coy. Hqrs. Canal Bank. C.25.a.8.2.	12/07/1917	15/07/1917
War Diary	Coy. Hqrs. "E" Camp. A. 30 Central	16/07/1917	23/07/1917
War Diary	Coy. Hqrs "E" Camp. A. 30 Central	20/07/1917	20/07/1917
War Diary	Coy Hqrs. "E" Camp. A. 30 Central	24/07/1917	27/07/1917
War Diary	E Camp. A. 30 Central	28/07/1917	31/07/1917
Miscellaneous	154th Machine Gun Company August 1917		
Heading	War Diary of 154th M.G. Coy. for Aug 1917 Vol 20		
Heading	Original War Diary of 154th Coy. M.G.C. for August 1917 Vol 20		
War Diary	Canal Bank C.25.a.8.2.	01/08/1917	01/08/1917
War Diary	Hqrs. Minty Farm Sheet 28 N.W. C.9.a.6.5.	02/08/1917	07/08/1917
War Diary	D Camp. A. 30 Central	08/08/1917	08/08/1917
War Diary	N Camp, St. Janster Biezen	09/08/1917	10/08/1917
War Diary	Hellebroucq	11/08/1917	23/08/1917
War Diary	N Camp, St. Janster Biezen.	24/08/1917	28/08/1917
War Diary	St. Janster Biezen	29/08/1917	29/08/1917
War Diary	Murat Camp B. 30.b.5.5. (Sheet 28 N.W.)	30/08/1917	31/08/1917
Miscellaneous	154th Machine Gun Company September 1917		
Heading	Original War Diary of 154th Coy. Machine Gun Corps Month of September, 1917 Vol. 21		
War Diary	Murat Camp B. 30.b. 5.5. (Sheet 28 N.W.)	01/09/1917	04/09/1917
War Diary	D Camp, A. 30 Central	05/09/1917	06/09/1917
War Diary	Coy. Hqrs. Cane Trench.	07/09/1917	12/09/1917
War Diary	Siege Camp	13/09/1917	19/09/1917
War Diary	Coy. Hqrs. Ferdinand Farm.	20/09/1917	22/09/1917
War Diary	Siege Camp	23/09/1917	24/09/1917
War Diary	108 Rue De Ypres Poperinghe	25/09/1917	28/09/1917
War Diary	Courcelles	29/09/1917	30/09/1917
Miscellaneous	Action of Machine Guns	20/09/1917	20/09/1917
Miscellaneous	154th Machine Gun Company October 1917		
War Diary	Courcelles-Le-Comte	01/10/1917	05/10/1917
War Diary	Carlisle Lines.	05/10/1917	05/10/1917
War Diary	Vis-En Artois Sector.	05/10/1917	05/10/1917
War Diary	Ref., Map. Sheet. 51 B 1:40,000	05/10/1917	05/10/1917
War Diary	Vis-En-Artois Sector L. Bde Sector	06/10/1917	08/10/1917
War Diary	Vis-En-Artois Trench Map Sheet 51 B SW. 2. 1:10,000	09/10/1917	09/10/1917
War Diary	Vis-En-Artois Sector. L Bde Sector	10/10/1917	12/10/1917
War Diary	Vis-En-Artois Trench Map: Sheet 51 B SW. 2. 1:10000	13/10/1917	13/10/1917
War Diary	Vis-En-Artois Sector. L. Bde	14/10/1917	14/10/1917

War Diary	Vis-En-Artois Trench Map. Sheet, 51B SW. 2. 1:10,000	14/10/1917	14/10/1917
War Diary	Vis-En-Artois Sector. L. Bde	14/10/1917	14/10/1917
War Diary	Vis-En-Artois Sector. L. Bde.	14/10/1917	16/10/1917
War Diary	Vis-En-Artois & Cerisy Tr., Maps. Sheet 51B SW 2 1:10000	16/10/1917	16/10/1917
War Diary	Vis-En Artois Sector L. Bde.	17/10/1917	20/10/1917
War Diary	Vis-En-Artois Tr. Map. 51 B. SW. 2. 1:10000	21/10/1917	21/10/1917
War Diary	Vis-En-Artois. L. Bde., Sector	21/10/1917	22/10/1917
War Diary	Vis-En-Artois Tr., Map. 51 B SW. 2 1:10,000	23/10/1917	23/10/1917
War Diary	Vis-En-Artois L. Bde. Sector	24/10/1917	26/10/1917
War Diary	Vis-En-Artois Tr., Map. 51 B. SW. 2. 1:10000	26/10/1917	26/10/1917
War Diary	Vis-En-Artois. L. Bde., Sector.	27/10/1917	27/10/1917
War Diary	Vis-En-Artois Tr., Map 51 B SW. 2. 1:10,000	27/10/1917	27/10/1917
War Diary	Vis-En-Artois Sector. Left. Bde.	28/10/1917	28/10/1917
War Diary	Vis-En-Artois Trench Map 51 B SW. 2. 1:10000	28/10/1917	28/10/1917
War Diary	Vis-En-Artois L Bde Sector	29/10/1917	30/10/1917
War Diary	Vis-En-Artois Tr. Map. 51b S.W. 2. 1:10000	31/10/1917	31/10/1917
War Diary	Vis-En-Artois L. Bde., Sector.	31/10/1917	31/10/1917
War Diary	Vis-En-Artois Tr., Map. 51B S.W. 2 1:10,000	31/10/1917	31/10/1917
War Diary	Vis-En-Artois L. Bde. Sector	31/10/1917	31/10/1917
Operation(al) Order(s)	154 Coy., Machine Gun Corps Operation Order No. 4 Appendix No. I	05/10/1917	05/10/1917
Map	Map "A" Appendix II		
Heading	154th Brigade. 51st Division. 154th Machine Gun Company- November 1917. Attached:- Report on Operations Cambrai		
Heading	War Diary 134 Coy. M.G. Corps. From 1st to 31st November 1917 Volume 24		
War Diary	Vis-En-Artois L. Bde, Sector.	01/11/1917	03/11/1917
War Diary	Vis-En-Artois Tr. Map., 51 B S.W. 2 1:10,000	03/11/1917	03/11/1917
War Diary	Avesnes Le-Comte	03/11/1917	16/11/1917
War Diary	Sheet 51c. 1:40,000		
War Diary	Avesnes Le-Comte		
War Diary	Sheet 51.c. 1:40000		
War Diary	Avesnes Le-Comte	16/11/1917	17/11/1917
War Diary	Bapaume.	17/11/1917	18/11/1917
War Diary	Lechelle	18/11/1917	19/11/1917
War Diary	Metz	20/11/1917	20/11/1917
War Diary	Sheet 57c 1:40000	21/11/1917	21/11/1917
War Diary	Sheet 57c SE. 1:20000	21/11/1917	21/11/1917
War Diary	Niergnies 1:20000	21/11/1917	21/11/1917
War Diary	Metz	21/11/1917	21/11/1917
War Diary	Flesquieres	21/11/1917	21/11/1917
War Diary	Niergnies TR. Map. 1:20000	21/11/1917	21/11/1917
War Diary	Flesquieres	22/11/1917	22/11/1917
War Diary	Niergnies 1:20000	22/11/1917	22/11/1917
War Diary	Flesquieres	22/11/1917	22/11/1917
War Diary	Map: Niergnies 1:20000	22/11/1917	22/11/1917
War Diary	Flesquieres	22/11/1917	22/11/1917
War Diary	Map Niergnies 1:20000	22/11/1917	22/11/1917
War Diary	Flesquieres.	23/11/1917	24/11/1917
War Diary	Map. Niergnies 1:20000	24/11/1917	24/11/1917
War Diary	Flesquieres.	24/11/1917	24/11/1917
War Diary	Metz	24/11/1917	24/11/1917
War Diary	Map. 57c 1:40000	24/11/1917	25/11/1917
War Diary	Treux	25/11/1917	25/11/1917

War Diary	Map: France. Amiens 17	25/11/1917	25/11/1917
War Diary	Treux (Map. Amiens. 17)	26/11/1917	30/11/1917
Operation(al) Order(s)	Report of Operation of 154 Coy. M.G. Corps. during period Nov 21st to 24th		
Miscellaneous	154th Machine Gun Company December 1917		
Heading	War Diary 154 Company, M.G. Corps Period December 1st to 31st 1917 Volume 24		
War Diary	Rocquigny	01/12/1917	01/12/1917
War Diary	Bertincourt	01/12/1917	01/12/1917
War Diary	Beugny	01/12/1917	02/12/1917
War Diary	Doignies	02/12/1917	02/12/1917
War Diary	Ref., Maps, Sheet 57c 1:40,000 57c N.E. 1. 1:20,000. Moeuvres. Special Sheet 1:20000	02/12/1917	02/12/1917
War Diary	Doignies. Coy, HQ J10d 6.1.	02/12/1917	02/12/1917
War Diary	Moeuvres 1:20000 Special Sheet	03/12/1917	03/12/1917
War Diary	Doignies Coy. H.Q. J 10 d 6.1.	03/12/1917	03/12/1917
War Diary	Moeuvres Special Sheet 1:20000	03/12/1917	03/12/1917
War Diary	Doignies Coy. H.Q. J 10 d 6.1	04/12/1916	04/12/1916
War Diary	Moeuvres Special Sheet 1:20,000	04/12/1916	04/12/1916
War Diary	Doignies Coy. HQ. J 10 d 6.1	04/12/1917	04/12/1917
War Diary	Moeuvres 1:20,000	05/12/1917	05/12/1917
War Diary	Doignies Coy. H.Q. J 10 d 6.1	05/12/1917	05/12/1917
War Diary	Moeuvres 1:20000	05/12/1917	05/12/1917
War Diary	Beugny	05/12/1917	06/12/1917
War Diary	Sheet 57c 1:40000	07/12/1917	07/12/1917
War Diary	Beugny	08/12/1917	12/12/1917
War Diary	Sheet 57c. 1:40000	12/12/1917	12/12/1917
War Diary	Beugny	13/12/1917	16/12/1917
War Diary	Line Coy. H.Q. J 2.b. Central	16/12/1917	17/12/1917
War Diary	Moeuvres 1:20000	18/12/1917	18/12/1917
War Diary	Line. H.Q. J 2 b Central.	17/12/1917	19/12/1917
War Diary	Moeuvres 1:20000	19/12/1917	19/12/1917
War Diary	Line. H.Q. J 2 b. Central.	20/12/1917	21/12/1917
War Diary	Moeuvres 1:20000	21/12/1917	21/12/1917
War Diary	Line HQ. J 2 b. central.	21/12/1917	22/12/1917
War Diary	Moeuvres 1: 20000	22/12/1917	22/12/1917
War Diary	Nr. Beugny 128.b.8.2.	23/12/1917	26/12/1917
War Diary	Sheet 57c 1:40000	26/12/1917	26/12/1917
War Diary	Beugny I.28b.8.2	26/12/1917	29/12/1917
War Diary	Sheet 57c 1:40000	29/12/1917	30/12/1917
War Diary	Line. Coy H.Q. J 10 d 6.1	31/12/1917	31/12/1917
War Diary	Moeuvres 1:20000	31/12/1917	31/12/1917
War Diary	Line. Coy. H.Q. J 10 d 6.1	31/12/1917	31/12/1917
War Diary	Moeuvres 1:20000	31/12/1917	31/12/1917
War Diary	Line Coy. HQ. J 10 d 6.1	31/12/1917	31/12/1917
War Diary	Moeuvres 1:20000	31/12/1917	31/12/1917
Operation(al) Order(s)	154 Machine Gun Company Operation Order No 5 Appendix No 1		
Miscellaneous	71st MGC		
Heading	War Diary Feb 1918 Appendix X.I. 154 M E Coy.		
Map	Appendix Showing own Positions.		
Heading	War Diary Feb. 1918 Appendix X.I. 154 M E Coy.		
Operation(al) Order(s)	154 Machine Gun Company Operation Order No. 6 App No. 2	22/12/1917	22/12/1917
Operation(al) Order(s)	Addenda No. 1 To Operation Order No. 6	22/12/1917	22/12/1917

Operation(al) Order(s)	154 Company Machine Gun Corps Operation Order No. 7	29/12/1917	29/12/1917
Heading	War Diary 154 Coy. M.G.C. Corps Period January 1st to 31st 1918 Volume 25		
War Diary	Line. S.W. of Moeuvres. Cox. H.Q. J 10 d 6.1.	01/01/1918	02/01/1918
War Diary	Moeuvres 1:20000	02/01/1918	02/01/1918
War Diary	Line. S.W. of Moeuvres. Coy. H.Q. J 10 d 6.1	02/01/1918	04/01/1918
War Diary	Moeuvres 1:20000	04/01/1918	04/01/1918
War Diary	Line. S.W. of Moeuvres	04/01/1918	06/01/1918
War Diary	Moeuvres 1:20000	06/01/1918	06/01/1918
War Diary	Line. S.W. of Moeuvres. Coy. H.Q. J 10 d 6.1	06/01/1918	07/01/1918
War Diary	Moeuvres 1:20000 Beugny. 1.28b. 8.2	07/01/1918	15/01/1918
War Diary	57.c. 1:40000	15/01/1918	15/01/1918
War Diary	Line. S.W. of Moeuvres. Coy. H.Q. J 10 d 6.1	15/01/1918	17/01/1918
War Diary	Map: Moeuvres 1:20000. Beugny 1 28b 8.2. Courcelles Le Comte. Map: 57c. 1:40000	17/01/1918	18/01/1918
War Diary	Courcelles Le-Comte.	19/01/1918	20/01/1918
War Diary	Pommier	20/01/1918	20/01/1918
War Diary	Basseux.	21/01/1918	31/01/1918
War Diary	Map. Lens. 11. 1:10000	31/01/1918	31/01/1918
War Diary	Basseux.	31/01/1918	31/01/1918
War Diary	Lens. 11. 1:100000	31/01/1918	31/01/1918
Heading	War Diary 154 Coy. Machine Gun Corps. From 1st February 1918 to 28th February 1918. Volume 26		
War Diary	Basseux	01/02/1918	01/02/1918
War Diary	Map 57c 1/40000 G.14.b.9.8	02/02/1918	07/02/1918
War Diary	Buchanan Camp	08/02/1918	11/02/1918
War Diary	Fremicourt	12/02/1918	19/02/1918
War Diary	Maps. Moevres 1/20000 Sheet 57c 1/40000 Line Coy. H.Q. J 10 d 6.1	20/02/1918	22/02/1918
War Diary	Line Coy. H.Q. J 10d 6.1	22/02/1918	28/02/1918

WO95/2888/2

154th Brigade Machine Gun Company

51ST DIVISION
154TH INFY BDE

154TH MACHINE GUN COY.
JAN 1916 - FEB 1918

51ST DIVISION
154TH INFY BDE

Army Form C. 2118

WAR DIARY
or
INTELLIGENCE SUMMARY

(Erase heading not required.)

51

CONFIDENTIAL

WAR DIARY

of

154 Inf Bde M.G. Coy

From 14-1-16 To 31-3-16

Vol I Vol II

Army Form C. 2118

WAR DIARY
or
INTELLIGENCE SUMMARY
(Erase heading not required.)

Instructions regarding War Diaries and Intelligence Summaries are contained in F.S. Regs., Part II. and the Staff Manual respectively. Title Pages will be prepared in manuscript.

Place	Date	Hour	Summary of Events and Information	Remarks and references to Appendices
Cardonette	14-1-16	-	154th Inf Bde Machine Gun Coy formed	awl.
"	14-1-16 to 6-2-16	-	Machine Gun training	awl.
La Neuville	7-2-16	-	Bde moves to new billeting area	awl.
"	8-2-16 to 28-2-16	-	Machine gun training	awl.
MIRVAUX	29-2-16 to 9-3-16	-	Bde moves up the line	awl.

1875 Wt. W593/826 1,000,000 4/15 J.B.C. & A. A.D.S.S./Forms/C. 2118.

Army Form C. 2118

WAR DIARY
or
INTELLIGENCE SUMMARY
(Erase heading not required.)

Instructions regarding War Diaries and Intelligence Summaries are contained in F.S. Regs., Part II. and the Staff Manual respectively. Title Pages will be prepared in manuscript.

Place	Date	Hour	Summary of Events and Information	Remarks and references to Appendices
A.22.B Sheet 51.B.NW1 Scale 1:20000	March 10		Brigade Machine Gun Company takes over positions from 25th Division, (French) two sections - comprising eight machine guns & Gunners being employed in the occupation of these points. The remaining two sections, also with eight machine guns, remain in Bde reserve at LOUEZ (L.10.B.3.7). Sheet 51C. Scale 1:40000.	Acctd.
"	11th		Situation normal. Bde M.G. Coy HQ & reserve guns remove to ETRUN (L.3d.0.3) Sheet 51C scale 1:40000).	
		4.15 pm	Hostile Rocket sent up at 4.15 p.m. bursting into two red lights. Nothing follows.	acn.
"	12th 8 p.m.		Airship passes over our lines flying very high in NNE direction. Our anti aircraft guns open fire, without any visible result.	
"	12th night		About 400 rounds fired from our machine guns during night. Range 1500. Indirect fire.	

WAR DIARY
or
INTELLIGENCE SUMMARY
(Erase heading not required.)

Army Form C. 2118

Instructions regarding War Diaries and Intelligence Summaries are contained in F. S. Regs., Part II. and the Staff Manual respectively. Title Pages will be prepared in manuscript.

Place	Date	Hour	Summary of Events and Information	Remarks and references to Appendices
A 22 B	Mar 13	1.15 pm	British Aeroplane is brought down at point due N.E of Abris de la Sablière (ref French map 23rd Division, scale 1:5000) by the enemy anti-aircraft guns. The machine broke up into three parts and fell into the enemy's lines.	AWM
"	14	10.35 pm	Enemy send up rocket which bursts into green stars; nothing follows	
		10.20 pm	Enemy heavy guns shell our batteries in neighbourhood of ANZIN with H.E. and Shrapnel.	AWM
"	15	9.15 am	at ROELINCOURT Enemy shell jump with H.E.	AWM
"	16	9.30 am	From 9.30 am till noon a large German working party is seen at 24 B.I.9. Our Artillery opens fire. Artillery active all forenoon.	
		night	Enemy open with three bursts of rapid fire in right sector.	AWM
"	17	5.30 am	Men are seen moving in open at large white mound A.24. On our guns firing one man is seen to fall and the remainder withdraw into trench.	
		9.50 pm	During bombardment by our heavy guns a large column of flame shoots upwards about eighty feet from a point well in rear and to the left of THELUS and is visible for about six seconds. It is suggested that magazine or oil reservoir	AWM

Army Form C. 2118

WAR DIARY
or
INTELLIGENCE SUMMARY
(Erase heading not required.)

Instructions regarding War Diaries and Intelligence Summaries are contained in F.S. Regs., Part II. and the Staff Manual respectively. Title Pages will be prepared in manuscript.

Place	Date	Hour	Summary of Events and Information	Remarks and references to Appendices
A.23.A.0.4. Sheet 51B.N.W.I	Mar 18th	3.20 p.m	Enemy working party seen and is dispersed by our Artillery.	
A.23.A.5.6. Sheet 51.B.N.W.	"	5.30 p.m.	Our artillery opens fire on enemy working party.	
"	"	10 pm to 10.20 pm	Enemy bombard front and support line in right sector with Trench mortars and grenades. Our Artillery replied with heavy and field guns. Rest of night quiet.	AWH
A.12. Sheet 51B NW Scale 1:20000	19th	2 p.m	A Grey motor is observed proceeding in the direction of Thelus on the road between Bois carré and Thelus. Thought by its size to be an ambulance car.	
A.22 B Sheet 51 B.N.W.I	"	5.10 pm	German Aeroplane – after being shelled by our Artillery & Aircraft guns – on returning at a great height over their lines drops one white rocket	
"	"	9.45 p.m	Enemy sends up a parachute rocket with four green lights. Nothing happens.	
"	"	Night	Quiet. Only slight rifle fire.	
"	"		R.E.'s finish emplacements at point 7.15.	AWH
B.13.C.44 Sheet 51B. NW.I	20th	5.30 p.m	Our Artillery disperse enemy working party.	
"	"	9.30 p.m	Searchlight observed from behind Thelus	
	"	2.15 am Sought	Trench observed from junction of Bryan trenches with trench leading to W position deepened	AWH
A.23.a.6.6.	21st	7.30 a.m	Two explosions – followed by clouds of black smoke – are observed in enemy reserve line at point N.E. of Sablière. Smoke continues all day.	
"	"	11.30 a.m	motor car is seen proceeding to THELUS from the direction of LES TILLEULS.	
B.13.d.1.9.	"	—	Several Germans are again seen at the Haystacks, walking about in the open.	
"	"	7.30 p.m to 8. p.m	Enemy send up several red rockets opposite our lines. Nothing happens	AWH

Army Form C. 2118

WAR DIARY
or
INTELLIGENCE SUMMARY
(Erase heading not required.)

Instructions regarding War Diaries and Intelligence Summaries are contained in F. S. Regs., Part II. and the Staff Manual respectively. Title Pages will be prepared in manuscript.

Place	Date	Hour	Summary of Events and Information	Remarks and references to Appendices
A 2.2 Sheet 51 B NW	March 22nd		Enemy very quiet all day. Weather very thick and observation not possible. During the night the enemy sent up an unusually large number of red lights, but no coloured lights. R.E.'s floor and strutt one of the gun emplacements in Grand Bollezeen at Pt. 712. (No. 3 position)	A.W.N.
"	23rd	11 am to 1 pm	Enemy Artillery Active on A.2 sub.sector. No damage was done	
"	"	evening	250 rounds fired at cross roads A.17.a.1.b (Sheet 51 B.N.W.1 Scale 1:10000.) Range 12,250 x Indirect Fire.	A.W.N.
"	"	night	Quiet.	
"	24th	Night	Quiet. Work continued on gun emplacement No. 2.	
"	25th	morning	A few shells fell in front of our Reserve line north of Rifle Rd. No damage.	
"	"	"	3 bycyclists and one motor cyclist seen on road from Bois Carré to Thelus.	
"	"	night	100 rounds fired during night at Bogan des Rapaces B.13.c.3.4. + 500 yds night. Emplacement built and radial mounting fixed for indirect fire.	A.W.N.
"	26th	night	Generally quiet. 500 rounds fired at Bogan des Rapaces. Observation post built at emplacement No. 8.	A.W.N.

Army Form C. 2118

WAR DIARY
or
INTELLIGENCE SUMMARY
(Erase heading not required.)

Instructions regarding War Diaries and Intelligence Summaries are contained in F. S. Regs., Part II. and the Staff Manual respectively. Title Pages will be prepared in manuscript.

Place	Date	Hour	Summary of Events and Information	Remarks and references to Appendices
A.22. Sheet 51 B.N.W	27th Night	8-8.30 p.m. Rayon 6 p.m. night	Enemy Artillery active, chiefly on Support trenches and BOYAU BIDOT. Emplacement for Rocket mounting begun in BOYAU BIDOT	AwH
	28th	7-10 p.m. 7.5 p.m. Night	Enemy machine guns active. Rocket sent up, bursting into red and green stars. Nothing follows. Work continued at emplacement in Boyau Bidot for rocket mounting.	AwH
	29th	Day. 7 p.m.	Generally quiet. Enemy artillery active on front of our left side, our artillery replying vigorously. During bombardment enemy continued to send up red star shells which burst into two green lights. One of these star shells was sent up from Trelus and a green flare from Fes Trilleuls. During bombardment German Heavy Guns flashes observed magnetic bearing 18 degrees from point 71.5 (E of N)	AwH
A.22. Sheet 51 B.NW	30th	Day.	Generally quiet. Hardly any movement observed in enemy lines. 250 rounds fired from No.8 at enemy aeroplane which had been flying low over our lines for some time. It immediately turned sharply back over enemy lines and did not return. No anti aircraft guns were firing at the time.	AwH
	31st	3.40 a.m. 4 p.m. 7.15 p.m. Night	Enemy exploded mine slightly to left of L2. 1250 rounds fired by W guns. Bombardment carried out by enemy on above. One red star shell is sent up by enemy and artillery immediately ceased fire. Work continued on new emplacement on Boyan Bidot	AwH

1875 Wt. W.593/826 1,000,000 4/15 J.B.C. & A. A.D.S.S./Forms/C.2118.

WAR DIARY
or
INTELLIGENCE SUMMARY

(Erase heading not required.)

Army Form C. 2118

Place	Date	Hour	Summary of Events and Information	Remarks and references to Appendices
A 22. Plut 51 C NW	31st		The general organisation of the Company during its first experience as a unit of trench warfare has proved satisfactory. The chief difficulty experienced has been the small number of gunners (four) allowed to each gun, which leaves no margin for casualties, and renders any considerable amount of work on emplacements etc. impossible. AWH.	

Original copy

Army Form C. 2118 51

WAR DIARY
or
INTELLIGENCE SUMMARY
(Erase heading not required.)

Confidential

War Diary

of

154th Inf Bde M.G. Coy

From 1st April 1916 To 30th April 1916

(Volume 2)

Army Form C. 2118

WAR DIARY
or
INTELLIGENCE SUMMARY
(Erase heading not required.)

Instructions regarding War Diaries and Intelligence Summaries are contained in F.S. Regs., Part II. and the Staff Manual respectively. Title Pages will be prepared in manuscript.

Place	Date	Hour	Summary of Events and Information	Remarks and references to Appendices
A 22 Sheet 51B.NW	April 1	-	Day generally quiet, with slight artillery activity.	
B.7.c.9.5.	"	-	Enemy have been working hard, the past two days on new work at B.7.c.9.5.	
B.7.d.5.2.	"	-	In the afternoon our heavy artillery registered some large works and dugouts (presumably a Headquarter of some kind) at cross roads B.7.d.5.2.	(WWM)
Boyau A	"	Night.	250 rounds fired on A.18.d.2.4. Work continued on new Emplacement in Boyau Bidot.	
A 22	2nd	-	Day and night quiet. Nothing to report. Work continued on Emplacement in BOYAU BIDOT, and new Battle Emplacement well started in East end of New Collecteur	(WWM)
"	3rd before dawn		Enemy sent up parachute flares in front of L.2.	
"		4.20	Enemy sent up red flares on left of L.2. and one red flare followed from direction of THELUS. Immediately followed by a short bombardment by Enemy artillery, our guns replying.	(WWM)

Army Form C. 2118

WAR DIARY
or
INTELLIGENCE SUMMARY
(Erase heading not required.)

Instructions regarding War Diaries and Intelligence Summaries are contained in F.S. Regs, Part II. and the Staff Manual respectively. Title Pages will be prepared in manuscript.

Place	Date	Hour	Summary of Events and Information	Remarks and references to Appendices
A.22.	Sept 4	—	Work continued on Emplacement in BOYAU BIDOT and excavation made for Battle Emplacement right of 219	
"	5	Day	Enemy very quiet during day	
A.22	"	4-7.30 p.m.	Enemy attacked with French mortars and Bombs on our front and support lines just right of LILLE ROAD. Our artillery opened fire. R.E.s completed new position in New Collecteur all but cementing. New position in BOYAU BIDOT is now completed.	CAMW
A.22	6	7.30 to 8 p.m.	Enemy shell SABLIÈRE with 77 mm from Boyau A. We fired 250 rounds on A.18.d.4.3.	
"	"	Night	Night quiet, suggestive of work being done by enemy. Work continued by engineers on emplacement in New Collecteur.	CAMW
"	7	10.30 to 12.30 a.m.	Our artillery intermittently shelled the enemy's front & support lines. Enemy particularly active all day with Grenades and French mortars.	
"	"	5 p.m.	Our Artillery retaliated, which caused the enemy to shell our Support line.	
"	"	Night	500 rounds were fired from "D" at A.24.7.8 and verbally 2 air fired 350 yards of French.	CAMW

1875 Wt. W593/826 1,000,000 7/15 J.B.C.&A. A.D.S.S./Forms/C.2118.

Army Form C. 2118

WAR DIARY
or
INTELLIGENCE SUMMARY
(Erase heading not required.)

Instructions regarding War Diaries and Intelligence Summaries are contained in F.S. Regs., Part II. and the Staff Manual respectively. Title Pages will be prepared in manuscript.

Place	Date	Hour	Summary of Events and Information	Remarks and references to Appendices
A.22	8	—	All day and night enemy were particularly active with grenades and trench mortars.	
"	"	8 to 8.30 pm	Our artillery shelled enemy's front line opposite M Sector	CWM
"	"	—	A rectangular board - painted in German Colours - was apparently for use by enemy's artillery, located at A.22.B.3.6. Bearing from A.22.d.5.5. is 13° left of North. The magnetic bearing from A.22.d.5.5. is 13° left of North.	CWM
"	"	—	Work continued at night on various gun emplacements	
A.22	9	Night	During night 1500 rounds fired at following targets:— A.17.d.4.7. A.18.a.2.8. A.12.c.8.0.	
"	"	8½ pm to 12 pm	German machine guns were particularly active along our front.	CWM
"	"	—	Work continued by Engineers.	
"	10	—	Enemy active with grenades all day	
"	"	6.30 to 7 pm	Enemy artillery heavily shelled left section of Collecteur	
"	"	Night	We fired 450 rounds at A.17.d.4.7; A.17.a.1.2. A.17.d.7.1.	CWM
"	"	7.45 pm	Hostile transport heard on Lille Road.	
"	"	8.20 pm	On our left enemy sent up 6 red rockets and immediately afterwards a green one. Nothing followed.	

Army Form C. 2118

WAR DIARY
or
INTELLIGENCE SUMMARY
(Erase heading not required.)

Instructions regarding War Diaries and Intelligence Summaries are contained in F.S. Regs., Part II. and the Staff Manual respectively. Title Pages will be prepared in manuscript.

Place	Date	Hour	Summary of Events and Information	Remarks and references to Appendices
A.22	April 11	5 p.m.	Enemy shelled the left of the Collecteur with heavies.	
"	"		There was a good deal of activity at Evening Stand-to with Trench mortars and Grenades.	
"	"		The enemy are digging a trench about A.22.b.5.5, a white tape being visible. We fired 500 rounds in short bursts between 7.30 p.m. and 10 p.m., after which our artillery shelled the place with shrapnel at irregular intervals till after 12 midnight.	(9)116
"	"	Night	750 rounds were fired at A.18.c.5.9 ; A.17.a.6.4 ; A.24.a.7.8	
"	"	"	Engineers continue work on No.1 & 2 Emplacements	
"	12	3.30 to 5 p.m.	Enemy's trench mortars active. Trench mortar located at A.22.B.9.5. 750 rounds fired at targets A.18.d.0.9. A.11.c.6.6. A.18.d.2.3.	
"	"	Night	52 red rockets & 26 green rockets are sent up by enemy	(9)116
"	"	10 p.m.	Work continued by R.E's at No.2 Gun emplacement.	
"	13	Morning afternoon	German Artillery active in the morning. Our Artillery active in the afternoon. Work continued on emplacement at LILLE ROAD	(9)116

WAR DIARY
or
INTELLIGENCE SUMMARY
(Erase heading not required.)

Army Form C. 2118

Place	Date	Hour	Summary of Events and Information	Remarks and references to Appendices
A 22	April 14	7 p.m.	Enemy shell Reserve.	
"	"	10 p.m.	Enemy send up two green rockets on our right bursting into 5 stars. Nothing follows.	
"	"	11.30 p.m.	Enemy shell reserve.	
"	15	7.50 p.m.	Red rockets are seen on right of No. 8 position. Nothing follows	
"	"	9.45 & 11.15 p.m.	Two aeroplanes cross and re-cross the lines	
"	"	8.10 p.m.	Transport is heard near BOIS CARRÉ	
"	"	Stand to (morning)	Motor transport is heard behind and slightly to left of THELUS	
"	"	Night.	1 gun fired from BOYAU A on A18d.40 – 3.4. During night expended 500 rounds	
"	"	"	R.8's work on various gun positions	
"	16	forenoon	Artillery active but little damage done to our trenches, their firing being chiefly directed towards ECURIE and ROCLINCOURT.	
"	"	5.15 p.m.	Lille Road shelled by enemy with heavy and 77 mm shells.	
"	"	12.15–1 p.m.	Artillery active.	
"	"	night.	No. 7 gun fired 250 rounds from BOYAU A on to A18d.0.9.	

Army Form C. 2118

WAR DIARY
or
INTELLIGENCE SUMMARY
(Erase heading not required.)

Instructions regarding War Diaries and Intelligence Summaries are contained in F. S. Regs, Part II. and the Staff Manual respectively. Title Pages will be prepared in manuscript.

Place	Date	Hour	Summary of Events and Information	Remarks and references to Appendices
A 22	Apl 17	5.30 p.m.	LILLE ROAD shelled by enemy	
"	"	7 p.m.	do	
"	"	night	500 rounds fired on A17a.1.2 and A17d.4.7 by our machine guns	(BWMB)
"	"	"	An enemy machine gun emplacement is suspected at A23.a.1.4.	
"	"	"	Work continues on emplacements &c	
"	18	-	Our machine guns fire on A18C.5.9 and A18 d.2.3	
"	"	7.30 to 8 p.m.	Enemy shell barrier on LILLE ROAD with heavy Artillery.	
"	"	7.30 to 7.45 p.m.	Enemy busy with trench mortars from 7.30 to 7.45 p.m.	
"	"	7.45 p.m.	Work continued on Observation Posts and Emplacements	(BWMB)
"	"	Night		
"	19	5.15 to 5.30 p.m.	Enemy shell left support trench near LILLE ROAD with shrapnel.	
"	"	10 to 10.30 p.m.	Artillery active beyond left sector.	
"	"	night	500 rounds fired from our machine guns at targets A17a.1.2 & A.17.d.4.7.	CAMB
"	"	"	Work continued on Emplacements & Observation Posts.	

1875 Wt. W593/826 1,000,000 4/15 J.B.C. & A. A.D.S.S./Forms/C. 2118.

WAR DIARY
or
INTELLIGENCE SUMMARY

(Erase heading not required.)

Army Form C. 2118

Instructions regarding War Diaries and Intelligence Summaries are contained in F. S. Regs., Part II. and the Staff Manual respectively. Title Pages will be prepared in manuscript.

Place	Date	Hour	Summary of Events and Information	Remarks and references to Appendices
A.22	Apl 20	11.15 am to noon	9 shells fired by enemy into Ecurie, five being blind shells.	
"	"	4 p.m.	Enemy active with H.E. & Shrapnel.	
"	"	Night	Our machine guns fired on A.12.c.8.0. and A.17.a.6.4.	
"	"	10 p.m.	A searchlight was seen bearing from Bois Carré. Morse signalling was also observed and the following letters translated. - AVEGEGSIXO: IIIMATITM: ISS: AKA: K: DEKA: TTTT: AR:	OMB
A.22	21	10.45 am	Two Germans seen walking on ROCLINCOURT - THELUS Road. One was wearing a khaki-coloured hat.	OMB
"	"	Night	500 rounds fired by our machine guns on A.24.a.7.8 & A.18.c.5.9.	
A.22	22	4.30 am to 5.30 am	Our Trench mortars and Stokes guns are active. Not much retaliation by the enemy.	OMB
A.22	23	10 p.m.	In conjunction with the 18 pounders we open fire at A.17.a.6.4. Showering to A.18.a.1.0.6.7. with three guns. This operation seems to have excited the enemy considerably as it was followed by strong Artillery & Trench mortar & enemy machine gun activity. We fired at B.13.c.0.4.	OMB
"	"	6 am		
"	"	8 pm to 9 pm	Searchlight is seen flashing skywards from direction of FARBUS WOOD	

Army Form C. 2118

WAR DIARY
or
INTELLIGENCE SUMMARY
(Erase heading not required.)

Instructions regarding War Diaries and Intelligence Summaries are contained in F.S. Regs., Part II. and the Staff Manual respectively. Title Pages will be prepared in manuscript.

Place	Date	Hour	Summary of Events and Information	Remarks and references to Appendices
A 2 2	Apr 24	—	Enemy active all day with Artillery and Trench mortars.	
"	"	8 p.m. to 10 p.m.	Enemy machine guns active.	
"	"	12 p.m. to 6 a.m.	At various times our machine guns vertically searched enemy trench railway from A 12 c 2.0. as trolley was thought to be heard at 11 p.m. Our machine guns also fired at A 14 d. 4.2. & traversed 250 yards.	C.O.M.B.
A 2 2	25	—	Enemy Artillery active all day, especially in forenoon, when our reserve trenches were shelled.	
"	"	Night	Our machine guns fired during night at points A 10 d. 8.0. and A 14 d. 4.2.	
"	"	6.30 to 7 p.m.	Our Artillery heavily shelled enemy trenches in front of M Sector.	C.O.M.B.
"	26	—	Enemy active with Trench mortars all day on left Sector	
"	"	4 p.m.	Enemy shell the Collecteur Trench	
"	"	8 p.m. 9 p.m.	Our machine guns fire on A 12 C. 2.0. vertically searching 400 yards also A 14 a. 3. 1. traversing 250 yards.	C.O.M.B.
"	"	3 —	Work continued on emplacements.	

Army Form C. 2118

WAR DIARY
or
INTELLIGENCE SUMMARY

(Erase heading not required.)

Instructions regarding War Diaries and Intelligence Summaries are contained in F.S. Regs., Part II. and the Staff Manual respectively. Title Pages will be prepared in manuscript.

Place	Date	Hour	Summary of Events and Information	Remarks and references to Appendices
A.22	27	3 a.m.	Our machine guns – in conjunction with the Artillery – fired on the Trolley line at A18.a.1.6. The enemy did not retaliate.	(9)M6
"	28	2 a.m.	A mine was sprung by enemy which we took to be about A.16.b.	
"	"	2.35 a.m.	A second mine was sprung on left battalion's front about A.16.d.	
"	"	3.30 a.m.	In each case enfilade fire was opened on support lines and communication trenches in these areas in case of massing for attack. Fire was maintained until 3.30 a.m. when situation became calm.	
"	"	6.30 p.m.	Gas gongs and hooter sounded. Troops – including machine gun teams – stood to until 8.15 p.m. Nothing followed.	(9)M6
"	"	8.30 & 10.30 p.m.	Bombing was heard in vicinity of the new mine crater.	
"	"	10 p.m.	A combined indirect machine gun "strafe" was carried out by the enemy on our sector. Effect unknown.	

Army Form C. 2118

WAR DIARY
or
INTELLIGENCE SUMMARY
(Erase heading not required.)

Instructions regarding War Diaries and Intelligence Summaries are contained in F. S. Regs., Part II. and the Staff Manual respectively. Title Pages will be prepared in manuscript.

Place	Date April	Hour	Summary of Events and Information	Remarks and references to Appendices
A 22	29	9.45 a.m.	An enemy aeroplane is brought down in our lines. A second aeroplane descends rapidly in to the German lines.	[initials]
"	"	4.45 p.m. to 8 p.m.	Enemy shell our gun positions at L A and L B with shrapnel.	
A 22	30	4 a.m.	Enemy shell the left section of COLLECTEUR with shrapnel.	[initials]
"	"	Night	Our machine guns fire A.18.a.16 ; A.11.d.17.05 ; A.19.b.1.5.	
"	"	"	Work continued on emplacements.	
A 22				

Army Form C. 2118.

WAR DIARY
or
INTELLIGENCE SUMMARY

(Erase heading not required.)

CONFIDENTIAL

Original WAR DIARY of
154th Inf Bde M G Coy

From 1st May 1916
To 31st May 1916

Volume 3

Vol 5

WAR DIARY
or
INTELLIGENCE SUMMARY
(Erase heading not required.)

Army Form C. 2118

Instructions regarding War Diaries and Intelligence Summaries are contained in F. S. Regs., Part II. and the Staff Manual respectively. Title Pages will be prepared in manuscript.

Place	Date	Hour	Summary of Events and Information	Remarks and references to Appendices
A 22 Roclincourt 51 B.N.W.1	1	9-11 pm	A combined "Strafe" by our Artillery and machine Guns is carried out. Points A.17.b.3.4; A.17.b.7.2; A.17.a.1.5 fired on until 11 pm. Three thousand rounds expended.	(Sgd) MB
"	"		Two enemy machine Gun emplacements located at A.23.d.14.8.2. and A.23.d.95.21.	
"	"	4.10 pm	Motor bar was seen yesterday travelling from Thelus through Bois Carré at high speed.	
"	"		Notice Board is located at A.23.d.14.92. bearing the following:- KUT EL MARA captured, 13000 Englishmen made prisoners.	
"	2	1-1.45 a.m	Searchlight is observed sweeping the sky from the direction of THELUS.	(Sgd) MB
"	"		Sniper's Post located at A.22.B.45.21. with cement opening. About 20 yards to right and left are snipers posts.	
"	"		R.E's work on emplacements	
"	3	3 am	Points A.12.a.55.26; A.11.b.60.66; A.12.a.0.5. (road front of Thelus) Enemy did not retaliate.	(Sgd) MB
"	"	8 pm	A shoot is carried out in conjunction with our 18 pounder Batteries on the enemy tracks at A.17.b.8.6. and A.17.b.95.85. from L.O.A and L.O.B. the Artillery fired two salvos of shrapnel and we fired 2000 rounds per gun between 8 and 10 pm.	
"	"		Searchlight observed from behind BOIS CARRE during night.	

Army Form C. 2118

WAR DIARY
or
INTELLIGENCE SUMMARY
(Erase heading not required.)

Instructions regarding War Diaries and Intelligence Summaries are contained in F. S. Regs., Part II. and the Staff Manual respectively. Title Pages will be prepared in manuscript.

Place	Date	Hour	Summary of Events and Information	Remarks and references to Appendices
A 22	4	6.15 to 6.30 pm	Enemy shell ABRIS CENTRAL and GRAND COLLECTEUR with 77 M M shells.	CWW6
"	5	(throughout)	Artillery activity on both sides.	
"	"	6 pm	Enemy shell ABRIS CENTRAL and SABLIERE.	
"	"	8-9 pm	Enemy fire several trench mortars and Shrapnel on S.24. Our Artillery retaliate with good effect.	CWW6
"	"	Night	Our machine Guns fire on targets A.17b.8.6; A.17a.27.07. A.17c.12.72. Expending 1500 rounds in all.	
"	"	"	Two trench mortar Emplacements located at A.23a.07.33. and A.23a.15.39.	
"	6	1.30 pm to 3 pm	Enemy fired several trench mortars. Our Artillery retaliate.	
"	"	7.30 pm to 8 pm	Enemy shell COLLECTEUR and ABRIS CENTRAL with 77 MM shells.	CWW6
"	"	Night	Indirect fire is carried out by our machine Guns on the LILLE ROAD at points A.16d.8.8. and A.17a.06.49. In conjunction with the Artillery we fire 2000 rounds.	

Army Form C. 2118

WAR DIARY
or
INTELLIGENCE SUMMARY
(Erase heading not required.)

Instructions regarding War Diaries and Intelligence Summaries are contained in F. S. Regs., Part II. and the Staff Manual respectively. Title Pages will be prepared in manuscript.

Place	Date	Hour	Summary of Events and Information	Remarks and references to Appendices
A 22	7 May		General Artillery activity during day on part of enemy	CMW
"	"	Night	Our machine guns fire on A.17.b.8.6 & A.17.b.9.5.85.	
"	8	8-11 p.m.	Our machine guns searched road from B.13.a.65.00 to Commandant's House	CMW
"	"	11 p.m.	Our Artillery fire three rounds at track behind Commandant's House and shell rounds at B.13.c.55.00 — Junction of B Petrake and Lantern, our machine guns traversing from A.18.b.1.0 to 15.19.6.32.55. No retaliation.	
"	"		Trench mortar located at A.23.a.9.1.	
"	9	12 noon	Our trench mortars carry out a "strafe".	MMM
"	"	2.15 p.m.	Enemy retaliate with trench mortars and also with 25 rounds of 4.2	
"	10	11 am to 1 pm	Enemy shell Bheiui Terre, near junction with L.2.3 between 11 am & 1 pm with whizz bangs and heavies. Damage slight.	MMM
"	"	8.50 p.m	Between 8.50 p.m. and 9.30 p.m. the sound of aerial motors was heard passing over our lines, and proceeded in the direction of THELUS, when lights were seen to be dropped.	
"	"	9 p.m	In conjunction with the Artillery and the M G Boys of M T N Sectors we carried out a shoot on the enemy's Trolley Line at A.17.b.3.4 and A.18.a.1.6 at B.7.d.6.2. Our artillery put 8 rounds of shrapnel on the new trench behind the house, which in apparently much used by their carrying parties.	MMM

WAR DIARY
or
INTELLIGENCE SUMMARY

(Erase heading not required.)

Army Form C. 2118

Instructions regarding War Diaries and Intelligence Summaries are contained in F. S. Regs., Part II. and the Staff Manual respectively. Title Pages will be prepared in manuscript.

Place	Date	Hour	Summary of Events and Information	Remarks and references to Appendices
A.22.	May 11	2.30 to 3.30 p.m.	Enemy Artillery active shelling our Support Trenches. We retaliate with Trench mortars and Field Guns	
"	"	Night	Owing to so many working parties being out it is impossible to fire our machine guns	
"	12	—	Our Artillery maintain a steady bombardment on K Sector during day.	
"	"	—	Enemy Active with Trench mortars during morning.	
"	"	9 p.m.	Our machine guns open fire on B.19.c.53.15 : B.19.d.25.46. A19.a.07.48.	
"	"	9.30 p.m. to midnight	Enemy machine guns keep up an active fire on our support lines.	
"	13	Forenoon	Enemy slightly active with Artillery, shelling our Support Trenches on left of L.1	
"	"	afternoon	Enemy very active with Trench mortars and Rifle Grenades. We retaliate with Trench mortars and Field Guns	
"	"	Night	Our machine guns fire on points B.25.a.00.78. and B.25.t.12.20	
"	14	2 p.m.	Support lines in the right of L.1 are shelled with Field Guns + 4.2 s. We retaliate with Trench mortars & Field Guns. A19.a.28.05 and A12.d.65.35	
"	"	Night	Our machine guns fire on points A.18.a.19.89 A19.a.28.05 and A12.d.65.35	
"	"	"	Two of our gun sections work on trench, narrowing parapets of sandbags for a distance of 20 yards in "W" trench.	

Army Form C. 2118

WAR DIARY
or
INTELLIGENCE SUMMARY
(Erase heading not required.)

Instructions regarding War Diaries and Intelligence Summaries are contained in F. S. Regs., Part II. and the Staff Manual respectively. Title Pages will be prepared in manuscript.

Place	Date	Hour	Summary of Events and Information	Remarks and references to Appendices
A 22	May 15	4.30 p.m.	Enemy fire a few shells on left batteleur at 4.30 p.m. No damage. Considerable artillery activity on both sides north of NEUVILLE ST VAAST	[signature]
"	"	8 p.m. to 11 p.m.	Our machine guns fire on A.18.d.2.3; A.24.a.7.8; A.17.d.4.7.	
"	16	6 p.m. – 8.30 p.m.	Our Artillery very active left of L.I.	[signature]
"	"	8-10 p.m.	Our machine guns fire on A.12.a.5.0; A.12.b.1.3; and road in front of THELUS	
"	"	4.15 p.m.	One of our aeroplanes is brought down and lands behind Écurie	
"	17	Dusk	A shoot is carried out with the co-operation of our 18 pounders on B.13.a.65.00 (junction of trenches and road) and on the Trolley line at A.18.a.10.62.	[signature]
"	"	12 midnight	We open fire at point B.13.a.85.75 where a new white mound has been observed. The enemy retaliate with machine guns and sniping, evidently trying to find our gun.	
"	"	9-12 p.m.	Lights are observed in the sky at different points, remaining there for about two minutes at a time. These were thought to be signalling operations from Observation balloons.	

WAR DIARY
or
INTELLIGENCE SUMMARY

(Erase heading not required.)

Army Form C. 2118

Instructions regarding War Diaries and Intelligence Summaries are contained in F. S. Regs., Part II. and the Staff Manual respectively. Title Pages will be prepared in manuscript.

Place	Date	Hour	Summary of Events and Information	Remarks and references to Appendices
A 22	May 18	6 p.m.	Six red balloons are seen rising from THELUS. One falls short in enemy's line; two fall at ROCLINCOURT: one behind ROCLINCOURT: and two fell on the LILLE ROAD.	
"	"	Night	It was noticed during the night that when enemy put up rocket with one red star, followed by rocket with two red stars their Artillery opened fire.	
"	"	Night.	From various points in sky, well behind enemy line, lights are observed flashing in and out. The humming of an aeroplane is also distinctly heard	
"	19	5.45 p.m	Enemy aeroplane drops three red balloons S.E of Sahure, which float in direction of Bevrie.	
"	"	9.20 p.m	Enemy searchlight is observed from behind THELUS. This remains stationary in the sky for nearly half an hour	
"	20	Afternoon	Enemy shell BONNAL and communication trenches. out of 23 shells 21 were "blinds."	

Army Form C. 2118

WAR DIARY
or
INTELLIGENCE SUMMARY
(Erase heading not required.)

Instructions regarding War Diaries and Intelligence Summaries are contained in F.S. Regs., Part II. and the Staff Manual respectively. Title Pages will be prepared in manuscript.

Place	Date	Hour	Summary of Events and Information	Remarks and references to Appendices
A 22	21	2 p.m.	Flash is observed on crest NE of LSA. Immediately afterwards Aeroplane crosses from enemy line over ours. About half an hour afterwards on flash re-appearing aeroplane flew back over enemy line. The enemy are using a machine gun which is much faster than one of our own.	
"	"	day	Artillery activity nil during day.	
"	"	1.30 p.m.	Enemy shell Bevrie	
"	"	6 p.m.	Enemy shell ROCLINCOURT	
"	"	Night	No firing by our machine guns owing to relief.	
"	"		Owing to 51st (H) Division taking over a portion of the front held by 25th Division, this Bde takes over a portion of M Sector (152 Bde) as far as Trench M.33.	
"	22	—	Arrangement for taking over a portion of M Section is cancelled until further orders.	
"	"	10 p.m.	We co-operated with Trench mortars and howitzers in firing on enemy's positions. Our guns traversed from A 22 B 75.60. to A 16 d.75.30. Searched from A 22 b.95.65 to A 22 A.17 c.27.12; and traversed from A 17 c.81.28 to A 24 a.20.85. 5000 rounds expended. Enemy artillery retaliated strongly in vicinity of LSE and the left battalion. This retaliation seemed to be entirely due to the combined fire which we put on the enemy.	

Army Form C. 2118

WAR DIARY
or
INTELLIGENCE SUMMARY
(Erase heading not required.)

Instructions regarding War Diaries and Intelligence Summaries are contained in F. S. Regs., Part II. and the Staff Manual respectively. Title Pages will be prepared in manuscript.

Place	Date	Hour	Summary of Events and Information	Remarks and references to Appendices
A 22	23	Shand to	Ball of fire is observed S.E. of L.S.B. Swayed about for ten seconds as though from Observation Balloon, and then disappeared. Artillery activity on the left during day.	
"	"	Night	We fire from L.O.D on to target A17a.15.55 (expending 500 rounds) in conjunction with the Artillery who fire 4 rounds on the LILLE ROAD at 10.45 p.m. We also fire from L.O.D on target A16d.85.90 expending 500 rounds.	
"	24	1 a.m.	Our Headquarters are moved to Abris du Moulin, and our guns extended so as to cover a portion of M. Sector.	
"	"	10 a.m.	Enemy shell LILLE ROAD and BOYAU CHARLES with 4.2's. Trench mortars active also during morning, but enemy does no damage.	
"	"	9 p.m.	In conjunction with the Artillery, who fire 4 rounds shrapnel, our machine guns fire on new tracks.	
"	25	forenoon	Enemy's trench mortars are active	
"	"	12 noon	Our field guns & Six Inch howitzers make a combined "strafe" on the enemy's trench mortar positions, and completely silenced them till evening.	
"	"	9.15 p.m	Enemy shell MADAGASCAR dump with 77 m.m. shells.	
"	"	9.30 p.m	Bombing attack on left of Divisional front.	
"	"	5 p.m.	A German is seen signalling with flags from the ridge just on the left of THELUS.	
"	"	Night	Our machine guns strafe points of enemy suspected movement.	

Army Form C. 2118

WAR DIARY
or
INTELLIGENCE SUMMARY
(Erase heading not required.)

Instructions regarding War Diaries and Intelligence Summaries are contained in F.S. Regs., Part II. and the Staff Manual respectively. Title Pages will be prepared in manuscript.

Place	Date	Hour	Summary of Events and Information	Remarks and references to Appendices
A 22	26	Day	Our field guns & howitzers fire on suspected trench mortar emplacements during day. Enemy's trench mortars also active during day.	[signature]
"	"	Night	Our machine guns fire on targets A24a. and A18d.0895. The artillery co-operate at intervals with shrapnel.	
"	27	Day	Enemy long range trench mortar is located by us this morning. It is seen firing and is pointed out to Officer of 8" Battery, who also spotted it from his O.P.	[signature]
"	"	Stand-to	Enemy bombard with Trench mortars; our artillery retaliate.	
"	"	9 p.m	In conjunction with the Artillery our machine guns fired on Trench Rly.	
"	28	1.10 a.m	A mine is exploded on left of Brigade front.	
"	"	7.30 a.m	Enemy shell SABLIERE with 4.2's.	
"	"	2.15 p.m	Our 8" howitzers fired 15 rounds at junction of the Boyau Torcoulers and mines, where a trench mortar was seen firing. This is believed to be the long distance trench mortar which was trying to reach the COLLECTEUR. A good deal of damage was done to the enemy's trenches.	[signature]
"	"	9.15 p.m	Heavy bombing exchanges	

1875 Wt. W593/826 1,000,000 4/15 J.B.C. & A. A.D.S.S./Forms/C. 2118.

Army Form C. 2118

WAR DIARY
or
INTELLIGENCE SUMMARY
(Erase heading not required.)

Instructions regarding War Diaries and Intelligence Summaries are contained in F.S. Regs., Part II. and the Staff Manual respectively. Title Pages will be prepared in manuscript.

Place	Date	Hour	Summary of Events and Information	Remarks and references to Appendices
A 22	29	8.30 p.m.	Our machine guns fire on Trench Crossing Sunken Road at B13b.35.70 which is apparently used by enemy reliefs. We also fire on B9a.85.15 to B13b. 4.5 (Trench).	
"	"	8.30 to 9 p.m.	Our artillery and trench mortars bombard the enemy trenches. Slight retaliation by enemy follows.	
"	30	Day	General artillery activity.	
"	"	4 p.m.	Enemy's trench mortars active.	
"	"	10 p.m.	In conjunction with the Artillery we bring enfilade fire to bear on the sunken road from B13a.70.00 to Commandant's House. We fire four belts from two guns.	
"	"	4 p.m. till dusk	The enemy seem to be using several machine guns in the vicinity of the Lille Road for firing at our aeroplanes. Its anti-aircraft guns were firing very little although our aeroplanes were almost continually over the enemy's lines.	
"	31	Day	Enemy very active with trench mortars during day.	
"	"	Night	We fire from two guns at A.17a.1.5, where a good deal of work is in progress. 1000 rounds expended.	
"	"	-		

Army Form C. 2118. 57

WAR DIARY
or
INTELLIGENCE SUMMARY

Vol 6

Confidential

Original WAR DIARY of 154th M.G. Coy

From 1/6/16 To 30/6/16

Volume IV

Army Form C. 2118

WAR DIARY
or
INTELLIGENCE SUMMARY
(Erase heading not required.)

Instructions regarding War Diaries and Intelligence Summaries are contained in F. S. Regs., Part II. and the Staff Manual respectively. Title Pages will be prepared in manuscript.

Place	Date	Hour	Summary of Events and Information	Remarks and references to Appendices
A 22 51.B.N.W1	June 1	Forenoon	What looks to be two forward field guns emplacements are seen at A.18.a.00.05. The earth is quite new and roof unfinished. These have been pointed out to the Officer of the 8in Battery.	
"	"	11 a.m.	Enemy aircraft are active. Two cross our lines at 11 a.m., one of which is almost invisible owing to its colour, which looked to be a very very pale green	
"	"	6-8 p.m.	An enemy machine is seen patrolling behind his lines	
"	"	8.30 p.m.	A heavy bombardment commences, becoming intense about 8 to 8.30 p.m. and continues up to midnight, when it starts to decrease.	
"	"	Night	We co-operate with Artillery, and enfilade the two trenches running from A.16.b.45.25 to A.16.b.40.70, firing 1000 rounds. There is very little retaliation to our Artillery.	
"	2	10 a.m.	Enemy aircraft are active	
"	"	Day.	Enemy are also active with trench mortars on right bollecour.	
"	"	8.30 to 10.30 p.m.	The enemy's machine guns sweep the support line with indirect fire	
"	"	9.30 p.m.	Our Artillery (field guns) and machine guns search the THELUS RD between BOIS CARRE WOOD and THELUS. No retaliation.	

WAR DIARY
or
INTELLIGENCE SUMMARY
(Erase heading not required.)

Army Form C. 2118

Instructions regarding War Diaries and Intelligence Summaries are contained in F. S. Regs., Part II. and the Staff Manual respectively. Title Pages will be prepared in manuscript.

Place	Date	Hour	Summary of Events and Information	Remarks and references to Appendices
A 22	June 3	3.35 am	A German aeroplane flies over our lines, fairly high. 20 shots are fired at it.	
	"	4 am	Six of our aeroplanes fly over the enemy's lines. The enemy open fire at them with anti-aircraft guns and machine guns.	
	"	8 pm	A deserter comes over, but is killed by fire from his own people when close to our line.	
	"	Night 8.30 pm to 9.30 pm	We carry out a combined strafe with Trench Mortar Batteries on enemy's line. The Lille Road is searched from the Dump to Thelus Road by one gun; from another gun we traverse and search trolley line; and from another gun the Communication trenches and ground on each side are searched from A 17.b.5.4 to Thelus Road. This strafe was also accompanied by artillery activity on our part.	

Army Form C. 2118

WAR DIARY
or
INTELLIGENCE SUMMARY
(Erase heading not required.)

Instructions regarding War Diaries and Intelligence Summaries are contained in F.S. Regs., Part II. and the Staff Manual respectively. Title Pages will be prepared in manuscript.

Place	Date	Hour	Summary of Events and Information	Remarks and references to Appendices
A22	June 4	3pm to 6pm	Artillery on both sides are very active in K Sector.	
"		9pm to 11pm	Two mines explode opposite K Sector. This was preceded a few minutes earlier by artillery activity on both sides. Trench mortars also took part. We fired from open emplacement in BOYAU "B" on enemy's support lines. This drew machine gun retaliation but after about seventy rounds the gun stopped.	Mull
"	5	9 pm to 12 midnight	Information having been received of possible enemy movement last night we keep up an intermittent fire on the enemy's communications in co-operation with the artillery. At 10.30 pm a fourth gun was directed on the Lille Road from A 17a.1.5 to A 11c.6.7. There was no retaliation of any sort whatever the enemy being particularly quiet all night. 5,500 rounds fired.	Mull
"	6	evening 9 p.m. 12.10 p.m.	In L Sector enemy active with he airy mortars. We search the Lille Road with bracketing fire from two guns. Artillery co-operate. In M Sector the enemy shell Sutherland Avenue with shrapnel and crumps. The emplacement at M.S.B in course of construction received a direct hit but is levelled to the ground.	Mull

1875 Wt. W593/826 1,000,000 4/15 J.B.C.& A. A.D.S.S./Forms/C.2118.

Army Form C. 2118

WAR DIARY
or
INTELLIGENCE SUMMARY

(Erase heading not required.)

Instructions regarding War Diaries and Intelligence Summaries are contained in F. S. Regs., Part II. and the Staff Manual respectively. Title Pages will be prepared in manuscript.

Place	Date	Hour	Summary of Events and Information	Remarks and references to Appendices
A 22	7	10.30 a.m.	Enemy shell trenches in vicinity of FERME de CARFE. Gun emplacement at this point was hit and wooden framework damaged.	
"	"	evening	Considerable trench mortar and artillery activity.	
"	"	9.30 pm	Our machine guns fire on the following targets:— A 17.b. 54 to A 18.a.1.6 and A 18.a.1.6 to A 12.c.4.8.	
"	8	Day	The day was marked by sudden activity of enemy's artillery. Most trenches in the sector came in for attention especially right COLECTEUR B. MORTIER and CHEMIN CREUX. Several heavy shells fall round our emplacement at "W", one of which destroys the wooden shutter at the loophole but doing no damage to the emplacement itself.	
"	"	Night	In co-operation with Artillery we fire on the South-eastern corner of Bois Carré. A 7. c. 5. 3.	
"	9	6.30 pm till dusk	Enemy's Observation Balloons seen. The usual three are observed behind THELUS.	
"	"	night	In consequence of enemy relief which is suspected, our machine guns co-operate with Artillery in firing small bursts at intervals between 9 pm & midnight at the following points:— Trench junction A 18d. 15. 85 A 24a. 66. 70 B 13 b. 5. 98	

WAR DIARY
or
INTELLIGENCE SUMMARY

(Erase heading not required.)

Army Form C. 2118

Instructions regarding War Diaries and Intelligence Summaries are contained in F.S. Regs., Part II. and the Staff Manual respectively. Title Pages will be prepared in manuscript.

Place	Date	Hour	Summary of Events and Information	Remarks and references to Appendices
A 22	10	8.30pm	A mine explosion is felt, but apparently some distance away.	
"	"	12 pm	Heavy trench mortaring in M Sector, to which Artillery retaliate.	
"	"	Night	Our machine guns carry out indirect fire on enemy communication B25a.00.10 to B25.b.20.20	
"	11	Night	Enemy trench mortars active.	
"	"	9 pm	Our machine guns fire on trench behind hedge; south side of THELUS : A11.b.5.7 to A12.a.5.0	
"	12	3.35pm	A mine was sprung on the left of the Bde Sector. Our artillery put down a barrage almost immediately.	
"	"	4.5pm	The enemy sends up a flare which bursts into two red lights. Immediately after this his heavy batteries are seen to put several "heavies" into our line.	
"	"	4.15pm	A white rocket is observed after which the enemy artillery seemed to cease fire.	
"	"	9 pm	Our machine guns fire on Sunken Road B.13.b.25.75 to B.13.c.50.60	

Army Form C. 2118

WAR DIARY
or
INTELLIGENCE SUMMARY
(Erase heading not required.)

Instructions regarding War Diaries and Intelligence Summaries are contained in F. S. Regs., Part II. and the Staff Manual respectively. Title Pages will be prepared in manuscript.

Place	Date	Hour	Summary of Events and Information	Remarks and references to Appendices
A22	13	4.25 p.m.	A mine was exploded at 4.25 p.m. to our left. Following this enemy are slightly active with Trench mortars but no apparent damage is done to our Sector	[signature]
"	"	9 p.m.	Our machine guns fire on the following targets:- A24 a 6.6.72. Trench Junction A24 a 6.5.72. to A18 d 10.90. Enfilading Road A 18 d. 10. 85. Junction of Trenches	
"	14	1.55 am	A mine is exploded to our left. Enemy Trench mortars active.	[signature]
"	"	2 am	Slight Trench mortar activity.	
"	"	Day	In conjunction with Artillery, who fired eight rounds shrapnel our machine guns fired on A17 d. 4. 2 to A 17 d. 4. 6 and also on A 17 d. 4. 5. 25 to ROCLINCOURT ROAD. (Time advanced 1 hour ie from 11 p.m.)	
"	15	—	Trench mortars and Stokes guns very active from our side. Enemy retaliate with Howitzers and do considerable damage to our support lines.	[signature]
"	"	10 p.m	Our machine guns fire on shallow Trench and Tramway A 24 d. 10. 43 to A 24 b 90. 45.	

WAR DIARY
or
INTELLIGENCE SUMMARY
(Erase heading not required.)

Army Form C. 2118

Place	Date	Hour	Summary of Events and Information	Remarks and references to Appendices
A.22	16	—	Enemy artillery active during forenoon.	
"	"	—	During afternoon our right front – especially right COLLECTEUR was heavily shelled by howitzers.	
"	"	6.30 p.m	Observation post at gun position LSB was blown in by a 5.9.	
"	"	8.40 p.m	In conjunction with Artillery 250 rounds were fired from LOA at Working Party at B7c.15.53.	
"	"	Night	1000 rounds – also in conjunction with Artillery – were fired at A16d.80.58 to A17a.12.86.	
"	17	2 a.m	Enemy shell our front with field guns.	
"	"	10.30 a.m	Enemy shell Boyau Charles.	
"	"	11 a.m	Enemy shell & trench mortar around LB position.	
"	"	—	During afternoon there is considerable aerial activity, a German battle plane is observed patrolling behind his lines. Four times this machine attacks our aeroplanes and drives them back.	
"	"	6.30 p.m	Six enemy machines cross our lines and were heavily shelled. One machine thereupon returns.	

Army Form C. 2118

WAR DIARY
or
INTELLIGENCE SUMMARY
(Erase heading not required.)

Instructions regarding War Diaries and Intelligence Summaries are contained in F.S. Regs., Part II. and the Staff Manual respectively. Title Pages will be prepared in manuscript.

Place	Date	Hour	Summary of Events and Information	Remarks and references to Appendices
A22	18	1.30 am	German machine guns are active. After the cease fire two distinct shots are heard, the sound coming from enemy lines. Nothing follows. The whistle sounded similar to our regulation pattern.	
"	"	—	Enemy artillery is considerably active during most of the day, doing considerable damage to our support trenches. Our field guns and trench mortars retaliate.	
"	"	3 pm	Twelve German aeroplanes cross our line, flying in direction of ARRAS. Soon after, seven of our battle planes cross to the enemy lines.	
"	"	3.15 pm	Our Hqrs are shelled with H.E's and trenches in vicinity damaged. One shell lands in BOYAU DU MOUTON and cuts telephone wires.	
"	"	4.40 pm	A British plane fights a duel with a Hun above the second and third German lines and after a brief fight is forced to descend in the enemy lines at A.23.a.7.8. Our Artillery fires on this point.	
"	"	5 pm	A man dressed in blue-grey uniform runs from trench to aeroplane but soon returned under heavy rifle fire. During night Lewis guns and our machine gun at LSA fire on point A.23.a.7.6.	

Army Form C. 2118

WAR DIARY
or
INTELLIGENCE SUMMARY
(Erase heading not required.)

Instructions regarding War Diaries and Intelligence Summaries are contained in F.S. Regs., Part II. and the Staff Manual respectively. Title Pages will be prepared in manuscript.

Place	Date	Hour	Summary of Events and Information	Remarks and references to Appendices
A.22	19	4.30 pm	Right COLLECTEUR is shelled by field guns.	~~
"	"	5 pm	Enemy shelled our lgrs in BOYAU DU MOUTON with H.E's. No damage.	
"	"	7.30 pm	Trench between MSC and MSD gun positions was shelled with shrapnel & H.E's. No damage of serious nature.	
"	"	11 pm	Our machine guns fired on the following targets expending 750 rounds:- A.18.a.12.62 to A.17.a.55.29 A.17.b.00.36 to A.18.a.12.62	
"	20	10.30 am	Enemy put several big shells round the Fermes deBaves and shrapnel into COLLECTEUR.	~~
"	"	afternoon	Trench mortars are active in the afternoon. Our mortars eventually draw strong retaliation from enemy field guns	
"	"	night	Our machine guns fire during night on enemy tracks from A.16.d.9.9 to A.14.a.1.5. From time to time during night we search the area round the fallen aeroplane	

WAR DIARY
or
INTELLIGENCE SUMMARY
(Erase heading not required.)

Army Form C. 2118

Place	Date	Hour	Summary of Events and Information	Remarks and references to Appendices
A 22	21	2.30 a.m.	Bomb Store near ROCLINCOURT exploded. Fire broke out and during night there is a continuous discharge of bombs & flarelights	
"	"	4 p.m.	Ferme des Dames receives a few rounds from enemy artillery	
"	"	Night	Our machine guns fire on enemy reserve trenches A17d.52.82 to A11d.68.45.	
"	22	Day	Very quiet.	
"	"	5.30 p.m.	Enemy commence to trench mortar the support line in RIGHT 2. Sector ? ? ? ? ?	
"	"	7pm to 8pm	Chemin creuse is heavily shelled with 5.9 shells.	
"	"	10.30 p.m.	When a rocket (red) breaking into several red lights is put up by the RIGHT COMPANY in support of RIGHT 2, the enemy immediately open with a slow barrage on the BONNAL between the LILLE ROAD and MORAY AVENUE. Our machine guns search SUNKEN ROAD towards the COMMANDANT'S HOUSE and maintain intermittent fire for an hour.	

Army Form C. 2118

WAR DIARY
or
INTELLIGENCE SUMMARY
(Erase heading not required.)

Instructions regarding War Diaries and Intelligence Summaries are contained in F. S. Regs., Part II. and the Staff Manual respectively. Title Pages will be prepared in manuscript.

Place	Date	Hour	Summary of Events and Information	Remarks and references to Appendices
A.22	23	12.1 a.m.	We open fire from three guns on A.11; A.12; A.19; A.18; and carry out a system of cross traversing fire. At each period of fire the three guns opened simultaneously, causing — at the points where the fire crossed — a strong barrage along various lines.	[signature]
"	"	1 a.m.	The enemy begin to retaliate with machine guns and respond with bursts of burst to our salvoes.	
"	"	3.45 a.m.	The last burst of fire lies with us.	
"	"	morning	During morning enemy search COLLECTEUR, BIDOT, and CHARLES behind COLLECTEUR. They may be searching for our MG emplacements.	
"	"	Afternoon	T.M. activity is very pronounced. Enemy also shell Right 2 with heavy shells and wound two of our men at the extreme left gun.	
"	"	Night	Our Machine Guns search A.18.a.48.00 to A.18.b.50.82. and A.18.a.15.90 to A.18.b.80.43. being tracks to communication trenches.	
"	"	12 midnight	Our artillery are called upon to suppress the enemy trench mortars. Enemy field guns immediately join in.	
"	"	—	Generally the enemy has been very jumpy and this may be due to the relief during this relief the previous night.	

WAR DIARY
or
INTELLIGENCE SUMMARY
(Erase heading not required.)

Army Form C. 2118

Instructions regarding War Diaries and Intelligence Summaries are contained in F.S. Regs., Part II. and the Staff Manual respectively. Title Pages will be prepared in manuscript.

Place	Date	Hour	Summary of Events and Information	Remarks and references to Appendices
A.22	24	Day	Intermittent shelling by trench mortars and guns.	
"	"	8.30 p.m. to 11.30 p.m.	Enemy Trench mortars very active	
"	"	10 p.m.	Our machine guns at LOA and LOC fire during night on A.11c.51.12 to A.11a.85.10 } Enfilading fire on communication A.10d.86.01 to A.10d.90.71 } trench.	
"	25	Dawn	Large German working party is seen near COMMANDANT'S HOUSE.	
"	"	12 noon	Our Stokes guns and mortars open fire on enemy's wire. Enemy Artillery retaliate immediately with 77 M.M. and 4.2's on our front trenches on the right and left of LILLE ROAD. Our Artillery open fire at 12.10 p.m.	
"	"	12.10	Our artillery again active	
"	"	after noon	Enemy retaliate on our front line trenches on account of combined activity by our T.M's & Artillery.	
"	"	10.30 p.m.	Our machine guns at LOA; LOB; LOC; LOD; LOE fire throughout the night with bursts of fire on enemy support lines and communication trenches.	
"	"	8 p.m.	One of our aeroplanes dropped incendiary bombs on two enemy observation balloons situated behind THELUS. One balloon is seen in flames.	

Army Form C. 2118

WAR DIARY
or
INTELLIGENCE SUMMARY
(Erase heading not required.)

Instructions regarding War Diaries and Intelligence Summaries are contained in F. S. Regs., Part II. and the Staff Manual respectively. Title Pages will be prepared in manuscript.

Place	Date	Hour	Summary of Events and Information	Remarks and references to Appendices
A 22	26	9 p.m.	Guns of division on our left commenced a steady bombardment lasting until midnight.	
"	"	Night	M G fire on enemy communications is carried out. There is practically no retaliation to our fire by enemy M G's.	
"	"	"	R.E's work on L.S.A.	
"	27	2 a.m. to 3 a.m.	Red and green rockets are used by enemy on right of Lille Road. Their purpose is not apparent.	
"	"	10 a.m.	Our T M's open fire on enemy's trenches. Retaliation by enemy artillery immediately followed.	
"	"	10.20 a.m.	Our Artillery open fire and keep up a fairly heavy fire all day.	
"	"	4 p.m.	The Huns retaliate on our T M's, and - for the first time since Sunday - fire 5.9's.	
"	"	Dusk	Commencing at dusk our M G's fire frequent bursts throughout the night on various sections of enemy lines. Enemy M. G. retaliation was very prompt.	
"	"	—	Though enemy's retaliation throughout the day was very prompt, yet his 77 MM ammunition seemed pretty poor. His howitzer ammunition was very much better, although there were a number of "duds".	

1875 Wt. W593/826 1,000,000 4/15 J.B.C. & A. A.D.S.S./Forms/C. 2118.

Army Form C. 2118

WAR DIARY
or
INTELLIGENCE SUMMARY

(Erase heading not required.)

Instructions regarding War Diaries and Intelligence Summaries are contained in F.S. Regs., Part II. and the Staff Manual respectively. Title Pages will be prepared in manuscript.

Place	Date	Hour	Summary of Events and Information	Remarks and references to Appendices
A 22	28	—	Both sides are active with Artillery and T M's during day.	
"	"	5.15 pm	Enemy shell Berthen Crene and left Collecteur with 77 M.M.	
"	"	6.45	The above two points are shelled with 5.9's. Battery appeared to be firing from FARBUS.	
"	"	9.30 pm	Our M G's fire in frequent bursts throughout the night on various points in enemy's lines	
"	29	3.40 am	Enemy artillery suddenly open fire on our front and support Trenches and continued at a very brisk rate till 4.30 a.m. Enemy T M's also fire. A bit of Spooner Avenue near Grand Collecteur is very badly damaged. Our Artillery retaliate.	
"	"	10.30 am	Our Artillery & T M's open fire on enemy support and front trenches. Enemy retaliate with 77 M M's and 4.2's shelling our support trench left of Lille Road	
"	"	3 pm	Wind being in our favour we let loose a smoke cloud which drifted with success towards enemy lines. Gas bombs at once sounded in his lines. Our Artillery along with T M's and machine guns open fire on enemy front and support lines doing considerable damage. Retaliation by enemy is mostly confined to firing on our front trenches, the supports, and communicating	

WAR DIARY
or
INTELLIGENCE SUMMARY
(Erase heading not required.)

Place	Date	Hour	Summary of Events and Information	Remarks and references to Appendices
A 22	29 (cont^d)	3 p.m. (cont^d)	Trenches hardly being touched.	
"	"	4.5 p.m.	We spring a mine in front of sap 32 and at the same time open fire on enemy lines with Artillery, Trench mortars and machine guns. A gas cloud is also sent over. Retaliation by enemy is not nearly as great as in the first phase.	
"	"	5.45 p.m.	Parados at gun position M S B is blown in. Gun undamaged. Our machine guns fire on various points in enemy line.	
"	"	Night		
"	30	3.30 a.m.	Enemy spring a mine near sap 29 and open fire on our front and support trenches. Our Artillery retaliate vigorously.	
"	"	Day.	Very quiet. MG Hyps are removed to Etrun	
"	"	8 p.m.	Ten box kites are observed in north-easterly direction.	
"	"	Night	Our machine guns fire on various points in enemy line. It is reported that enemy have a large party out repairing trenches to sout to right of Lille Rd. Our artillery & Lewis guns keep up a steady fire.	

51st Highland Division.

154th BRIGADE MACHINE GUN COMPANY

JULY 1916

(Original)

Confidential Vol 1

WAR DIARY
of
154th M.G. COY

From 1-7-16 To 31-7-16

(Vol. 5)

INTELLIGENCE SUMMARY

(Erase heading not required.)

Place	Date	Hour	Summary of Events and Information	Remarks and references to Appendices
A.22.B Sheet 51B NW	July 1	9.45 a.m.	Over 20 enemy aeroplanes fly over our lines in batches of five proceeding in a south-westerly direction.	
"	"	10.30 to 11 p.m.	Enemy spring a mine just in front of K. Sexton. Their Artillery & Trench mortars at once open fire on our support trenches. Our Artillery retaliate and keep on bombarding enemy trenches for nearly an hour.	✓✓✓
"	"	12 mid-night	Our field guns and trench mortars open fire at enemy trenches in front of L. Sexton. Retaliation follows with 77 M.M's.	
"	"	Night	Our machine guns fire during night on enemy support lines.	
"	2	12.20 a.m.	Four enemy searchlights are active in front of M. Sexton.	
"	"	11 a.m. to 12 noon	Enemy shell trench between M.S.B and M.S.D. Gun emplacements with 77 M.M's.	✓✓✓
"	"	3-4 p.m.	Enemy trench mortars are active chiefly about M.S.C and M.S.D.	
"	"	Night	Our machine gun fire during night on enemy support trenches to right of Lille Road.	

INTELLIGENCE SUMMARY

(Erase heading not required.)

Instructions regarding War Diaries and Intelligence Summaries are contained in F.S. Regs., Part II. and the Staff Manual respectively. Title Pages will be prepared in manuscript.

Place	Date	Hour	Summary of Events and Information	Remarks and references to Appendices
A.22	3	1.40 a.m.	A few red and green star shells are observed on our right. Nothing follows.	
"	"	6 a.m.	Six of our aeroplanes fly over in direction of THELUS.	
"	"	11.45 a.m.	Enemy damage our support line between MSB and MSC with trench mortars and 77 M.M's	
"	"	11.30 p.m.	Our machine guns fire on points B.13.b.4.5 and A.11.b.26.42 where enemy working parties are sometimes seen.	
"	4	Day	Intermittent shelling and trench mortar activity throughout the day.	
"	"	12.30 p.m.	Enemy shell our support line with 77 M.M's and trench mortars chiefly between MSB and MSD.	
"	"	7.15 p.m.	Enemy trench mortars fired on support line	
"	"	11 p.m.	Our machine guns fired on the following points:— A.18.a.12.62 to A.12.a.55.27 A.17.b.00.36 to A.18.a.12.62 A.18.a.12.62 to A.17.b.00.36.	

INTELLIGENCE SUMMARY

(Erase heading not required.)

Instructions regarding War Diaries and Intelligence Summaries are contained in F. S. Regs., Part II. and the Staff Manual respectively. Title Pages will be prepared in manuscript.

Place	Date	Hour	Summary of Events and Information	Remarks and references to Appendices
A 22	5	5-6 pm	Heavy Bombing.	Q.o.P
"	"	11-12.30am	Our machine guns fired on A17a6.3 to A19.t.5.8. and A19.t.5.8. to A18a.20.85 — Enemy's track area from trolley line to dump	
"	6	forenoon & afternoon	Enemy shell and trench mortar support line between MSB and MSC during forenoon and afternoon	Q.o.P
"	"	9.30 pm	Enemy put up 4 white flares from right of 503 crater. Nothing follows	
"	"	10.30 - 12.30 am	Indirect fire is carried out from 10.30 pm to 12.30 am by our M G's on A13a.70 to A13t.26.70 (Road leading to Commandants House) and A18c.30.85 to A18t.50.85 (Track area to Support line).	
"	7	—	Intermittent shelling and trench mortaring.	
"	"	6-7 pm	Enemy direct their artillery and trench mortars chiefly on support line from MSB to MSD.	Q.o.P
"	"	10.30 pm to midnight	Indirect fire is carried out by our machine guns on Lille Rd. (A19a.10.50 to A11a.65.25	

INTELLIGENCE SUMMARY

(Erase heading not required.)

Instructions regarding War Diaries and Intelligence Summaries are contained in F.S. Regs., Part II. and the Staff Manual respectively. Title Pages will be prepared in manuscript.

Place	Date	Hour	Summary of Events and Information	Remarks and references to Appendices
A.22	8	after noon	Our Trench mortars and Stokes guns are very active. Enemy retaliate by shelling our support trenches with 77 M.M's.	ADS
"	"	day	Considerable aerial activity by both sides during the day.	
"	"	Night	Indirect fire is carried out by our M.G's on trenches behind hedge – south east of Thelus.	
"	9	—	Enemy shell our trenches intermittently with field guns.	
"	"	9.45 pm	A white rocket is observed in easterly direction. Nothing follows.	ADS
"	"	10.15 pm	Two green lights followed by a red one are observed west of THELUS. Nothing follows.	
"	"	Night	Indirect fire carried out by our Machine guns on two points where enemy working parties have been observed.	
"	10	Day	Enemy shell our lines intermittently throughout the day.	ADS
"	"	10.30 pm	Enemy shell Kill Road dump with 77 M.M shells	
"	"	10-11 pm	Indirect fire is carried out by our M.G's on targets A.17.b.95.05 to A.18.c.85.18 (Communication Trench) and A.16.b.23.97 to A.10.d.20.48 (Support lines).	

INTELLIGENCE SUMMARY

(Erase heading not required.)

Summaries are contained in F. S. Regs., Part II. and the Staff Manual respectively. Title Pages will be prepared in manuscript.

Place	Date	Hour	Summary of Events and Information	Remarks and references to Appendices
A 22	11	forenoon	Our Trench mortars and Stokes guns are very active during early part of forenoon. Enemy retaliate & do some damage.	
"	-	afternoon	Enemy Trench mortars are exceedingly active. Our field guns retaliate.	
"	12	12 a.m. to 2 a.m.	Indirect fire is carried out by our M.G's on target A.17.a.10.48 to A.11.a.62.50 (Lille Road)	
"	"	12 midnight	181st M G Coy relieve 154th M G Coy from Trenches	
Etrun	13	-	Limbers packed ready for removal to back area	
Etrun Berlin le Vert	14	11 a.m.	154th M G Coy remove to Berlin le Vert.	
Berlin le Vert Brévillers	15	4 a.m.	154th M G Coy remove to Brévillers	
Brévillers Bernaville	16	9 a.m.	154th M G Coy remove to Bernaville	
Bernaville	17	-	Company training	
do	19	-	do.	
Meaulte	20	-	154th M G Coy remove to MEAULTE (Transport left for Flesselles at 6 p.m.)	

INTELLIGENCE SUMMARY

(Erase heading not required.)

Instructions regarding War Diaries and Intelligence Summaries are contained in F.S. Regs., Part II. and the Staff Manual respectively. Title Pages will be prepared in manuscript.

Place	Date	Hour	Summary of Events and Information	Remarks and references to Appendices
S. 19 d Sheet 57C France	July 21	—	During the evening one section proceed to the front line, and remainder of Company to support line. (Mametz Wood)	Lyas
"	22	—	Heavy shelling all day.	
"	"	—	Our section in front line is relieved by another section of this Coy; heavy shelling being met on the way up to the front line	Lyas
"	"	10 p.m	An attack is started on the right.	
"	23	1.30 a.m	The Batty to which our front line section is attached viz: 4 Gordons attacked. The German line is reached but owing to the failure of the attack on the flanks the ground gained could not be held. Under the circumstances our machine guns could not be moved forward.	Lyas
"	"	Night	Heavy shelling continues	
"	"	6 a.m.	The Germans leave their trench on the left of the wood. Two of our machine guns open fire and quickly drive them back. Expended some 1000 rounds S.A.A	
"	"	—	During the morning two of our guns are subjected to heavy shelling, and during retaliation a number of our own artillery shells fall short. (continued)	

INTELLIGENCE SUMMARY

Instructions regarding War Diaries and Intelligence Summaries are contained in F.S. Regs., Part II. and the Staff Manual respectively. Title Pages will be prepared in manuscript.

(Erase heading not required.)

Place	Date	Hour	Summary of Events and Information	Remarks and references to Appendices
S.19.d (57c)	23 (cont)	10 a.m.	One of our artillery shells fell short and smashes one of our M.G's; also killing one man. The remaining guns were then temporarily withdrawn to the wood.	initials
"	"	–	Remainder of day fairly quiet.	
"	"	6 p.m.	Section in front line returns to bivouacs in Mametz Wood. Another section relieves.	
"	24	5 a.m.	Enemy shell ground behind BAZENTINE-LE-GRAND and to either flank at intervals of half an hour; his intention apparently being to silence our Batteries.	initials
"	"	12 noon	Situation quiet.	
"	"	6 p.m.	Slight artillery activity by enemy on ground behind High Wood, mainly with shrapnel which is of inferior quality.	
"	25	Night	Fierce artillery duels all night; also heavy rifle and machine gun fire on both sides. Our Vickers guns claim many certain casualties.	initials
"	"	Day	Situation normal. cont!	

1875 Wt. W593/826 1,000,000 4/15 J.B.C.&A. A.D.S.S./Forms/C. 2118.

INTELLIGENCE SUMMARY

(Erase heading not required.)

Instructions regarding War Diaries and Intelligence Summaries are contained in F.S. Regs., Part II. and the Staff Manual respectively. Title Pages will be prepared in manuscript.

Place	Date	Hour	Summary of Events and Information	Remarks and references to Appendices
S.19.d.	July 25 (Cont'd)	6 p.m.	The 4th Seaforths send out three patrols which advance 200 yards in front of wood. They capture three strong posts and consolidate them.	Q.s.B
"		9.20.	An attack, followed previously by bombardment — artillery and mortar — is made by Seaforths on strong post in right of wood. This attack fails.	
"	26	—	Whole Company is relieved from front line and supports and proceeds to bivouacs just in front of MEAULTE.	Q.s.B
MEAULTE	24-31	—	Company remain in reserve.	Q.s.B

Q.S.Donogrued Lt.
On Officer Commanding
154th Machine Gun Coy

1875 Wt. W593/826 1,000,000 4/15 J.B.C. & A. A.D.S.S./Forms/C. 2118.

154th Brigade
51st Division.

154th BRIGADE MACHINE GUN COMPANY

AUGUST 1 9 1 6:::

Vol 8
Army Form C. 2118
154 M.G.C
DIV 17

WAR DIARY
or
INTELLIGENCE SUMMARY
(Erase heading not required.)

Place	Date	Hour	Summary of Events and Information	Remarks and references to Appendices
MEAULTE	August 1	-	M G Coy in reserve to 152nd & 153 Bdes	WRS
MAMETZ WOOD	2	-	Coy proceed to Support Line (MAMETZ WOOD)	WRS
"	3-5	-	Artillery on both sides very active. Enemy puts a barrage from time to time on support line.	WRS
DERNACOURT	6	-	Coy is relieved and proceed to DERNACOURT.	WRS
"	7	-	Guns and limbers cleaned.	WRS
POULLANVILLE	8	-	Transport remove to POULLANVILLE	WRS
BELLIFONTAINE	9	-	Transport continue journey on to BELLIFONTAINE. M.G. Sections proceed by train and road as far as BELLIFONTAINE	WRS
LYNDE	10/11	-	Transport & M G Sections proceed by train to STEENBECQUES and march to billets at LYNDE	WRS
do.	12/13	-	Guns and limbers cleaned.	WRS

WAR DIARY
or
INTELLIGENCE SUMMARY
(Erase heading not required.)

Army Form C. 2118

Place	Date	Hour	Summary of Events and Information	Remarks and references to Appendices
LYNDE ARMENTIÈRES	14	—	Company proceeds to Armentières. Transport and cyclists move off from Lynde at 3.45 p.m. and remainder entrain at Ebblingham during afternoon	WRS
ARMENTIÈRES	15	5 a.m.	Three sections of the Coy. proceed into the line. One section remains in reserve at Armentières.	
"	"	4 a.m.	No. 4 Emplacement is knocked out by enemy trench mortar. Two men are killed and one wounded. (As this position has been knocked out on two occasions recently, another position on the right of it has been sited and built)	
"	"	9–11 a.m.	Enemy shell and trench mortar our front and support line.	WRS
"	"	10 p.m. & 10.45 p.m.	Two of our machine guns search the enemy's wire and parapet.	

Army Form C. 2118.

WAR DIARY
or
INTELLIGENCE SUMMARY
(Erase heading not required.)

Instructions regarding War Diaries and Intelligence Summaries are contained in F. S. Regs., Part II. and the Staff Manual respectively. Title Pages will be prepared in manuscript.

Place	Date	Hour	Summary of Events and Information	Remarks and references to Appendices
ARMENTIERES	16	Day.	Enemy quiet	
"		Night	At intervals enemy are active firing on our wire with machine gun. From our own gun on the left of the Sector we fire 500 rounds. On the right of the Sector we are unable to fire owing to working parties being out.	WRS
"	17	Day.	Quiet. Enemy fire a little with 77 M.M guns. One Vickers gun is withdrawn from no.9 position in front line and replaced by a Lewis gun.	WRS
"		Night	Our machine guns fire during night on enemy front line.	WRS
"	18	Day.	Enemy quiet. A little artillery and trench mortar activity is shown at times.	WRS
"		Night	Enemy is busy with his machine gun and rifle fire.	WRS
"	19	10.30 a.m.	A few trench mortars are sent over by enemy on to our front and support line.	WRS
"		Night	Quiet.	
"	20	8.30 p.m. — 12 midnight	Enemy machine gun fire, Trench parapet on left of our front intermittent	WRS

WAR DIARY
or
INTELLIGENCE SUMMARY

(Erase heading not required.)

Army Form C. 2118.

Place	Date	Hour	Summary of Events and Information	Remarks and references to Appendices
ARMENTIERES	Aug 21	12 midnight to 4.30 a.m.	Enemy machine guns traverse parapet on left of our front intermittently.	
"	"	(Day)	Quiet	
"	"	8 - 8.30 p.m.	Enemy traverse the parapet of front line with M.G. fire.	
"	"	10.45 p.m.	Enemy send up one green rocket on the right of our sector which remains stationary in air for 15 minutes several seconds. Our Artillery open fire on enemy's front line for five minutes	10 R.L.
"	"	11 p.m. to midnight	Enemy very active with trench mortars and rifle grenades. Our 2" mortars retaliate	
"	22	Midnight to 1 a.m.	Enemy trench mortars active.	
"	"	9 p.m.	A green rocket went up well behind the enemy's lines. Nothing follows.	
"	"	11 p.m. to 11.30	We fire 250 rounds S.A.A. into PREMESQUES in co-operation with our Artillery.	10 R.L.

Army Form C. 2118.

WAR DIARY
or
INTELLIGENCE SUMMARY

(Erase heading not required.)

Instructions regarding War Diaries and Intelligence Summaries are contained in F. S. Regs., Part II. and the Staff Manual respectively. Title Pages will be prepared in manuscript.

Place	Date	Hour	Summary of Events and Information	Remarks and references to Appendices
ARMENTIERES	23	1 a.m.	Our Artillery shell enemy trenches. Enemy retaliate with Trench mortars.	
"	"	morning	Quiet	
"	"	3 p.m.	Enemy shell our Support trenches	
"	"	3.30 p.m.	Enemy active with Trench mortars	
"	"	10 p.m.	Vertical searching is done by our guns on Crenesque Rd. in co-operation with Artillery	
"	"	10.20 p.m.	Rifle shells and junction of two roads in front of this town are swept with overhead fire. Enemy M.G. replies from Crenesque Rd. his bullets striking our parapet.	W.R.S.
"	24	9 p.m.	We fire 500 rounds on Ruelle de la Nove.	
"	"	8.30 p.m. to 9.30 p.m.	Indirect fire is carried out on Crenesque Village in co-operation with our Artillery.	W.R.S.
"	"	9.30 p.m.	One of our aircraft is brought down by the enemy. It descends in our own lines	

WAR DIARY
or
INTELLIGENCE SUMMARY

(Erase heading not required.)

Army Form C. 2118.

Place	Date	Hour	Summary of Events and Information	Remarks and references to Appendices
Armentieres	Aug 25	11 a.m.	German Aeroplane comes over our lines and a man is seen leaning over the side, evidently taking photographs. We open fire on him and he withdrew out of range.	NoRS
"	"	4 p.m.	Our trench mortars open fire. Enemy retaliate with 77 M.M.'s causing some damage to trench.	NoRS
"	"	Night	Enemy active with machine guns during night.	NoRS
"	26	9 a.m.	Our Coy is relieved by 152 M.G. Coy. Company proceeds to billets in Armentieres	NoRS
ARMENTIERES to BAILLEUL	27	10.30 a.m.	Coy proceeds to training camp at Bailleul	NoRS
"	"	6 p.m.	M. Guns cleaned	
"	28	7-8 a.m.	Gun and further cleaning	
"	"	9-9.30	Kit inspection	
"	"	9.30-10	O.C's inspection	
"	"	10-11	Squad Drill	
"	"	11-12	Company Drill	
"	"	12-12.45	and Signallers Class	

Army Form C. 2118.

WAR DIARY
or
INTELLIGENCE SUMMARY

(Erase heading not required.)

Instructions regarding War Diaries and Intelligence Summaries are contained in F. S. Regs., Part II. and the Staff Manual respectively. Title Pages will be prepared in manuscript.

Place	Date	Hour	Summary of Events and Information	Remarks and references to Appendices
BAILLEUL	29	7-7.45	Squad Drill	
"	"	9 am	Laying out kit	
"	"	9.30	60's inspection	
"	"	11 am	Ceremonial Parade	W.R.S.
"	"	2.30 pm	Inspection of Guns and Spare Parts	
"	"	2 pm	Lecture to Sergeants	
"	30	7-8	Short Route march	
"	"	9 am	Laying out kits	
"	"	9.20 am	Rifle and Helmet inspection	
"	"	9.30 am	6O's Inspection	
"	"	10-10.30	Gas Drill	
"	"	10.45-11.45	Gun Drill	
"	"	11.45-12.45	Company Drill	
"	"	2-3 pm	Lecture to NCO's and Officers Riding	W.R.S.

Army Form C. 2118.

WAR DIARY
or
INTELLIGENCE SUMMARY
(Erase heading not required.)

Place	Date	Hour	Summary of Events and Information	Remarks and references to Appendices
Brilleul	Aug 31	7 a.m.	Route march	W.R.S.
"	"	9 a.m.	Inspection of Rifles and box respirators	
"	"	9.15	100's Inspection	
"	"	9.45	Packing of limbers and cleaning of guns and equipment	
"	"	11 a.m.	First Aid lecture by M.O.	
"	"	12 noon	Company drill	
"	"	2 p.m.	Lecture to Sergeants. Junior Officers riding	
"	"	4 p.m.	Night operations	

W.R. Sutherland 2nd Lieut.
for Officer Commanding
154 M G Coy

Confidential

(Original)

WAR DIARY
of
154th Coy M.G.C.

From 1/9/16 to 30/9/16

Vol 9

WAR DIARY or INTELLIGENCE SUMMARY

Army Form C. 2118.

154th Coy M.G.C.

Place	Date	Hour	Summary of Events and Information	Remarks and references to Appendices
Bailleul	Sept 1	7AM	Route March	C.W.J. Capt
"		9AM	Inspection of Rifles Smoke Helmets	
"		9.15	C O's Inspection	
"		9.45	Gun Drill and Orders	
"		11.15	Company Drill	
"		12	Maxim Officers Lecture	
"		2PM	Lecture to Sergeants Junior Officers Roring	

Army Form C. 2118.

WAR DIARY
or
INTELLIGENCE SUMMARY

(Erase heading not required.)

Instructions regarding War Diaries and Intelligence Summaries are contained in F. S. Regs., Part II. and the Staff Manual respectively. Title Pages will be prepared in manuscript.

Place	Date	Hour	Summary of Events and Information	Remarks and references to Appendices
Balleul Armentières	2.9.16	9.30AM	Packing Limbers	
"	"	1.30PM	Coy. Proceeds to Armentières	
"	"	5PM	Coy arrives in Armentières	

Army Form C. 2118.

WAR DIARY
or
INTELLIGENCE SUMMARY

(Erase heading not required.)

Instructions regarding War Diaries and Intelligence Summaries are contained in F. S. Regs., Part II. and the Staff Manual respectively. Title Pages will be prepared in manuscript.

Place	Date	Hour	Summary of Events and Information	Remarks and references to Appendices
Armentières	3	8.15 AM	Three and a half sections (14 Guns) proceed into the Line and relieve the 68th Brigade. ½ Section remains in reserve in Armentières	
"	"	Night	Very quiet. Our Guns search the enemys front line Communication trenches	
"	4	11.15 AM	Our Artillery & Trench Mortars Bombard enemys front line trench on right of Brigade front. Very little Retaliation	
"	"	2.30 PM	Enemy put some heavy Trench Mortars in Bunkenham Farm	
"	"	6 PM	Enemys aeroplanes covered at Le Bizet	
"	"	Night	Generally quiet	

2449 Wt. W14957/M90 750,000 1/16 J.B.C. & A. Forms/C.2118/12.

WAR DIARY
or
INTELLIGENCE SUMMARY

Army Form C. 2118.

Place	Date	Hour	Summary of Events and Information	Remarks and references to Appendices
Armentières	5	Morning	Quiet.	
"		4 P.M.	Enemy put on two on to Barkenham Farm intermittently for half an hour.	
"		night	Very Quiet	
"	6	11 A.M.	The enemy sent over half a dozen shells on the Hindenburg at La Toquet station. Our field guns retaliated on enemy front line.	
"		3 P.M.	Enemy shelled Paternoster Road, and damaged French and Machine Gun position, wounding one man. A dug out was also blown in by a 4.2 Shell	
"		6.15 P.M.	An Aeroplane was brought down in flames inside the enemy's lines. It is uncertain whether it was a Bristol or a German Plane. From position near Carter Farm, we fired 500 rounds on to Bridge our river at C.11.c.45.62. This drew retaliation	
"		night	Between 8 PM & 11 PM our artillery were very active between on enemys line about C.4.a.65	

Army Form C. 2118.

WAR DIARY
or
INTELLIGENCE SUMMARY
(Erase heading not required.)

Instructions regarding War Diaries and Intelligence Summaries are contained in F. S. Regs., Part II. and the Staff Manual respectively. Title Pages will be prepared in manuscript.

Place	Date	Hour	Summary of Events and Information	Remarks and references to Appendices
Armentières	7	Morning	At 3 A.m. a working party was noticed repairing damage done by our Artillery. This party was dispersed by our Vickers fire, situated in front of Entrenched de Bordeau. A Carrier pigeon flew over our lines in the direction of Armentières.	
"	"	6 p.m.	Our trench mortars and artillery have a combined strafe on the enemy front line opposite 6/4 p. What appears to be a M G Emplacement is knocked out.	
"	"	Night	Quiet	
"	"	7.30 p.m. 7.45 8 p.m.	Enemy shell Armentières. M G H.qrs 43 Rue Nationale are twice hit. Most of the shells fall about this quarter of the town	
"	8	Morning	154 M G Coy are relieved by 58th Bde and proceed to billets in Armentières. Relief complete at 2.15 p.m.	[signature]

Army Form C. 2118.

WAR DIARY
or
INTELLIGENCE SUMMARY

(Erase heading not required.)

Place	Date	Hour	Summary of Events and Information	Remarks and references to Appendices
Armentières	Sept 9	8.30 a.m.	We take over line from 153rd M.G. Coy.	
"	"	5.30 p.m.	A small mine is blown up by us under enemy's lines at 619 a 40.2.3, followed by a small bombardment. No retaliation follows.	
"	"	5.45 p.m.	Our trench mortars open fire. Enemy retaliates with his heavy trench mortars on T 48-49.	
"	"	11.30 p.m.	We fire 450 rounds S.A.A. from T 88 gun position into the above mentioned mine crater in conjunction with the trench mortars. In retaliation the enemy send over three or four trench mortars, which do no damage.	AWB

Army Form C. 2118.

WAR DIARY
or
INTELLIGENCE SUMMARY

(Erase heading not required.)

Place	Date	Hour	Summary of Events and Information	Remarks and references to Appendices
Armentières	Sept 10	6.15 a.m	Our field guns - in conjunction with Stokes and 2" Trench mortars - bombard enemy front line until 6.50 a.m.	
"	"	4 a.m	Enemy retaliate with minenwerfer shells, most of them landing South Africa trench. As a result of this bombardment the M.G. dugout is buried and two rifles and 8 belt boxes, containing ammunition, lost.	
"	"	6 p.m	Enemy send four minenwerfer shells into the Orchard. No damage	
"	"	10.15 p.m	Our trench mortars and field guns shell the enemy front line. No retaliation.	CWB
"	"	Night	From two of our M.G's we fire intermittently on X Roads La Doulette and the area round L'Aventure. 1500 rounds.	

Army Form C. 2118.

WAR DIARY
or
INTELLIGENCE SUMMARY
(Erase heading not required.)

Instructions regarding War Diaries and Intelligence Summaries are contained in F. S. Regs., Part II. and the Staff Manual respectively. Title Pages will be prepared in manuscript.

Place	Date	Hour	Summary of Events and Information	Remarks and references to Appendices
ARMENTIERES	Sept 11	4 p.m. – 6 p.m.	Enemy are busy with Trench Mortars about Hobbs Farm, doing damage to trenches in vicinity.	
"	"	4 p.m.	Two carrier pigeons come over from German lines and fly in direction of Armentieres.	
"	"	5 p.m.	Our Stokes mortars open fire, and the enemy retaliates, his fire being mainly concentrated on the Orchard and Tiji.	
"	"	6.15 p.m.	The enemy send up one red rocket about quarter left of S.P.Z. Nothing happens.	
"	"	10 p.m.	We fire 1000 rounds from River post position at Chastel Farm.	
"	"	10 – 11	L'Aventure X Road area is fired on from gun position in Subsidiary c.28.c.40.65. 1000 rounds expended.	
"	"	10.15	An enemy working party is distinctly heard about half right from gun position T88. Gun T88 is brought into action and 850 rounds fired at party.	
"	"	10.30 – 11.30	M.G. at Try Pan position searches road from c.12.c.25.00 to X Roads c.18.d.6.5. 1000 rounds S.A.A. expended.	
"	"	11 p.m.	We fire from rear gun position T88 in conjunction with Trench Mortars, 850 rounds at Chicken Run and Mine Crater.	
"	"	11 p.m.	From position T65 we traverse along enemy parapet & wire from rear gun position	

WAR DIARY
or
INTELLIGENCE SUMMARY.

(Erase heading not required.)

Army Form C. 2118.

Place	Date	Hour	Summary of Events and Information	Remarks and references to Appendices
ARMENTIERES	Sept 12	10.30 a.m.	Enemy bombard terrain about ORCHARD and FIT 1 with minenwerfers and small aerial torpedoes	
"	"	4-5 p.m.	Our Trench mortars are very active and also our field guns in shelling enemy front and support trenches	
"	"	8.30 – 9.30 p.m.	1000 rounds S.A.A. are fired from M G at Fry Pan position on to Rue Ouraine Ferme	
"	"	9.30 p.m. to 12	Enemy machine guns are more active during the night than they have been hitherto. Two guns fire down our Trolley line at irregular intervals. Bullets seen to go fairly high.	
"	13	4.30 a.m.	M.G. at position S.S.84 fires 1000 rounds on German 3rd line c.23.d 9.0. to c.24.d. 25.80.	
"	"	4.5 a.m. 8.10 11.45 12.30	Our T.M's supported by Artillery, open fire on enemy lines, doing considerable damage. Enemy retaliate at 8.15 and 8.30 a.m. with Minenwerfers and field guns	
"	"	3 p.m.	Enemy put about a dozen heavy mortars into the vicinity of Rohts Farm, doing damage to our trenches.	

(Continued)

Army Form C. 2118.

WAR DIARY
or
INTELLIGENCE SUMMARY
(Erase heading not required.)

Place	Date	Hour	Summary of Events and Information	Remarks and references to Appendices
ARMENTIERES	Sept 13 (Cont:)	6.5 p.m 7.15	We again bombard the enemy, our M.G's opening fire on area behind where our trench mortars and Artillery were firing. No retaliation followed by enemy.	
"	"	6 p.m	Our M.G's also fire 500 rounds from gun position S84 at C24a.76.29 to C24d.25.82.	
"	"	10 p.m	1000 rounds S.A.A. are fired from River Post position at road from Ferme du Bluets to C24 c.55.82.	
"	"	—	Position of minenwerfer that fires into area at Hobbs farm has been located, the true bearing from C22d.5.6 is 56. Position has also been observed from another point. True bearing is being obtained.	CWS.

Army Form C. 2118.

WAR DIARY
or
INTELLIGENCE SUMMARY

(Erase heading not required.)

Instructions regarding War Diaries and Intelligence Summaries are contained in F. S. Regs., Part II. and the Staff Manual respectively. Title Pages will be prepared in manuscript.

Place	Date	Hour	Summary of Events and Information	Remarks and references to Appendices
ARMENTIERES	Sept 14.	11 a.m.	Our Artillery in conjunction with the Trench mortars carry out ten minutes bombardment on enemy front line. Enemy does not retaliate.	
"	"	12 noon	Enemy send over a number of minenwerfer shells and Grenades mostly all coming into our front and support trenches around Pont Ferm.	
"	"	3.35 pm	After the 3.35 pm phase enemy retaliate very severely with Heavy mortars by shelling Orchard, South Africa trench, Porirua canal & Fiji position.	
"	"	6.20 pm	Our Artillery and TM's carry out a combined shape on enemy front line	
"	"	8.30 pm	Our M.G. at Pt Schroding position fires 1000 rounds at Trench Railway c 24 d.58.40 to c 19 c. 28.00. Given Sgt	
"	"	6.20 pm	500 Rounds are fired from Fairy Ram position at target c 24 a.78 d to c 24 c. 23.80	
"	"	—	Compass bearings are taken of the enemy heavy Trench mortars which has been located from two different points, and the same communicated to the Artillery Liaison Officer.	

Army Form C. 2118.

WAR DIARY
or
INTELLIGENCE SUMMARY
(Erase heading not required.)

Place	Date	Hour	Summary of Events and Information	Remarks and references to Appendices
ARMENTIERES	Sept 15	5.30 a.m.	1000 rounds are fired from Tiny Paw position on to German Third Line C.18.c.4.5 to C.13.c.31.15.	
"	"	6.30 a.m.	500 rounds are fired from River Post at Road C.12.C.90.00 to D.13.a.50.00. 1000 rounds are also directed on enemy Assembly Trenches at C.30.c.50.50.	
"	"	3.30 p.m.	There is an exchange of trench mortars, the enemy also retaliating with rifle grenades. Considerable damage is done to trench on each side of gun T82. Stroq at this point is wrecked.	
"	"	5.40 p.m.	500 rounds are fired from S.24 at Assembly Trenches about C.24.c and C.30.a. 800 rounds are also fired on Road C.30.a.19.50 to C.30.a.65.15.	
"	"	8.35 p.m.	Firing is done from River Post position at road from Farm du Chastel to C.18.c.4.7.	
"	"	8.55 p.m.	Fire is opened by our guns on enemy parapet. Firing, in conjunction with our artillery continued until 9.10 p.m. Enemy retaliation was weak.	

Army Form C. 2118.

WAR DIARY
or
INTELLIGENCE SUMMARY

(Erase heading not required.)

Instructions regarding War Diaries and Intelligence Summaries are contained in F. S. Regs., Part II. and the Staff Manual respectively. Title Pages will be prepared in manuscript.

Place	Date	Hour	Summary of Events and Information	Remarks and references to Appendices
ARMENTIERES	16	12.15 a.m.	Several minenwerfers come over and do further damage to the front line trenches to the right of T.82.	
"	"	9.30am	Our Artillery and T.M's open fire on enemy lines for two minutes.	
"	"	10.45am	Our M.G at Pt Subsidiary position fires 500 rounds on each occasion on C.23.d.9.0. to C.24.c.5.6	
"	"	3pm	Two observation balloons are sent up by the enemy. One remains in the air for about half an hour only, the other descends at 4pm.	
"	"	5pm	Our heavy Artillery fire on enemy lines	
"	"	4.45pm	Indirect fire is opened by gun at Frying Pan position, and at 7.13 pm by gun on Panama Canal Bank.	
"	"	8 - 8.15	At Subsidiary gun fires as per plane Y. 1450 rounds are expended. Enemy give very little retaliation.	
"	"	8.15	M.G. S.S.84 open a fire on to Road from Frelinghien C.11.d.7.43 to C.18.t.9.0.50.	
"	"	8.30pm	Fire is opened from position on parapet in trench 85 on to C.17.d.10.05 to C.23.c.90.90. This is continued in short bursts till rocket fires up at 8.50pm. There is very little retaliation, only a few Trench Mortars being sent across.	[signature]

2449 Wt. W14957/M90 750,000 1/16 J.B.C. & A. Forms'C.2118/12.

Army Form C. 2118.

WAR DIARY
or
INTELLIGENCE SUMMARY
(Erase heading not required.)

Instructions regarding War Diaries and Intelligence Summaries are contained in F. S. Regs., Part II. and the Staff Manual respectively. Title Pages will be prepared in manuscript.

Place	Date	Hour	Summary of Events and Information	Remarks and references to Appendices
ARMENTIÈRES	Sept 1st	Day	At intervals our artillery fire on enemy front line and also well behind it.	
"	"	4.30 p.m	Our Artillery - in conjunction with trench mortars-bombard German line opposite T84. There is no retaliation.	
"	"	5 p.m.	The enemy trench mortared is about T.78 and S.78. minenwerfers. Small mortars and sting bombs are sent over. Our Stokes, 2" mortars and field guns silence the enemy.	
"	"	8.15 p.m.	We fire 500 rounds on C.11.d.8.4.43 to C.18.b.8.0.50 from gun position SS84.	
"	"	10.15 p.m. to 11 p.m	1000 rounds SAA are fired from the Cemetary Right Indirect position on to C.30.b.45.51.	
"	"	10.30 p.m	A searchlight is observed operating behind the enemy lines	
"	"	Night	The enemy appears to be in a state of nerves all night and there is a good deal of Rifle & MG fire	

Army Form C. 2118.

WAR DIARY
or
INTELLIGENCE SUMMARY

(*Erase heading not required.*)

Instructions regarding War Diaries and Intelligence Summaries are contained in F. S. Regs., Part II. and the Staff Manual respectively. Title Pages will be prepared in manuscript.

Place	Date	Hour	Summary of Events and Information	Remarks and references to Appendices
ARMENTIERES	Sept 18	12.45 a.m. to 1.30 a.m.	A heavy bombardment by our Artillery took place on our right.	
"	"	Day	Very quiet	
"	"	2-4 p.m.	Our field gun fires several rounds on enemy front line.	
"	"	11 p.m.	A T.M. Strafe starts on our right and our Stokes 2" and field guns fire for about 5 minutes. The enemy opposite us evidently stood to as they opened rifle and M.G. fire, keeping it up for several minutes.	
"	"	11.45 p.m.	A similar strafe is commenced with same results from the enemy.	[signature]

2449 Wt. W14957/M90 750,000 1/16 J.B.C. & A. Forms/C.2118/12.

Army Form C. 2118.

WAR DIARY
or
INTELLIGENCE SUMMARY
(Erase heading not required.)

Instructions regarding War Diaries and Intelligence Summaries are contained in F. S. Regs., Part II. and the Staff Manual respectively. Title Pages will be prepared in manuscript.

Place	Date	Hour	Summary of Events and Information	Remarks and references to Appendices
ARMENTIERES	19 Sept.	Day	Our Artillery fire at irregular intervals. Enemy active with minenwerfers.	
"	"	9 a.m.	do.	
"	"	3.30 p.m.	Gun at River post position searches enemy third line in front of La Houlette.	
"	"	9.30–10	Gun at Try Pan position searches enemy third line in front of Rue du Bhastel. This gun is subject to heavy sniping by enemy throughout the night.	
"	"	10–11 pm	Gun at Cemetery subsidiary position searches road from L'Aventeur to le Temple.	AB.
"	"	11.40 pm		

Army Form C. 2118.

WAR DIARY
or
INTELLIGENCE SUMMARY

(Erase heading not required.)

Instructions regarding War Diaries and Intelligence Summaries are contained in F. S. Regs., Part II. and the Staff Manual respectively. Title Pages will be prepared in manuscript.

Place	Date	Hour	Summary of Events and Information	Remarks and references to Appendices
ARMENTIERES	Sept 20	11-12 noon	Enemy Minenwerfers are exceedingly active. Our Stokes and 2" mortars retaliate doing considerable damage to enemy trenches	
"	"		Day and night quiet	
"	21	12.30 a.m.	One of our aeroplanes destroyed an enemy Observation balloon.	
"	"	10 p.m.	Our Lewis guns are active all along the front. Enemy keep up a steady rifle fire.	
"	"	10.30 p.m. to 12.15 p.m.	We fire 1000 rounds S.A.A. from Rt Subsidiary Gun Position on to target C.24.c.50.85 to C.24.d.0.5.	
ARMENTIERES ERQUINGHEM	22 Morning		We are relieved by 8th Australian M G Coy and proceed to billets at Erquinghem	
"	"	Afternoon	Cleaning of guns	
ERQUINGHEM	23	6.45 a.m.	Rifle & bayonet inspection.	
		9 a.m.	Gas Drill	
		10 a.m.	Company proceeds to Armentieres for firing of new respirators by Gas Officer.	C.W.S.
		2 p.m.	" " " " "	
		3.30 p.m.	Kit inspection	

Army Form C. 2118.

WAR DIARY
or
INTELLIGENCE SUMMARY
(Erase heading not required.)

Instructions regarding War Diaries and Intelligence Summaries are contained in F. S. Regs., Part II. and the Staff Manual respectively. Title Pages will be prepared in manuscript.

Place	Date	Hour	Summary of Events and Information	Remarks and references to Appendices
ERQUINGHEM	24	10 a.m.	Church Parade	
ERQUINGHEM ESTAIRES	25	8.30 a.m.	Company proceed to Estaires	
"	"	2 p.m.	Cleaning of limbers	
ESTAIRES	26	9 a.m.	Company is inspected while in column of route by Army Commander.	
"	"	2 p.m.	Cleaning of limbers and overhauling of gun equipment.	
"	27	9 a.m.	Route march	
"	"	9 a.m.	C.O's inspection and company drill.	
"	"	10.30 a	Cleaning and overhauling of gun equipment and vehicles.	
"	"	12 noon	Specialists Signallers and Range Takers on special duty	
"	"	12 noon	Gun drill	
"	"	2 p.m.	Overhauling of gun equipment.	

WAR DIARY
or
INTELLIGENCE SUMMARY
(Erase heading not required.)

Army Form C. 2118.

Instructions regarding War Diaries and Intelligence Summaries are contained in F.S. Regs., Part II. and the Staff Manual respectively. Title Pages will be prepared in manuscript.

Place	Date	Hour	Summary of Events and Information	Remarks and references to Appendices
ESTAIRES	28	4 a.m.	Short route march	
"	"	9 a.m.	C.O's inspection. Coy and Army drill	
"	"	10 a.m.	Gun drill	
"	"	11 a.m.	Immediate action. Specialists on special duty	
"	"	12 a.m.	Gas drill	
"	"	2 p.m.	Overhauling of gun equipment	
"	29	4 a.m.	Short Route march	
"	"	9 a.m.	C.O's inspection.	
"	"	9.30 a.m.	Tactical scheme. M.G's in attack.	
ESTAIRES FIENVILLIERS	30	9.30 -11 a.m.	Transport and remainder of Coy proceed to entraining station (MERVILLE). Detrain at CANDAS (FIENVILLIERS) and march to billets at FIENVILLIERS	

A.F. Doual Capt
Officer Comm'g.
154 M.G. Coy

Army Form C. 2118.

WAR DIARY
or
INTELLIGENCE SUMMARY

Confidential

ORIGINAL
WAR DIARY
of
154th COY. M.G.C.
from 1st Oct 1916
To 31st Oct 1916

WAR DIARY or INTELLIGENCE SUMMARY

Army Form C. 2118.

Place	Date	Hour	Summary of Events and Information	Remarks and references to Appendices
FIENVILLERS	1	9.30 a.m.	C.O.'s inspection	A05
"	"	10 a.m.	Cleaning guns and limbers	A05
"	2	9 a.m.–1 p.m.	Company field operations	A05
Fienvillers Thievres	3	10 a.m.	Company removes to Thievres	A05
Thievres Bus-les-Artois	4	11.30 a.m.	Company removes to Bus Wood	A05
Bus	5	9 a.m.	C.O.'s inspection	
"	"	9.30	Gun cleaning	
"	"	10.30 a.m.	Physical training	A05
"	6	7.15 a.m.	Short Route march	
"	"	9 a.m.	C.O's parade	
"	"	9.20	Company and Arms drill	
"	"	10.30 a.m.	Gun drill in attack. Range takers and signallers on special work.	A05
"	"	11.30 a.m.	Mechanism and of Immediate Action	

Army Form C. 2118.

WAR DIARY
or
INTELLIGENCE SUMMARY
(Erase heading not required.)

Instructions regarding War Diaries and Intelligence Summaries are contained in F.S. Regs., Part II. and the Staff Manual respectively. Title Pages will be prepared in manuscript.

Place	Date	Hour	Summary of Events and Information	Remarks and references to Appendices
BUS	7	7.15 am	Physical training	
"	"	9 am	C.O's parade	
"	"	9.30 am	Sections in attack	
"	"	11.30 am to 12.30	Immediate action	Als.
"	"	1.30 pm	Bde field operations	
BUS COLINCAMP	8	12.30 pm	1 Section proceeds to trenches to relieve 152nd Coy	
"	"	1 pm	Hqrs and 3 Sections remove to COLINCAMP PS in relief of 152nd Coy	Als.
COLINCAMP	"	Afternoon	Our artillery shows considerable activity. Enemy retaliate with shrapnel and some heavy shells	
"	"	Night	Quiet	

WAR DIARY
or
INTELLIGENCE SUMMARY

(Erase heading not required.)

Army Form C. 2118.

Place	Date	Hour	Summary of Events and Information	Remarks and references to Appendices
COLINCAMPS K.25.c.9.3 Sheet 57D NE	9	12.30 am to 1.15 am	The enemy send over about a dozen minenwerfers	
"	"	Forenoon & Afternoon	Our field and heavy guns are active, shelling enemy trenches all along our front.	
"	"	5-6 p.m.	The enemy shell HEBUTERNE	A.AS.
"	"	9.45 p.m.	Enemy mortars are very active, most of them falling in the vicinity of No.1 gun in front trench.	
"	"	Night	No firing is done by our M.G's owing to patrols and working parties being out.	
"	"	"	During the day and night work was continued on dug-outs and emplacements. Two frames were also completed.	

Army Form C. 2118.

WAR DIARY
or
INTELLIGENCE SUMMARY
(Erase heading not required.)

Instructions regarding War Diaries and Intelligence Summaries are contained in F. S. Regs., Part II. and the Staff Manual respectively. Title Pages will be prepared in manuscript.

Place	Date	Hour	Summary of Events and Information	Remarks and references to Appendices
COLINCAMPS K 25. c. 7. 3	10	Early morning	Generally quiet.	
"	"	—	Throughout the day and night our Artillery are very active especially around neighbourhood of SERRE. Enemy does not retaliate to any extent on our front system of trenches, but sends quite a number of shells into our rear lines.	Nos.
"	"	4 p.m.	From V.1. Gun position a thin stream of light (green) is observed in a S.E direction, being sent up at intervals. This is followed by bright red flare, which appears several times.	
"	"	—	Our machine guns do not fire during night owing to patrols and so many working parties being out.	
"	"	—	Work done. Four frogs emplaced and trenches deepened leading to them. Work on dug-outs continued.	

WAR DIARY
or
INTELLIGENCE SUMMARY

(Erase heading not required.)

Army Form C. 2118.

Place	Date	Hour	Summary of Events and Information	Remarks and references to Appendices
COLINCAMPS K25c.7.c	11	9am	Enemy send over several Minenwerfers in the vicinity of our V.1 Gun position	AAS.
"	"	10am	Our heavy guns and field guns are active during the greater part of the day. Work done:- Work continued on dug-outs.	
"	"			
COLINCAMPS	12	4am	Rapid fire is heard on our left.	AAS.
"	"	4am–5.30am	Our machine gun at position V.1 traverses enemy trench from point K.17.d.5.2. to K.24.c.8.5. 750 rounds are expended.	
"	"	2pm	Our Artillery bombard enemy lines, considerable retaliation at COLINCAMPS	
"	"	4pm	M.G. section and 1gun are relieved by 153rd bn and proceed to Billets at LOUVENCOURT.	
"	"	9pm	Remaining section in the line is also relieved by 153 bn and proceeds to LOUVENCOURT.	

Army Form C. 2118.

WAR DIARY
or
INTELLIGENCE SUMMARY

(Erase heading not required.)

Place	Date	Hour	Summary of Events and Information	Remarks and references to Appendices
LOUVENCOURT	13	Morning	Cleaning up.	
"	"	2.30 p.m.	Squad & Arm Drill	
"	14	9.15 a.m.	Short period of Physical training	
"	"	9 a.m.	C.O.'s Inspection Company Drill	
"	"	10 a.m.	Gas drill	
"	"	10.30 a.m. to 12.30	Arm Drill (attack)	
"	"	2.15 p.m.	Lecture	
"	15	Morning	Church Parade	

Army Form C. 2118.

WAR DIARY
or
INTELLIGENCE SUMMARY

(Erase heading not required.)

Instructions regarding War Diaries and Intelligence Summaries are contained in F. S. Regs., Part II. and the Staff Manual respectively. Title Pages will be prepared in manuscript.

Place	Date	Hour	Summary of Events and Information	Remarks and references to Appendices
LOUVENCOURT	16	7.15	Physical Training	
"	"	9 a.m.	C.O.'s Inspection & Company Drill	
"	"	9.30 a.m.	Guns in attack	
LOUVENCOURT FORCEVILLE	17	9.30 a.m.	Company removes to FORCEVILLE	
FORCEVILLE LEALVILLERS	18	9.30 a.m.	Company removes from FORCEVILLE to LEALVILLERS.	
LEALVILLERS	19	morning	Cleaning Guns & Immediate Action	
"	"	afternoon	ditto	
"	20	9 a.m.	Physical Training	
"	"	10 a.m.	Inspection & Company Drill	
"	"	11 a.m.	Gun drill and Immediate Action (mechanism) Immediate Action for attached men	
"	"	2.30	Checking and cleaning of gun equipment.	

WAR DIARY
or
INTELLIGENCE SUMMARY

(Erase heading not required.)

Army Form C. 2118.

Place	Date	Hour	Summary of Events and Information	Remarks and references to Appendices
LEALVILLERS	21	9 a.m.	Physical Training	
"	"	10 a.m.	C.O's Inspection. Inspection of Gas Helmets. Company Drill	
"	"	11 a.m.	Gun Drill	
"	"	2 p.m.	Filling belts and overhauling ammunition	
MAILLY MAILLET WOOD	22		One Section proceeds into the line	*signature*
"	"	12.30 pm	Remainder of Company proceed to MAILLY WOOD	
"	"	2 pm	Another Section proceeded into the line	
"	"	2 pm	Our Artillery and Trench mortars concentrate an intense fire upon BEAUMONT HAMEL and enemy front line wire, which appears to cause considerable damage. Enemy retaliate with a few shells near our Essex St Gun hut, but no damage is done.	
"	"	6.30 pm 9.30 pm	Intermittent artillery fire is carried on, the enemy replying with minenwerfers.	*signature*

Army Form C. 2118.

WAR DIARY
or
INTELLIGENCE SUMMARY

(Erase heading not required.)

Instructions regarding War Diaries and Intelligence Summaries are contained in F. S. Regs., Part II. and the Staff Manual respectively. Title Pages will be prepared in manuscript.

Place	Date	Hour	Summary of Events and Information	Remarks and references to Appendices
AUCHONVILLERS	2/3	12 midnight to 12.30 a.m.	Our Artillery are especially active	
"	"	do	The enemy bombard our Fanwick Trench Gun position with minenwerfers and Sling Bombs. Seaforth trench is also bombarded. No damage is done.	
"	"	5 a.m.	Our Artillery open a heavy bombardment which lasts until 6.15 a.m. when the enemy retaliate with 4" M.M. shells	
"	"	"	During the night our M.G's fire on German Second line wire.	
"	2/3 (cont.)	11 a.m.	Four of our guns then fire on enemy wire to prevent its being repaired. Firing continues until the haze clears away.	
"	"	2 p.m.	Enemy open a heavy bombardment with large calibre shells on our front and support lines. This continues with varying intensity until 4.30 p.m. Considerable damage is done to our Redeye St and Seaforth trenches, two brust stoves being blown	

2449 Wt. W14957/M90 750,000 1/16 J.B.C. & A. Forms/C.2118/12.

Army Form C. 2118.

WAR DIARY
or
INTELLIGENCE SUMMARY
(Erase heading not required.)

Instructions regarding War Diaries and Intelligence Summaries are contained in F. S. Regs., Part II. and the Staff Manual respectively. Title Pages will be prepared in manuscript.

Place	Date	Hour	Summary of Events and Information	Remarks and references to Appendices
AUCHONVILLERS	8/3 (cont'd)	4 pm	Our Essex Street trench is rendered untenable owing to the damage caused.	
"	"	5.30 pm	A huge fire is observed on our right	
"	"	4 pm to 10 pm	All our machine guns co-operate with the Artillery in concentrating fire upon the enemy's lines.	
"	"	Night	During the night four of our guns fire on enemy's second line wire and also on gap to right of BEAUMONT HAMEL	

Army Form C. 2118.

WAR DIARY
or
INTELLIGENCE SUMMARY

(Erase heading not required.)

Instructions regarding War Diaries and Intelligence Summaries are contained in F. S. Regs., Part II. and the Staff Manual respectively. Title Pages will be prepared in manuscript.

Place	Date	Hour	Summary of Events and Information	Remarks and references to Appendices
AUCHONVILLERS	4	4.30 am	The enemy bombard the right of our Sector with heavy shells.	
—	—	5 am – 6.15 am	Our guns co-operate with the Artillery in concentrating fire upon the enemy lines. As soon as fire is opened four red rockets are sent up from rear of enemy lines.	
—	—	6 am	Our Artillery are very active and in retaliation enemy heavily bombard our right doing considerable damage.	
—	—	10 am	White City is shelled by heavy guns. No damage. During the day dug out at our 20.9 gun was blown in and one casualty caused. Damage was also done to the trench.	
—	—	10.30 pm	Our Artillery heavily shell the enemy's lines. Enemy retaliated with 44 m.m. shells.	

2449 Wt. W14957/M90 750,000 1/16 J.B.C. & A. Forms/C.2118/12.

WAR DIARY
or
INTELLIGENCE SUMMARY
(Erase heading not required.)

Army Form C. 2118.

Place	Date	Hour	Summary of Events and Information	Remarks and references to Appendices
AUCHONVILLERS	25	—	During the early morning our 86 Trench was shelled with accuracy by the enemy and he is evidently registering thereon. Our guns fired during the morning to prevent the enemy repairing his wire. Bursts of fire were continued until the haze cleared away.	
"	"	5.30 a.m	Our Artillery bombarded the enemy's lines. Retaliation was only slight.	
"	"	Day	Artillery on both sides shelled intermittently during the day.	
"	"	3 p.m to 4 p.m	The enemy shell the White City causing considerable damage to FORTH AVENUE trench on each side of and in the neighbourhood of our gun position there.	
"	"	4.30 p.m to 6.30 p.m	The enemy shell along 86 TRENCH and afterwards in the WHITE CITY causing great damage to the trench in the immediate vicinity of our KING STREET GUN position.	
"	"	4.30 p.m to 10 p.m	White City is shelled	

WAR DIARY
or
INTELLIGENCE SUMMARY

(Erase heading not required.)

Army Form C. 2118.

Instructions regarding War Diaries and Intelligence Summaries are contained in F. S. Regs., Part II. and the Staff Manual respectively. Title Pages will be prepared in manuscript.

Place	Date	Hour	Summary of Events and Information	Remarks and references to Appendices
MEHONVILLERS	26	Night	Owing to various working parties out in front only 1000 rounds SAA are fired.	
		5 am to 6 am	Each machine gun fired in bursts during lulls in Artillery fire.	
		6 am to 4.30 am	The enemy retaliate with 5.9's on our FOURTH AVENUE Gun position.	
		—	During the remainder of the morning firing is carried on spasmodically by both sides	
		3 p.m.	A squadron of enemy aeroplanes engages with ours and several duels take place, the result being that at about 3.30 p.m. three of ours are forced to descend inside our lines. Two enemy planes are brought down in our lines, one being partially in flames.	
		6 p.m.	Our Artillery bombard the enemy lines with shells and mortars	
		6.30 p.m.	Enemy retaliate a number of shells falling in the vicinity of the White b.h.	

(Cont.)

Army Form C. 2118.

WAR DIARY
or
INTELLIGENCE SUMMARY
(Erase heading not required.)

Instructions regarding War Diaries and Intelligence Summaries are contained in F. S. Regs., Part II. and the Staff Manual respectively. Title Pages will be prepared in manuscript.

Place	Date	Hour	Summary of Events and Information	Remarks and references to Appendices
AUCHONVILLERS	26 (cont'd)	8pm to 8.45	The enemy send over some heavy shells round the trolley line in rear of WHITE CITY.	
"	-	-	During the night 2000 rounds are fired from the KING STREET and 86 TRENCH guns.	
"	27	5 am to 6.15 a.m.	All our guns fire in bursts during lulls in artillery fire.	
"	"	11 am	Enemy shell AUCHONVILLERS for about half an hour	
"	"	12.30 pm	Fourth Avenue and neighbouring trenches are heavily shelled	
"	"	2 pm	Our field guns shoot considerable activity. Shortly after the enemy put a heavy barrage on FOURTH AVENUE and thence on to the TROLLEY LINE in the rear of the WHITE CITY.	
"	"	3.30 pm	The enemy lift their barrage further back on to 86 TRENCH, doing some damage to the trench and destroying two recently made M.G. emplacements.	
"	"	4 pm	During to heavy shelling the FOURTH AVENUE GUN is withdrawn	
"	"	5.15 pm Night	Gun at 86 TRENCH is withdrawn to one of the newly made emplacements. Our M.G's fire intermittent on BEAUCOURT ROAD and STATION ROAD	

WAR DIARY
or
INTELLIGENCE SUMMARY
(Erase heading not required.)

Army Form C. 2118.

Place	Date	Hour	Summary of Events and Information	Remarks and references to Appendices
	26	—	During the early part of the morning the enemy are fairly active putting some heavy shells into the WHITE CITY and AUCHONVILLERS till about 10.30 a.m.	
		11 a.m.	Enemy searches Essex Street and continues active until noon.	
		Noon	Gun in fort over to the enemy trenches and into BEAUMONT HAMEL. His artillery immediately ceases. Two shells fall in the vicinity of FOURTH AVENUE but nothing more is observed till about 3.30 p.m. when some heavies are heard passing overhead in the direction of AUCHONVILLERS and MAILLY MAILLET.	
		Noon to 3 p.m.	We search with M.G. fire WAGON and STATION ROADS in order to catch any parties of men who might be leaving the trenches. We also search his trenches and the steep ground behind the village. 10000 rounds S.A.A. are expended.	
		—	Late in the afternoon the enemy artillery become active and send over some heavies apparently searching for the batteries behind AUCHONVILLERS.	
		6 – 7	Enemy put some shells along 88 TRENCH towards its junction with SECOND AVENUE, a 5.9 landing on Battalion Hqrs — now used as Coy Hqrs — and bursting on the dug out but causing no injuries.	
		Night	From the KING STREET gun we fire 2000 rounds into the enemy 2nd line wire	

Army Form C. 2118.

WAR DIARY
or
INTELLIGENCE SUMMARY
(Erase heading not required.)

Instructions regarding War Diaries and Intelligence Summaries are contained in F. S. Regs., Part II. and the Staff Manual respectively. Title Pages will be prepared in manuscript.

Place	Date	Hour	Summary of Events and Information	Remarks and references to Appendices
	29	5 am to 6.15	We co-operate with the Artillery in keeping up a continuous fire on the enemy trenches.	
		—	During the early part of the morning our Artillery bombard the enemy lines for over an hour. Very little retaliation follows. Later in the morning the enemy send over some heavy shells in the direction of AUCHONVILLERS and also to the rear of it.	
		2 pm to 2.30	The enemy artillery does considerable damage to the trench by our KING ST. Gun position and destroys a quantity of machine gun equipment.	
		5.20 to 6 pm	The enemy subject 66 and 68 TRENCHES to heavy artillery fire, much damage being done.	
		—	At intervals during the night artillery is active on both sides.	
		—	Continuously throughout the night our machine guns fire on enemy second and third line wire opposite Divisional sector.	
	30	5 am to 6.15 am	The usual co-operation with our Artillery is carried out from 5 am to 6.15 am, our machine guns firing in bursts during lulls in the Artillery fire. 12,500 rounds SAA are expended in all.	

Army Form C. 2118.

WAR DIARY
or
INTELLIGENCE SUMMARY

(Erase heading not required.)

Instructions regarding War Diaries and Intelligence Summaries are contained in F. S. Regs., Part II. and the Staff Manual respectively. Title Pages will be prepared in manuscript.

Place	Date	Hour	Summary of Events and Information	Remarks and references to Appendices
	30 (cont)	—	Owing to the inclemency of the weather very few shells came over until late in the morning.	
		12 noon	The enemy again shell 86 and 88 trenches with 5.9's and seems to concentrate his fire (as he did the day before) more especially at the junction of SECOND AVENUE and 88 TRENCH. Damage is done to the trenches.	
		12.45	Our howitzers retaliate whereupon the enemy cease.	
		2-3 pm	Our field guns are extremely active on to the enemy lines.	
		4.30 pm	The enemy send heavies on to SECOND AVENUE. At this time the company is relieved and proceeds to RAINCHEVAL.	
RAINCHEVAL	31	—	Company clean up clothing and equipment.	

Sm Birlayh Lieut
for Officer Commanding
154th M.G. Coy

Army Form C. 2118.

WAR DIARY
or
INTELLIGENCE SUMMARY.
(Erase heading not required.)

Confidential

Original War Diary of 154th Coy. M.G.C.

From 1/11/16 to 30/11/16

Army Form C. 2118.

WAR DIARY
or
INTELLIGENCE SUMMARY.
(Erase heading not required.)

Instructions regarding War Diaries and Intelligence Summaries are contained in F. S. Regs., Part II. and the Staff Manual respectively. Title pages will be prepared in manuscript.

Place	Date	Hour	Summary of Events and Information	Remarks and references to Appendices
RAINCHEVAL	Nov 1916 1	9 a.m.	Physical training	
		10 a.m.	C.O's Inspection	
		10.30 a.m.	Cleaning of guns and equipment.	S/Lt L^ns
	2	9-12	Cleaning of guns and equipment	AR
	3	9 a.m.	Physical training	
		10 a.m.	C.O's inspection	AR
		10.30	Cleaning of guns and equipment	

Army Form C. 2118.

WAR DIARY
or
INTELLIGENCE SUMMARY.
(Erase heading not required.)

Instructions regarding War Diaries and Intelligence Summaries are contained in F. S. Regs., Part II. and the Staff Manual respectively. Title pages will be prepared in manuscript.

Place	Date	Hour	Summary of Events and Information	Remarks and references to Appendices
AUCHONVILLERS	4	9 a.m.	Company moves from RAINCHÉVAL to the trenches	
"	"	4.30 p.m.	Our Artillery conduct a thirty minutes bombardment. The enemy retaliate vigorously on ESSEX TRENCH, 86 and 88 TRENCHES, WHITE CITY, and AUCHONVILLERS.	
"	"	—	There is much aerial activity by our planes during the afternoon.	Ap.
"	"	6 p.m.	The enemy are very active with minenwerfers	
"	"	8.30 p.m.	3 Red Rockets are observed on our right. Nothing follows.	
"	"	9.30 p.m. 10.30 p.m.	The enemy send over shells on to 86 and 88 trenches.	
"	"	—	During the night we fire 3250 rounds on enemy second line wire.	
"	5	—	Morning very quiet	
"	"	3.30 p.m.	Enemy send over about forty 4.2's by WHITE CITY and in front of 86 TRENCH	Ap.
"	"	—	Evening very quiet	
"	"	—	From dusk till midnight we fired on enemy wire and on to WAGGON RD.	

WAR DIARY
or
INTELLIGENCE SUMMARY.
(Erase heading not required.)

Army Form C. 2118.

Place	Date	Hour	Summary of Events and Information	Remarks and references to Appendices
AUCHONVILLERS	6	—	From midnight to dawn we fire on enemy wire expending in all during the night 9250 rounds S.A.A.	
"	"	10.45 A.M.	Enemy shell LANDWITH TRENCH and ALBERT TRENCH.	
"	"	1 PM to 1.15 PM	Our Artillery heavily bombard the enemy lines.	
"	"	Afternoon	SECOND AVENUE is shelled and MINENWERFERS put into SEAFORTH TRENCH. Some damage being done. Several enemy observation balloons are seen	
"	"	3.30 P.M.	The enemy shell AUCHONVILLERS.	
"	"	10-11 P.M.	A large fire is observed. The direction appears to be about 5 miles southwards. Shortly afterwards three large explosions are heard behind our lines.	
"	"	Night	During the night our machine guns fire 23500 rounds S.A.A. on to enemy wire, covering the whole Divisional front. Firing is also carried out on to WAGGON ROAD and STATION ROAD	R.W.

Army Form C. 2118.

WAR DIARY
or
INTELLIGENCE SUMMARY.
(Erase heading not required.)

Instructions regarding War Diaries and Intelligence Summaries are contained in F. S. Regs., Part II. and the Staff Manual respectively. Title pages will be prepared in manuscript.

Place	Date	Hour	Summary of Events and Information	Remarks and references to Appendices
AUCHONVILLERS	4	12.40 P.M.	A corporal reports that he saw a zeppelin returning over to the enemy lines, going very slowly and flying low.	
"	"	Forenoon	Enemy is comparatively quiet	
"	"	Noon	Enemy shells WHITE CITY with "whiz-bangs" from a battery which appears to be very close.	
"	"	after noon	Both ours and the enemy Artillery are active.	
"	"	5.45 P.M.	Our Artillery bombards the enemy's lines heavily for about half an hour. Our machine guns co-operate according to scheme, firing 28,500 rounds during the night. Enemy retaliation is slight at first on 88 TRENCH front and support lines. Later enemy shell 88 TRENCH with 6.9's, also communication trenches - especially SECOND AVENUE. This is continued up to 11 p.m. and considerable damage is done including the burying of a gun and tripod.	G.W.

Army Form C. 2118.

WAR DIARY
or
INTELLIGENCE SUMMARY.
(Erase heading not required.)

Instructions regarding War Diaries and Intelligence Summaries are contained in F. S. Regs., Part II. and the Staff Manual respectively. Title pages will be prepared in manuscript.

Place	Date	Hour	Summary of Events and Information	Remarks and references to Appendices
AUCHONVILLERS	8 Nov	Night	Our machine guns fire on enemy Second Line Wire.	
"	"	A.M.	Enemy send over a number of shells at various points without inflicting much damage.	
"	"	3.30 PM to 5.30 PM	Enemy shell AUCHONVILLERS every two minutes with 4.9 in. ∞	
"	"	5.30 PM to 6.30 PM	Enemy shell AUCHONVILLERS intermittently.	
"	"	—	Artillery (ours) carry out some wire cutting during the day	
"	"	Night	Our machine guns fire on enemy Second Line Wire, Tracks, and WAGGON ROAD firing in all 21,000 rounds S.A.A.	W.R.
"	9	11.30 AM	Enemy shell TRENCH 88 with shells of various calibres	
"	"	Afternoon	Our Artillery are active	
"	"	3.30 PM to 5 PM	A large number of long range shells are sent over by the enemy	
"	"	6 PM.	Our Artillery open a short bombardment on enemy lines to our left.	K.R.

Army Form C. 2118.

WAR DIARY
or
INTELLIGENCE SUMMARY.
(Erase heading not required.)

Place	Date	Hour	Summary of Events and Information	Remarks and references to Appendices
AUCHONVILLERS	9 (Con/d)	—	There is much aerial activity during the day. German planes attempt to cross our lines but are pursued away by 11 of our own. During the afternoon the enemy has 11 Observation Balloons up.	
"	"	9 p.m.	An aeroplane is heard coming from the German lines and passes over ours. It can be heard flying about for 15 minutes.	WK.
"	10	midnight to 2 A.M.	The enemy fire a number of gas shells to our right. Some however land near our gun positions but a favourable wind disperses the clouds of gas.	
"	"	night	Our machine guns fire in enemy second line wire and Waggon Road. 19500 rounds SAA are fired in all	
"	"	—	Our Artillery is fairly active during the day. Enemy retaliate, shelling AUCHONVILLERS and the vicinity of ST JOHN'S ROAD	WT
"	"	afternoon		
"	"	10 PM to 12 midnight	Enemy shell AUCHONVILLERS and positions behind with gas and tear shells necessitating the use of respirator.	
"	"	9.30 P.M.	Aerial motors are heard and antiaircraft shells are seen bursting behind our lines	

Army Form C. 2118.

WAR DIARY
or
INTELLIGENCE SUMMARY.
(Erase heading not required.)

Instructions regarding War Diaries and Intelligence Summaries are contained in F. S. Regs., Part II. and the Staff Manual respectively. Title pages will be prepared in manuscript.

Place	Date	Hour	Summary of Events and Information	Remarks and references to Appendices
AUCHONVILLERS	11	Night	Our machine guns fire 32,450 rounds during the night on to LEAVE TRENCH, enemy 2nd line wire, and tracks and roads behind the lines.	
"	"	"	Enemy machine guns are active	
"	"	12 mid night to 1.30 AM	Enemy shell gun positions behind AUCHONVILLERS with gas and tear shells.	
"	"	2AM to 6AM	AUCHONVILLERS is shelled with gas shells.	
"	"	—	Our machine guns are active both day and night owing to misty weather.	
"	"	—	24,000 rounds S.A.A. are fired in all.	
"	"	—	Our Artillery are active during the morning & afternoon	R.T.
AUCHONVILLERS	12	"	General Artillery activity during day	
"	"	2 p.m.	Enemy shell Whites trench and Auchonvillers with 5.9's	
"	"	Night	Our machine guns fire 21,000 rounds on enemy second line wire	R.T.

Army Form C. 2118.

Instructions regarding War Diaries and Intelligence Summaries are contained in F. S. Regs., Part II. and the Staff Manual respectively. Title pages will be prepared in manuscript.

WAR DIARY
or
INTELLIGENCE SUMMARY.
(Erase heading not required.)

Place	Date	Hour	Summary of Events and Information	Remarks and references to Appendices
AUCHONVILLERS BEAUMONT HAMEL	Nov 1931 to 19th	—	It is stated that one of the reasons for the failure of the attack on Beaumont Hamel on 1st July was that an intense machine gun fire was opened on our troops advancing over the enemy front lines. This fire came from the high ground behind BEAUMONT-HAMEL which was outside the British artillery barrage line. The success of the recent attack depended to a considerable extent on these guns being kept out of action, so it was decided to cover the whole ridge with intense machine gun fire from the rear British lines from zero hour, and to lift in four phases until the ultimate objective was attained. In this case machine guns were the most suitable weapon to knock out or keep under the enemy guns as it was supposed — and this has subsequently been proved, that the enemy guns on the ridge were not in covered emplacements against which machine gun fire would be comparatively useless, but were concealed in shell holes and by natural features on the ground. Positions were chosen several days in advance for guns of the	

Army Form C. 2118.

WAR DIARY
or
INTELLIGENCE SUMMARY.
(Erase heading not required.)

Instructions regarding War Diaries and Intelligence Summaries are contained in F. S. Regs., Part II. and the Staff Manual respectively. Title pages will be prepared in manuscript.

Place	Date	Hour	Summary of Events and Information	Remarks and references to Appendices
BEAUMONT-HAMEL	13th to 14th (contd)		Division and these were placed for the most part in the British third line; sixteen guns of the 154 M G Coy being in the centre and responsible in the first phase for the lower slopes of the ridge immediately behind BEAUMONT-HAMEL from where the most fire was expected and where enemy machine guns had already been located. The margin of safety over the heads of our own troops being extremely small a great deal of work had to be put in on the emplacements so that cocking of the tripods might be avoided, vibration reduced to a minimum and general stability increased to the maximum under the circumstances. The establishment of a machine gun Coy provides four French mountings which are very stable and give the maximum of accuracy for overhead or indirect fire, and these were of the greatest use. It was hoped to register the guns on Y day but this was found impossible - except in one case - owing to unfavourable weather conditions.	B.D.

2353 Wt. W2544/1454 700,000 5/15 D. D. & L. A.D.S.S./Forms/C. 2118.

Army Form C. 2118.

WAR DIARY
or
INTELLIGENCE SUMMARY.
(Erase heading not required.)

Instructions regarding War Diaries and Intelligence Summaries are contained in F. S. Regs., Part II. and the Staff Manual respectively. Title pages will be prepared in manuscript.

Place	Date	Hour	Summary of Events and Information	Remarks and references to Appendices
BEAUMONT HAMEL	Nov 13th to 14th (contd.)	—	On zero day fire was carried out according to scheme and — as far as the 154th Coy was concerned — without a hitch. The first two phases continued for 40 minutes, and, during this time, not a single enemy machine gun came into action along the Divisional front with the exception of advanced line positions which were not covered by our fire. This is confirmed by the Infantry. According to scheme, the guns were out of action for 1 hour and 10 minutes, and during this time several enemy guns came into action, but these were silenced when the third phase began and our guns lifted on to the top of the ridge. After the capture of BEAUMONT HAMEL a considerable quantity of machine gun equipment and belt boxes were found scattered along the ridge. Prisoners also state that they found it impossible to leave BEAUMONT-HAMEL owing to the machine gun barrage. On the night of zero day when our troops were occupying a hastily dug	[signature]

2353 Wt. W2544/1454 700,000 5/15 D.D.&L. A.D.S.S./Forms/C. 2118.

Army Form C. 2118.

WAR DIARY
or
INTELLIGENCE SUMMARY.
(Erase heading not required.)

Instructions regarding War Diaries and Intelligence Summaries are contained in F. S. Regs., Part II. and the Staff Manual respectively. Title pages will be prepared in manuscript.

Place	Date	Hour	Summary of Events and Information	Remarks and references to Appendices
BEAUMONT-HAMEL	Nov 13th to 14th	—	line beyond BEAUMONT-HAMEL a barrage was ordered by the Brigade 450 yards in advance of our line to keep down possibility of a counter-attack. In fifteen minutes this line was under barrage fire which was continued throughout the night. This fire was probably a greater deterrent to the enemy than a shrapnel barrage would have been, and it was maintained for twelve hours without intermission. This was possible owing to the large number of guns – 16 in action – and to the comparative smallness of the Divisional front. In general it was thought these operations have conclusively demonstrated the efficacy of machine gun fire for barrage purposes. Sufficient time for preparation however, must be available in order to make thoroughly stable positions for the mountings, otherwise such a margin of safety has to be allowed that it is impossible to barrage at all closely to our own troops.	W.B.

Army Form C. 2118.

WAR DIARY
or
INTELLIGENCE SUMMARY.
(Erase heading not required.)

Instructions regarding War Diaries and Intelligence Summaries are contained in F. S. Regs., Part II. and the Staff Manual respectively. Title pages will be prepared in manuscript.

Place	Date	Hour	Summary of Events and Information	Remarks and references to Appendices
BEAUMONT HAMEL	Nov 13th to 17th	—	Until comparatively recently any kind of machine gun fire over the heads of our own troops was disliked by the Infantry, partly no doubt owing to the fact that they were unaccustomed to it and also unfortunately owing to casualties having been caused by inaccurate fire. This feeling on the part of the Infantry has now disappeared and, on the contrary, those of the Infantry to whom we have spoken since the attack, say that — quite apart from the actual help they received — the great volume of machine gun fire overhead gave them considerable confidence.	ST6
"	18th	—	Several artillery activity during day.	KN
"	19th	11 am	152 M G Coy relieve 154 M G Coy.	
MAILLY WOOD		12 noon	154 Coy proceed to bivouacs at MAILLY WOOD	ST6

Army Form C. 2118.

WAR DIARY
or
INTELLIGENCE SUMMARY.
(Erase heading not required.)

Instructions regarding War Diaries and Intelligence Summaries are contained in F. S. Regs., Part II and the Staff Manual respectively. Title pages will be prepared in manuscript.

Place	Date	Hour	Summary of Events and Information	Remarks and references to Appendices
MAILLY WOOD	Nov 20	—	Cleaning of clothes and equipment	5¾
"	21	—	Cleaning of guns and equipment & 60's Inspection	5¾
"	22	9 AM	Physical Training	
		10.15 AM	60's Inspection	
		10.30 AM	Immediate action & mechanism	5¾
VARENNES	23	9 AM	Company moves to new billets at VARENNES	5¾
PUSHEVILLERS	24	9.15 AM	Company moves to new billets at PUSHEVILLERS	5¾
"	25	9 AM	Cleaning guns and Immediate Action	5¾
		10.30 AM		
"	"	11 AM	Two Sections are attached to 153 MG Coy, proceeding to VARENNES	
"	"	11-12.30	Mechanism	
		2-3 pm	Filling belts and cleaning equipment	

2353 Wt. W2514/1454 700,000 5/15 D. D. & L. A.D.S.S./Forms/C. 2118.

Army Form C. 2118.

WAR DIARY
or
INTELLIGENCE SUMMARY.
(Erase heading not required.)

Instructions regarding War Diaries and Intelligence Summaries are contained in F. S. Regs., Part II. and the Staff Manual respectively. Title pages will be prepared in manuscript.

Place	Date	Hour	Summary of Events and Information	Remarks and references to Appendices
PUSHEVILLERS	Nov 26	11 AM	Company proceed to Bromwell Huts, AVELUY. (W17 b.o.8 - Sheet 57D)	WM
(Sheet 57D W17 S.O.8) AVELUY	27	9 AM	Filling Belts and re-packing limbers	WM
Sheet 57D W.18	28	9 AM	Company remove to Ouillers Huts	WM
"	"	2.30 PM	Inspection of Rifles and improving paths around billets. Filling Belts	
"	29	8.45 AM	Inspection of Rifles	WM
"	"	9 AM to 10.30 AM	Cleaning of guns and equipments Mechanism (draft men).	
"	"	10.45 AM to 12.30 AM	Immediate Action	
"	"	2.30 PM	Improving paths around billets. Filling Belts.	

Army Form C. 2118.

WAR DIARY
or
INTELLIGENCE SUMMARY.
(Erase heading not required.)

Instructions regarding War Diaries and Intelligence Summaries are contained in F. S. Regs., Part II. and the Staff Manual respectively. Title pages will be prepared in manuscript.

Place	Date	Hour	Summary of Events and Information	Remarks and references to Appendices
West of D W18	Nov 30	9 A.M.	Feet Rubbing	
"	"	9 A.M.	Inspection	
"	"	9.15 to 12.30	Cleaning Ammunition & Refilling Belts	
"	"	3.30 P.M.	Bath parade	

W. A. White
2nd Officer Comdg.
154 M. G. Coy

Vol 12.   154/51

154 Coy. M.G.C.

December 1916

Army Form C. 2118.

WAR DIARY
or
INTELLIGENCE SUMMARY.
(Erase heading not required.)

Instructions regarding War Diaries and Intelligence Summaries are contained in F. S. Regs., Part II. and the Staff Manual respectively. Title pages will be prepared in manuscript.

Place	Date	Hour	Summary of Events and Information	Remarks and references to Appendices
W.18 Ovillers huts	Dec 1	9 AM	Inspection	
		9.15 AM to 10.30	Cleaning guns and equipment	
		10.30 to 12.30	Fatigue	
	2	9 AM	Inspection	
		9.15 to 10.30	Cleaning guns, equipment & ammunition	
		10.30 to 12.30	Relaying trench boards and building cookhouses. Teams 1-6 proceed to line	
	3	9 AM	Blankets rolled	
		noon	Teams 7-12 proceed to trenches. Teams 13-29 proceed to barracks. Holiday this Avine.	
		4.57 PM	Our right group of indirect fire guns is shelled heavily. Night 5000 rounds are fired on to enemy tracks & roads.	

Army Form C. 2118.

WAR DIARY
or
INTELLIGENCE SUMMARY.
(Erase heading not required.)

Instructions regarding War Diaries and Intelligence Summaries are contained in F. S. Regs., Part II. and the Staff Manual respectively. Title pages will be prepared in manuscript.

Place	Date	Hour	Summary of Events and Information	Remarks and references to Appendices
R.29 Central	4	Morning	Considerable aerial activity. Several planes try to cross our lines but are quickly driven back.	
		2.30 p.m.	Report from gun team in position on ridge to right of 10th Avenue that a "pip squeak" battery which fired a salvo every hour on to the ridge (from the direction of the centre of LOUPART WOOD) ceased fire when our howrs opened on LOUPART WOOD.	
		Night	Night firing is carried out as usual on to the East and West MIRAUMONT ROADS and tracks behind the German lines. Bursts of fire were also carried out during the afternoon. 10000 rounds fired in all. Work done. Emplacements & Shelters built. Trenches cleared. A telephone line laid between guns in KENORA TRENCH and bmy Headquarters	

WAR DIARY
or
INTELLIGENCE SUMMARY.

(Erase heading not required.)

Army Form C. 2118.

Place	Date	Hour	Summary of Events and Information	Remarks and references to Appendices
R29E4d	5	—	Past 24 hours have been very quiet. Enemy	
		Night	During the night our machine guns fire on enemy tracks & roads	
	6	9 P.M	Enemy send up thin red rockets from the direction of LE SARS	
		Night	9170 rounds are fired during the night on to outskirts of PYS and MIRAUMONT and tracks behind the line. Work done. Several alternative emplacements strongly sheltered erected, trenches revetted and cleared	
	7	—	Past 24 hours quiet	
		4.15PM	Enemy shell ALBERT-BAPAUME ROAD near POZIERES.	
		Night	6770 rounds are fired during the night on to tracks & communication trenches in the enemy's lines.	

Army Form C. 2118.

WAR DIARY
or
INTELLIGENCE SUMMARY.
(Erase heading not required.)

Place	Date	Hour	Summary of Events and Information	Remarks and references to Appendices
R 29 Central	8	—	General artillery activity during day.	
		6-7pm	Enemy artillery very active. Between 6 & 7pm the Sunken Road and ground behind R 29 Central is shelled intermittently. During the night our machine guns fire 10000 rounds on to German reserve line, communication trenches and roads around PYS and MIRAUMONT.	MB
	9	Day	Remainder of "B" Coy in line are relieved from trenches	
AVELUY WOLSELEY HUTS	10	1pm	"B" Company remove to reserve billets at BOUZINCOURT	
BOUZINCOURT	11	9:00 AM	C.O's Inspection	
		10 - 12.30	Overhauling guns and equipment.	
		1.45	Bath Parade.	

Army Form C. 2118.

WAR DIARY
or
INTELLIGENCE SUMMARY.
(Erase heading not required.)

Instructions regarding War Diaries and Intelligence Summaries are contained in F. S. Regs., Part II. and the Staff Manual respectively. Title pages will be prepared in manuscript.

Place	Date	Hour	Summary of Events and Information	Remarks and references to Appendices
BOUZINCOURT	Dec 12	9:30 AM	CO's Inspection.	
		10 AM to 12:30	Cleaning gun equipment &c	
"	13	9:30 AM	CO's Inspection	
		9:45 AM to 12:30	Belt filling and cleaning ammunition	
"	14	9:30 AM	CO's Inspection	
		9:45 AM	Route march	
		2 PM to 3 PM	Belt filling	
"	15	9:30 AM	CO's Inspection	
		9:45 AM to 12:30	Cleaning Equipment and packing limbers	

Army Form C. 2118.

WAR DIARY
or
INTELLIGENCE SUMMARY.
(Erase heading not required.)

Instructions regarding War Diaries and Intelligence Summaries are contained in F. S. Regs., Part II. and the Staff Manual respectively. Title pages will be prepared in manuscript.

Place	Date	Hour	Summary of Events and Information	Remarks and references to Appendices
WOLSELEY HUTS AVELUY	16	10AM	Company moves from BOUZINCOURT to WOLSELEY HUTS, AVELUY.	
"	17	9AM to 12.30	Cleaning surroundings of huts and laying trench boards.	
		3.30PM	C.O's Inspection.	
"	18	9AM	M.O's inspection	
		9.15AM	Fatigues	
		9.45AM	Rangefinders parade.	
"	19	7.60AM	1 Officer & N.C.O & 18 men proceed as fatigue party to trenches	
		9.30AM	C.O's Inspection	
		9.45AM	Overhauling gun equipment, filling belts, & cleaning ammunition.	

Army Form C. 2118.

WAR DIARY
or
INTELLIGENCE SUMMARY.
(Erase heading not required.)

Instructions regarding War Diaries and Intelligence Summaries are contained in F. S. Regs., Part II. and the Staff Manual respectively. Title pages will be prepared in manuscript.

Place	Date	Hour	Summary of Events and Information	Remarks and references to Appendices
WOLESEY HUTS AVELUY	20	9.30am	Inspection of Respirators	
"	"	1pm	Company relieves 153rd bn in line	
R29 Central	"	Night	During the night roads and tracks behind the enemy's line are searched. Also frequent bursts are fired on the trolley line at R11B. Rounds fired 4000	
R29 Central	21	Morning	Two enemy planes are brought down by our anti-aircraft guns.	
"	"	Night	During the night our machine guns fire 5000 rounds on to roads and tracks behind the enemy line. Frequent bursts are also fired on to crescent trench and the trolley line in R11B.	
"	"		Work done. Trenches cleared and trench boards laid. Material for shelter carried up to No.1 gun position. Telephone wire re-laid to KENORA TRENCH	

WAR DIARY
or
INTELLIGENCE SUMMARY.
(Erase heading not required.)

Army Form C. 2118.

Place	Date	Hour	Summary of Events and Information	Remarks and references to Appendices
R 29 bet 4	22	—	Artillery activity normal.	
"	"	12 noon to 2 p.m.	Enemy search Artillery Lane with Field and Heavy Guns.	JB
"	"	After noon	During the afternoon and evening COURCELETTE, THE VALLEY, and positions in front of our left barrage guns are heavily shelled with 5.9's.	
"	"	Night	Work done. Work started on trench and shelter at No.1 Gun position. Trench cleared at No. 6 and 7 positions. Small supply of S.A.A. and Bombs carried up to 1 2 3 4 5 positions.	
"	23	Night	During the night of 22/23rd our machine guns expend 5000 rounds. — Targets engaged, — East and West.	
"	"	4 AM to 9 AM	MIRAUMONT ROADS and CREST TRENCH. COURCELETTE is heavily shelled. THE VALLEY is also steadily bombarded from 8 AM to 1 P.M.	JB
"	"	2.45 PM to 3.36 PM	Enemy shell the QUARRIES and battery positions to the left of Bde Hqrs with 5.9's.	

Cont⁺

WAR DIARY
or
INTELLIGENCE SUMMARY.
(Erase heading not required.)

Army Form C. 2118.

Place	Date	Hour	Summary of Events and Information	Remarks and references to Appendices
R29 Cent.	23	Night 10 pm	Our machine guns fire 6000 rounds upon roads, tracks and communication trenches behind the enemy lines, also upon the trolley line at R11.B. Work done carrying up of material for No.1 position completed. Further supply of reserve S.A.A. and bombs carried to gun positions in Kenora Trench. In the other gun positions the teams are only able to keep down the water, owing to the flooded state of the ground.	
"	24	Day	Enemy artillery less active. Some aerial activity on both sides.	
"	"	Night	Our machine guns expend 5000 rounds on East and West MIRAUMONT ROADS and MIRAUMONT TRENCH. Work done Sap dug for new shelter at No.1 position. Sandbags & material carried up to KENORA and 4 & 5 positions in DESIRE TRENCH.	

Army Form C. 2118.

WAR DIARY
or
INTELLIGENCE SUMMARY.
(Erase heading not required.)

Instructions regarding War Diaries and Intelligence Summaries are contained in F.S. Regs., Part II. and the Staff Manual respectively. Title pages will be prepared in manuscript.

Place	Date	Hour	Summary of Events and Information	Remarks and references to Appendices
Ragbenkal	25 Day		Enemy artillery active	
"	"	11 AM	Enemy shell COURCELETTE and Battery positions about R 29. with heavy guns.	JB
"	"	12 NOON	Our machine guns fire 8000 rounds SAA on to roads, tracks and communication trenches in enemy lines.	
"	"	Night	Work done. Clearing and re-building of trench at position 6 & 7.	
"	26 Day		Enemy artillery normal	JB
"	"	-	During afternoon and evening the boy is relieved by 152 M.G.boy. Proceed to billets at Wolseley Huts.	
WOLSELEY HUTS	2nd	10 AM	Feet Inspection	JB
"	"	-	During remainder of day men clean clothing and equipment	

WAR DIARY
or
INTELLIGENCE SUMMARY.
(Erase heading not required.)

Army Form C. 2118.

Place	Date	Hour	Summary of Events and Information	Remarks and references to Appendices
BOUZINCOURT	28	10 AM	Company remove to Billets at BOUZINCOURT.	B
"	29	9.30 AM	C O's Inspection	B
"	"	9.45 AM	Cleaning guns and equipment.	
"	"	10.45	Bathing parade	
"	"	2-3 p.m.	Cleaning guns and equipment	
"	30	9.30 a.m.	C.O.'s Inspection	B
"	"	9.45	Gas Helmet Drill	
"	"	10.30	Cleaning Guns & Equipment	
"	"	2-3	Route March	
"	31	a.m.	Church Parade	B

Ayleigh Bow M,
for Officer Commanding
154th M.G. Company

On His Majesty's Service.

154th Machine Gun Company.

January 1917.

WAR DIARY
or
INTELLIGENCE SUMMARY.
(Erase heading not required.)

Army Form C. 2118.

CONFIDENTIAL
No 21(A)
HIGHLAND
DIVISION

CONFIDENTIAL

ORIGINAL
WAR DIARY
of
154TH COY M.G.C.
From 1/1/17 To 31/1/17
Vol I

Army Form C. 2118.

WAR DIARY
or
INTELLIGENCE SUMMARY.
(Erase heading not required.)

Instructions regarding War Diaries and Intelligence Summaries are contained in F. S. Regs., Part II. and the Staff Manual respectively. Title pages will be prepared in manuscript.

Place	Date	Hour	Summary of Events and Information	Remarks and references to Appendices
BOUZINCOURT	Jan. 1		C.O's Inspection	Egypt
BOUZINCOURT	Jan. 2	9.30 a.m. 9.45 to 10.30 2 pm to 3.	C.O's Inspection Belt filling & packing of Limbers Route March	Egypt
BOUZINCOURT	3	9.45 a.m.	Route March to billets at Wolseley Huts, Ovillers.	Egypt
OVILLERS	4	9.30 a.m. 9.45	C.O's Inspection Gun Cleaning Relaying of Trench Roads & Constructing of Beds.	Egypt
OVILLERS	5	9.30 a.m. 9.45 to 10.30	C.O's Inspection Improving of Billets.	Egypt
OVILLERS	6	9.30 a.m. 9.45	C.O's Inspection Immediate Action Construction of Beds.	Egypt

Army Form C. 2118.

WAR DIARY
or
INTELLIGENCE SUMMARY.
(Erase heading not required.)

Instructions regarding War Diaries and Intelligence Summaries are contained in F. S. Regs., Part II. and the Staff Manual respectively. Title pages will be prepared in manuscript.

Place	Date	Hour	Summary of Events and Information	Remarks and references to Appendices
OVILLERS	Jan 7		Divine Service	
R.29 CENTRAL	8	6:30 p.m.	Company relieves 153rd Company in line	
		NIGHT	Enemy artillery activity below normal. The night was very quiet. The usual night firing was carried on.	
R.29 Central	9	9:30 a.m.	Four enemy aeroplanes seen very high over their own lines	
			Work done :— Repairs to dug-out in R.29 Central and continuation of work on dug-out in Stenota trench and No.1 position.	
			Our artillery was very active during the day — enemy retaliation practically nil. The night was very quiet.	
		NIGHT	Machine Guns fired 5000 rounds during the night on to EAST & WEST MIRAUMONT ROADS and roads round PYS.	
R.29 Central	10		During the early hours of the morning we appeared to start a very heavy bombardment away to the left in the direction of BEAUMONT HAMEL.	
		NIGHT	Work done :— Entrance to deep dug-out at No.4 position cleared & deepened. Trench cleared & deeper.	

Army Form C. 2118.

WAR DIARY
or
INTELLIGENCE SUMMARY.
(Erase heading not required.)

Place	Date	Hour	Summary of Events and Information	Remarks and references to Appendices
R.29 Central	11	11 a.m.	Two German aeroplanes flew over our lines.	Appx
		4 p.m.	One German 'plane flew over our lines, the observer which fired his machine gun at the sunken road in R.29 Central.	
		NIGHT	Roads & tracks behind enemy lines were searched by our machine guns. Expenditure :- 6,000 rounds S.A.A.	
R.29 Central	12	6.30 a.m.	In cooperation with the machine gun company on our left we enfiladed a German communication trench in order to assist the 182nd Brigade to raid the enemy trenches. Expenditure - 4,000 rounds S.A.A.	Appx
		DAY	Very low visibility; hostile artillery activity normal. Quiet.	
		NIGHT	Our machine guns fired 6,000 rounds on to roads, tracks behind the line & enemy reserve line.	
		"	Work done:- NOT Trenches cleared of trench boards laid. Dug-outs cleaned of during the night. The company was relieved by the 7th Company moved to billets at RUBEMPRE.	
RUBEMPRE	13			Appx
DOMESMONT	14	9.30 a.m.	Company commences route march to DOMESMONT	Appx
NEUF MOULIN	15	9.30 a.m.	Whole Company proceeds by route march to NEUF MOULIN.	Appx

A.5834. Wt. W4973/M687 750,000 8/16 D. D. & L. Ltd. Forms/C.2118/13.

WAR DIARY
or
INTELLIGENCE SUMMARY.
(Erase heading not required.)

Army Form C. 2118.

Place	Date	Hour	Summary of Events and Information	Remarks and references to Appendices
NOLETTE	16	10 a.m.	Company marches to billets at NOLETTE	[sgd]
NOLETTE	17	9.30 a.m. 10 " 10.30 noon	C.O's Inspection Kit Inspection Gun Cleaning & N.C.O's parade Saluting Drill	[sgd]
Do.	18	9 a.m. 9.15 9.45 10.45 to 12.45	C.O's Inspection Saluting Drill Re-packing of kit bags Cleaning guns & equipment	[sgd]
Do.	19	9 a.m. 9.15 10.40 12.45	C.O's Inspection Squad Drill Cleaning of guns, etc.	[sgd]
Do.	20	8.45 a.m. 9.10 10.11 11 noon	C.O's Inspection Squad Drill Mechanism & Immediate action Gun Drill Physical Training	[sgd]

Army Form C. 2118.

WAR DIARY
or
INTELLIGENCE SUMMARY.
(Erase heading not required.)

Instructions regarding War Diaries and Intelligence Summaries are contained in F. S. Regs., Part II. and the Staff Manual respectively. Title pages will be prepared in manuscript.

Place	Date	Hour	Summary of Events and Information	Remarks and references to Appendices
NOLETTE	21		Sunday. Divine Services.	C of A
Do	22	8.45 a.m.	C.O.'s Inspection	C of A
		9.	Company Drill	
		10.	Immediate action	
		11.	Gun Drill	
		noon	Route March	
		2 p.m.	Communication Drill for N.C.O.'s	
Do	23	9 a.m.	C.O.'s Inspection	C of A
		9.15	Company Drill	
		noon	Stripping	
Do	24	9.30 a.m.	C.O.'s Inspection	C of A
		11	Inspection of Company by G.O.C.	
Do	25	9 a.m.	C.O.'s Inspection	C of A
		9.15	Company Drill	
		10	Gun "	
		11	Immediate Action	
		noon	Physical Training	

Army Form C. 2118.

WAR DIARY
or
INTELLIGENCE SUMMARY.
(Erase heading not required.)

Instructions regarding War Diaries and Intelligence Summaries are contained in F.S. Regs., Part II. and the Staff Manual respectively. Title pages will be prepared in manuscript.

Place	Date	Hour	Summary of Events and Information	Remarks and references to Appendices
NOLETTE	26	9 a.m.	C.O.'s Inspection	
		9.15	Company Drill	
		10 to 12.45	Extended Order Drill	
		2 "	Lecture to N.C.O.'s	
Do	27	9 a.m.	C.O.'s Inspection	
		9.30 to noon	"A" & "B" Sections Revolver Practice, etc.	
		"	"C" & "D" Gas Drill, Bomb throwing, Gun Laying, Indication & Recognition of Targets.	
		noon	Physical Training	
Do	28		Sunday 8.30 a.m. Batt. Parade Divine Services	
Do	29	9 a.m.	C.O.'s Inspection	
		9.15	Revolver Practice (Remainder of "A" & "B" Sections)	
		"	Route March ("C" & "D" & part of "A" Sections)	
		"	Gun Drill	
		12/10 p.m.	Physical Training	

A.5834 Wt.W4973/M687 750,000 8/16 D.D.&L.Ltd. Forms/C.2118/13.

Army Form C. 2118.

WAR DIARY
or
INTELLIGENCE SUMMARY.
(Erase heading not required.)

Instructions regarding War Diaries and Intelligence Summaries are contained in F.S. Regs., Part II. and the Staff Manual respectively. Title pages will be prepared in manuscript.

Place	Date	Hour	Summary of Events and Information	Remarks and references to Appendices
NOLETTE	30	9 a.m.	C.O.'s Inspection	J.O.M.A.
		9.15 to noon	C. & D. Lectures — Revolver Practice "A" & "B" — Gas Drill, Bomb Throwing, Gun Laying, Indication & Recognition of Targets. Physical Training.	
NOLETTE	31	9 a.m. to 1 p.m.	Recent Drafts — Range (Firing) Table "C". Remainder of Coy. — Tactical Handling.	J.O.M.A.

J.O. Hughes Lt
for Officer Commanding
164th Coy. M.G.C.

On His Majesty's Service.

154th Machine Gun Company

February 1917.

Army Form C. 2118.

WAR DIARY
or
INTELLIGENCE SUMMARY.
(Erase heading not required.)

Confidential

Original
WAR DIARY
of
154th Coy. M.G.C.
from 1/2/17 to 28/2/17
Vol 2

Army Form C. 2118.

WAR DIARY
or
INTELLIGENCE SUMMARY.
(Erase heading not required.)

Instructions regarding War Diaries and Intelligence Summaries are contained in F.S. Regs, Part II. and the Staff Manual respectively. Title pages will be prepared in manuscript.

Place	Date Feb.	Hour	Summary of Events and Information	Remarks and references to Appendices
NOLETTE	1	9 a.m. to 1 p.m. 9 to 12 12 to 1	Recent Drafts — Range Firing Table "C". Reminder of Coy. — Route March. Lecture to N.C.O's.	O.B.S.
NOLETTE	2	9 a.m. to 1 p.m. 9 a.m. 6 p.m.	Recent Drafts — Range Firing Table "C". Remainder — Tactical Scheme. C.O's Inspection. Lecture.	O.B.S.
NOLETTE	3	9 a.m. 9.15 a.m. to 1 p.m.	C.O's Inspection Recent Drafts — Range Firing Table "C" Remainder — Rolt Polling, Packing of Limbers, Gun Equipment Inspection.	O.B.S.
NOLETTE	4 SUN		Divine Services.	O.B.S.
NOLETTE	5	1.15 p.m.	Company proceed by route march to FOREST D'ABBAYE	O.B.S.
FOREST D'ABBAYE	6	8.30 a.m.	Company march to ACQUET	O.B.S.
ACQUET	7	10.30 a.m.	Company march to billets at BOFFLES.	O.B.S.

Army Form C. 2118.

WAR DIARY
or
INTELLIGENCE SUMMARY.
(Erase heading not required.)

Instructions regarding War Diaries and Intelligence Summaries are contained in F. S. Regs., Part II. and the Staff Manual respectively. Title pages will be prepared in manuscript.

Place	Date	Hour	Summary of Events and Information	Remarks and references to Appendices
BOFFLES	8	9.45 a.m.	Company proceed by route march to NUNCQ.	OBS
NUNCQ	9	9.45 a.m.	Company march to billets at ORLENCOURT	OBS
ORLENCOURT	10	9.30 a.m.	Inspection of Rifles & Box Respirators Gun Cleaning	OBS
ORLENCOURT	11	9.45 a.m.	Company move by route march to billets at CAUCOURT.	OBS
CAUCOURT	12	9 a.m. 9 a.m. 10 a.m. 11 a.m.	C.O.'s Inspection Physical Training Gun & Equipment cleaning Fitting of Gas Helmets & Gas Drill.	OBS
CAUCOURT	13	9.15 a.m. 9.30 a.m. 11.30	"A" and "B" Sections — Inoculation "C" and "D" — Physical Training. 10.30 — Lecture to N.C.O.s. Immediate Action.	OBS

WAR DIARY
or
INTELLIGENCE SUMMARY.

Army Form C. 2118.

Place	Date	Hour	Summary of Events and Information	Remarks and references to Appendices
	FEB.			
CAUCOURT	14	9 a.m.	Rifle Inspection by Section Officers.	A.S.T.
		9.15 a.m.	"C" and "D" Sections — Inoculation.	
CAUCOURT	15	9.15 a.m.	Inoculation for those not yet been inoculated.	A.S.T.
CAUCOURT	16	9 a.m.	Section Inspection.	A.S.T.
		9.15 a.m.	Gun Cleaning.	
CAUCOURT	17	9.30 a.m.	C.O.'s Inspection (Dress:- Full Marching Order)	A.S.T.
		10.15	Gun Drill	
		11.30	Immediate Action & Gun Cleaning.	
CAUCOURT	18	8 a.m. 9.15 a.m. noon	Divine Services.	A.S.T.
CAUCOURT	19	9.30 a.m.	Inspection by Section Officers	A.S.T.
		9.45 a.m.	Physical Training	

WAR DIARY
or
INTELLIGENCE SUMMARY.
(Erase heading not required.)

Army Form C. 2118.

Place	Date	Hour	Summary of Events and Information	Remarks and references to Appendices
	FEB			
CAUCOURT	19 (continued)	11 a.m.	Immediate Action	AST.
		noon	Gun Cleaning	
		2.30 to 4.15	Paraded to Baths.	
CAUCOURT	20	9.30 a.m.	Rifle Inspection	AST.
		9.45	Gas Drill	
		10.30	Physical Training	
		11.30 to 12.30	Immediate Action.	
CAUCOURT	21	9.30	Inspection	AST.
		9.45	Gas Drill	
		10.30	Physical Training	
		11.30 to 12.30	Immediate Action.	
CAUCOURT	22	9.30 a.m.	Inspection and Route March.	AST.
		11.30	Gun Cleaning	

Army Form C. 2118.

WAR DIARY
or
INTELLIGENCE SUMMARY.
(Erase heading not required.)

Instructions regarding War Diaries and Intelligence Summaries are contained in F. S. Regs., Part II. and the Staff Manual respectively. Title pages will be prepared in manuscript.

Place	Date	Hour	Summary of Events and Information	Remarks and references to Appendices
CAUCOURT	23	9.30 a.m. to 10.30	Gas Drill	CRS
		10.30 to 11.30	Immediate Action	
		noon	Company Parade – Marching Order without packs.	
CAUCOURT	24	9.30 a.m.	Inspection	CRS
		10 a.m.	Running Drill	
		11 a.m.	Immediate Action	
		noon	Gun Cleaning	
CAUCOURT	25	1 p.m.	Company march off to billets at ACQ.	CRS
ACQ	26	9 a.m.	Company Inspection followed by route march to billets at ANZIN	CRS
		9.15	Gun Drill	
		10.30	Physical Training	
		11.30	Immediate Action	

T/134. Wt. W708-776. 50000. 4/15. Sir J. C. & S.

WAR DIARY or INTELLIGENCE SUMMARY.

Army Form C. 2118.

Place	Date	Hour	Summary of Events and Information	Remarks and references to Appendices
ACQ SHEET 51 B.N.W. A.28.a.	27	9 a.m.	Company leave billets at ACQ to relieve 152 M.G. Coy. on front between ROCLINCOURT & LILLE RD. Indirect fire schemes were carried out by us on tracks & trench tramways behind the enemy's lines during the night	O.S.
		3.5 p.m.	Enemy aeroplanes crossed our lines & attacked one of our planes. After a very short engagement one was seen to fall in flames. Unable to state if enemy's or our own. Artillery activity was normal. About 1 p.m. enemy shelled vicinity of "G" Dugout with 77 m.m. H.E. shells. About 3.45 p.m. two 4.2 shells fell close to corner of ECURIE AV. ECURIE was also shelled with 77 m.m. H.E. shells about 7 p.m. (about 3 rounds).	
		about 8 p.m.	BIDOT TRENCH slightly damaged by enemy artillery about 8 p.m. WORK DONE. Cleaning trench round gun positions, levelling floors of frogs, renewing fire steps.	

WAR DIARY
or
INTELLIGENCE SUMMARY.
(Erase heading not required.)

Army Form C. 2118.

Place	Date	Hour	Summary of Events and Information	Remarks and references to Appendices
A.28a.	28	NIGHT	During the night we carried out indirect fire on to enemy dumps, overland routes. 6,000 rounds were fired in all. The enemy was seen exposing himself quite frequently in his front & support lines opposite our right sector. No large parties were seen however. During the morning & afternoon enemy's artillery was very quiet.	O.R.
		9.45pm	Enemy shelled about A.22', A.2.2 with 5.9"s. Work done. About 15 yards of MOUTON AVENUE cleared & traits revetted. Latrines altered & repaired. 4 ore built. Trenches round emplacements cleared & deepened.	

C.S. Armoth 2/Lt
for Officer Commdg.
154th Coy. M.G.C.

On His Majesty's Service.

154th Machine Gun Company

March 1917

Army Form C. 2118.

WAR DIARY
or
INTELLIGENCE SUMMARY.
(Erase heading not required.)

Confidential

ORIGINAL
WAR DIARY
of
154TH COY M.G.C.
11/9/14 to 31/10/16
Vol 16

WAR DIARY
or
INTELLIGENCE SUMMARY.
(Erase heading not required.)

Army Form C. 2118.

Place	Date	Hour	Summary of Events and Information	Remarks and references to Appendices
A28a (Sheet 51 BNW)	March 1911	6 PM 4.55	Enemy machine gun searches LILLE ROAD at intervals.	
"	1	Night	Indirect fire is carried out during the night and early morning on trench junctions and ground around battalion H.qrs at A.17.a.3.5.65. We fire 7500 rounds	
"	"	11 A.M	We fire on a working party at about A.17.d.4.2. The party disappear, after which a mist descends and no further observation is possible.	
"	"	afternoon	Enemy aircraft active	
"	"	—	Artillery (Our own) Normal. (Enemy) Very quiet. Average number of shells 20.	
"	"	—	Work done. Cleaning ECURIE AVENUE to gun position. Entrance to dug-outs repaired and revetted, and one indirect fire emplacement repaired. Continuation of work on MOUTON AVENUE.	
"	"	Night	Our MG's fire on trench railways and tracks behind the enemy line.	

WAR DIARY
or
INTELLIGENCE SUMMARY.
(Erase heading not required.)

Army Form C. 2118.

Place	Date	Hour	Summary of Events and Information	Remarks and references to Appendices
A 28a	1917 mar 2	—	Very low visibility during day.	
"	"	Afternoon	Our heavy artillery and field guns are active during the afternoon	
"	"	2 PM to 4 PM	Enemy Artillery very active, special attention being paid to LILLE ROAD and ECURIE with 77 mm HE and 4.2's. Some fell in the vicinity of PETITE COLLECTEUR – no damage	
"	"	9 PM to midnight	Searchlight sweeps our right sector from the direction of the COMMANDANT'S HOUSE	
"	"	Night	We fire 6250 rounds from our MG's on trench railways and tracks behind the enemy line	
"	"	—	Work done Trench rebuilt for ten yards round No.5 Gun position in ECURIE. Emplacements repaired and cleaned.	

Army Form C. 2118.

WAR DIARY
or
INTELLIGENCE SUMMARY.
(Erase heading not required.)

Instructions regarding War Diaries and Intelligence Summaries are contained in F. S. Regs., Part II. and the Staff Manual respectively. Title pages will be prepared in manuscript.

Place	Date	Hour	Summary of Events and Information	Remarks and references to Appendices
A28a	Mar 3	4AM to 6AM	Enemy searchlight sweeps our right sector from the direction of the COMMANDANT'S HOUSE.	
"	"	Early morning	As soon as our MG near LILLE ROAD opens fire the enemy retaliates on the road.	
"	"	2 PM	Two men are seen walking about near the NINE ELMS.	
"	"	afternoon	Artillery (our own) Our heavies are active. do. (enemy's) Very quiet. Approx. number of rounds fired – 50. About 25 4.2's are fired in the vicinity of No.1 Gun, evidently searching for our trench mortars which had been firing there during the day.	
"	"	—	A white tape has been observed between the enemy second and third line from A.23.d.5.5 to A.30.a.3.8. About 50 yards of trench has now been dug along this.	
"	"	Night	Our MG's fire 5000 rounds indirect on to enemy trench junctions & dumps; also tracks around THELUS.	
"	"	6 PM to midnight	Enemy MG as usual fires on the LILLE ROAD at intervals from 6 PM to midnight. All bullets are going high and to the left, and do no apparent damage.	

Army Form C. 2118.

WAR DIARY
or
INTELLIGENCE SUMMARY.
(Erase heading not required.)

Place	Date	Hour	Summary of Events and Information	Remarks and references to Appendices
A28a.	Mar 4	Early morning	Our MG's fire on to enemy trench junctions and dumps - also tracks around THELUS.	
"	"	"	Enemy MG fires on the LILLE ROAD at intervals. Fire is observed in enemy lines at about A11d.9.3. Our machine guns expend 260 rounds direct fire on to this and continue to search the area around during the night.	
"	"	5.30 PM		
"	"	Night	We fire 6000 rounds on to ground round Batt? dgrs in the enemy line and also on overland tracks.	
"	"	"	Work done. Trench cleared round 26.1 gun position. Rubbish on top of 60y Hqrs in MOUTON AVENUE collected and buried. Improvements made to latrine and trench entrance to same.	

WAR DIARY
or
INTELLIGENCE SUMMARY.

(Erase heading not required.)

Army Form C. 2118.

Place	Date	Hour	Summary of Events and Information	Remarks and references to Appendices
A.28.a	Mar 5	MIDNIGHT to 6.30 A.M.	Our M.G's fire on to ground round Bn. Hqrs in the enemy line and also on overland tracks.	
"	"	6.10 A.M.	A raid is successfully made on the enemy's trenches in A.23.d. and A.30.a. Enemy retaliation for our raid is very feeble. Two and a half minutes elapsed from the time his first S.O.S. went up till the first shell came from his guns. He appeared to pay particular attention to the junction of Avenue A and the GRAND COLLECTEUR, where he kept up a brisk fire with 5.9 shells. He sent a large number of 77 mm shells into the junction of AVENUE A and RIPPERT AVENUE but not much damage was done. He appeared to put nothing into our front line. Prisoners taken:- 1 Officer & 20 O.R. 1 MG captured.	
"	"	6-7 A.M.	Our own artillery are very active.	
"	"	10.5 P.M. to 11 P.M.	Enemy artillery open up a bombardment with 77 mm's and 4.2's. on the front line and COLLECTEUR. Most of the shells fall short of the COLLECTEUR by about 15 yards. Our artillery	(Cont?)

Army Form C. 2118.

WAR DIARY
or
INTELLIGENCE SUMMARY.
(Erase heading not required.)

Instructions regarding War Diaries and Intelligence Summaries are contained in F. S. Regs., Part II. and the Staff Manual respectively. Title pages will be prepared in manuscript.

Place	Date	Hour	Summary of Events and Information	Remarks and references to Appendices
A28a	Mar 5 (con)	Night	Our M.G's fire 6250 rounds on to trench railways and ground behind enemy lines. Enemy M.G. fires across the LILLE RD. WORK DONE Trench round No1 position cleaned & deepened. Trench boards laid round gun position in the MONASTERY at ECURIE.	
"	"	-		
A28a.	"	6 A.M.	During the early morning our M.G's fire on to trench rly's & ground behind enemy lines.	
"	"	After noon.	Enemy fire several "MINNIES". One of their trench mortars is located about A22B3.7.	
"	"	"	Aircraft active. Artillery on both sides very quiet. Approx. number of rounds fired – 50.	
"	"	Night	Indirect fire scheme is carried out – 6000 rounds fired in all. WORK DONE. Repairs to indirect fire position in Avenue A. Cleaning trench round gun positions.	

Army Form C. 2118.

WAR DIARY
or
INTELLIGENCE SUMMARY.
(Erase heading not required.)

Instructions regarding War Diaries and Intelligence Summaries are contained in F. S. Regs., Part II. and the Staff Manual respectively. Title pages will be prepared in manuscript.

Place	Date	Hour	Summary of Events and Information	Remarks and references to Appendices
A 28 a.	4	Day	One of the enemy is seen to leave a trench about A 22 B 5.3. He went out of sight about 20 yards behind this point. Close observation is kept here but no further movement is seen.	
"	"	—	During the afternoon our heavies bombard the enemy front line.	
"	"	3.45 P.M.	Enemy fire about 30 5.9 shells into the area around the COLECTEUR and WEDNESDAY AVENUE. Some damage is done to our trenches. This is apparently retaliation for our trench mortar activity. Some attention is also paid to the SABLIÈRE	
"	"	Night	4500 rounds fired during the night on to enemy dumps and trenches behind the lines. Our trench mortars in the right subsector are very active. Enemy machine guns sweep the parapet of the COLECTEUR in the left sub-sector at intervals during the night, commencing at about 8 P.M.	
"	"	"	Work done. Cleaning trenches round gun positions and repairing 5 yards of trench knocked in by enemy artillery near 26.1 gun	

WAR DIARY
or
INTELLIGENCE SUMMARY.
(Erase heading not required.)

Army Form C. 2118.

Instructions regarding War Diaries and Intelligence Summaries are contained in F.S. Regs., Part II. and the Staff Manual respectively. Title pages will be prepared in manuscript.

Place	Date	Hour	Summary of Events and Information	Remarks and references to Appendices
A.28a.	8	1/1 a.m.	Three enemy 'planes brought down one of ours in flames – well inside the German lines. About 30 of the enemy were seen round our aeroplane when it fell but were not within rifle & machine gun range.	
"	"	Day.	A suspected wood dump has been located at about A.12.C.3.4.	
"	"	Noon	A working party was seen at A.12.d.9.9 fired on	
"	"	Aftn.	Our artillery was ordered. The enemy artillery shelled "G" Dump with 4.2"s late in the afternoon.	
"	"	Night	Indirect fire scheme was carried out on to trench railways & tracks behind enemy lines. 6,500 rounds were fired. Completion of repairs to Indirect Fire Position. Work done. AVENUE "A". Trenches cleaned round gun position. New latrine made near No. 5 gun.	
A.28a.	9	1 p.m.	An enemy working party is reported at A.12.d.99. Our machine guns open fire on it. Good observation is possible & the party is seen to disperse, apparently into a trench adjacent. A larger party is also seen but out of range.	

WAR DIARY or INTELLIGENCE SUMMARY.

Army Form C. 2118.

Place	Date	Hour	Summary of Events and Information	Remarks and references to Appendices
A.28.c.	9	Night	Our artillery is active & the party is dispersed by them. Indirect fire schemes are carried out on enemy roads, communication trenches & dumps. 8,000 rounds of ammunition are expended. Work done. Mud cleared away round gun positions since the thaw this morning.	
A.28.a	10	Morning	Enemy aircraft is active this morning, two of our a/c't lines being brought down within an hour. The tail of one of our planes is shot away.	
"		3 a.m	Our artillery is fairly quiet whilst the enemy is more than usually active, carrying out a heavy bombardment well do our right.	
"		10 a.m		
"		Night	Indirect fire is carried out on to enemy overland tracks & dumps. 7,500 rounds are used.	
"	10		Work done. Repairs to covered emplacement in WESTERN TRENCH. Reserve S.A.A. made up from dumps.	

WAR DIARY
or
INTELLIGENCE SUMMARY.
(Erase heading not required.)

Army Form C. 2118.

Place	Date	Hour	Summary of Events and Information	Remarks and references to Appendices
A.28a.	11	10:15	A man is observed walking over the open entering the trench at A.18d.12.	
"	"		The artillery on both sides more active than usual.	
"	"	Night	Indirect fire schemes are being carried out by us on roads & communication trenches in enemy lines. S.A.A. Expended 6,500 rounds.	
"	"		Enemy machine gun as usual is searching ground around "G" Dump with indirect fire.	
"	"		Work done. Trench cleared round gun positions. New roof made at emplacement R.1.	
A.28a	12	Morn'g	Our artillery is fairly active on our left, whilst the enemy is very quiet.	
"	"	Night	We search the enemy's tracks, roads & dumps with indirect fire. S.A.A. expended 7,000 rounds.	
"	"		Work done. Mordon trench cleared from Company Headquarters to junction with MAIN AVENUE 3.	
"	13	3 a.m. to 5 a.m.	Enemy bombards the sector on our left with Trench Mortars & after attempts to raid out trenches but is repulsed with rifle & machine gun fire.	

WAR DIARY
or
INTELLIGENCE SUMMARY.
(Erase heading not required.)

Army Form C. 2118.

Place	Date	Hour	Summary of Events and Information	Remarks and references to Appendices
A.28a.	13	aftn.	500 rounds were fired at hostile aircraft. Work done. Trenches revetted & cleared round all gun positions.	
"	14	5a.m.	During enemy bombardment on the right divisional front our gun at S.1 position shot the enemy front line on our divisional front under fire. No enemy were seen. The enemy bombardment lasted about 40 minutes.	
A.28a.		Night	6,500 rounds are fired on to enemy overland routes and tracks. Enemy machine guns are active, sweeping the parapet of the PETIT COLLECTEUR & searching the LILLE ROAD. Artillery on both sides is very quiet. Work done. New alternative emplacement for M.G.1 & N°2 position in ECURIE. Trenches cleared round gun positions.	
"	15	Early morng.	M.G. fire 7,000 rounds on to trench railways & overland tracks behind the enemy's lines.	
"		3 p.m.	A German aeroplane flies very high over ANZIN. Fire opened on all	

WAR DIARY
or
INTELLIGENCE SUMMARY.
(Erase heading not required.)

Army Form C. 2118.

Place	Date	Hour	Summary of Events and Information	Remarks and references to Appendices
A.28.a.	15		were seen. Our archies fired at them with no apparent result. Enemy machine guns are again active on LILLE ROAD and COLLECTEUR.	
"		aft.	Our artillery was active during the afternoon. Enemy artillery also very active. Particular attention was paid to the BARRICADE	
"			Work done. Trench at front Machine Gun Company Headquarters cleaned & revetted; trench heads lifted & sump dug.	
A.28.a.	16	Morn.	Our machine gun fire on to tracks behind the enemy's lines in the early morning.	
		Aftn.	The Company is relieved by 153rd Machine Gun Coy & proceed to BRAY.	
BRAY.	17	9.45 a.m.	The Company proceeds by route march to LA COMTE	
LA COMTE	18	10 a.m.	Kit Inspection.	
		5 p.m.	Divine Service.	
		9 a.m.	C.O.'s Inspection.	
LA COMTE	19	9.15	Gun Cleaning & packing of limbers.	
		2.30 p.m.	Company drilled.	

WAR DIARY
or
INTELLIGENCE SUMMARY.
(Erase heading not required.)

Army Form C. 2118.

Place	Date	Hour	Summary of Events and Information	Remarks and references to Appendices
LA COMTE	20	9 a.m.	Inspection by Sections	
		9.15	Gas Drill	
		9.45	Rifle Cleaning & Filling	
		2.15 p.m.	Lecture by Section Officers	
LA COMTE	21	8.45 a.m.	Inspection by Section Officers	
		9.15 to 10.15	Physical Training. 10.30 a.m. Judging Distance. Range Cards.	
		2.15 p.m.	Company Drill	
LA COMTE	22	9.45 a.m.	Company proceed by route march to billets at MAROEUIL.	
MAROEUIL	23	9 a.m.	C.O.'s Inspection	
		9.30 a.m.	Gun Cleaning	
		10.30 a.m.	Immediate Action	
			One Section proceeds into line to build emplacements.	

WAR DIARY
or
INTELLIGENCE SUMMARY.
(Erase heading not required.)

Army Form C. 2118.

Place	Date	Hour	Summary of Events and Information	Remarks and references to Appendices
MAROEUIL	24	9 a.m.	Inspection by Section Officers.	
		9.30	Physical Training	
		10.30	Immediate Action	
MAROEUIL	25	9.15 a.m.	Inspection	
		9.45 a.m. 9.46 a.m.	Divine Services.	
MAROEUIL	26	9 a.m.	Inspection.	
		9.15	Company Drill	
		10.30	Physical Training	
		11.30	Gun Drill	
		2.15	Attached men - Mechanism, Last draft: - Gas Drill.	
		10 P.M.	Fatigue party.	
MAROEUIL	27	4 P.M.	Section Officers Inspection	
	"	2.30 p.m.	Fatigue Party.	
MAROEUIL	28	7.50 a.m. 2 p.m.	Whole Company paraded for Baths.	

Instructions regarding War Diaries and Intelligence Summaries are contained in F. S. Regs., Part II. and the Staff Manual respectively. Title pages will be prepared in manuscript.

Army Form C. 2118.

WAR DIARY
or
INTELLIGENCE SUMMARY.
(Erase heading not required.)

Instructions regarding War Diaries and Intelligence Summaries are contained in F. S. Regs., Part II. and the Staff Manual respectively. Title pages will be prepared in manuscript.

Place	Date	Hour	Summary of Events and Information	Remarks and references to Appendices
	MARCH			
MAROEUIL	29	7 a.m.	Fatigue Party.	
		4 p.m.	Inspection by Section Officers.	
MAROEUIL	30	9 a.m.	Inspection by Section Officers	
		9.15	Company Drill	
		10.30	Physical Training	
		11.30 a.m.	Gun Drill.	
MAROEUIL	31	9 a.m.	Inspection by Section Officers	
		9.15	Company Drill	
		10.30	Physical Training	
		11.30 a.m.	Gun Drill.	

[signature]
Officer commanding 154 Machine Gun Company.

On His Majesty's Service.

154/51

154th MACHINE GUN COMPANY

APRIL MONTH 1917

Army Form C. 2118.

WAR DIARY
or
INTELLIGENCE SUMMARY.
(Erase heading not required.)

Instructions regarding War Diaries and Intelligence Summaries are contained in F. S. Regs., Part II. and the Staff Manual respectively. Title pages will be prepared in manuscript.

Place	Date	Hour	Summary of Events and Information	Remarks and references to Appendices
			CONFIDENTIAL ORIGINAL WAR DIARY of 154 Company M.G.C. From 1·4·17 to 30·4·17. VOL. 16	

Army Form C. 2118.

WAR DIARY
or
INTELLIGENCE SUMMARY.
(Erase heading not required.)

Instructions regarding War Diaries and Intelligence Summaries are contained in F.S. Regs., Part II. and the Staff Manual respectively. Title pages will be prepared in manuscript.

Place	Date	Hour	Summary of Events and Information	Remarks and references to Appendices
	APRIL.			
MAROEUIL	1	9 a.m. & 10:30 a.m. & 4:30 p.m.	Divine Services. Enemy shells MAROEUIL during the early evening.	
MAROEUIL	2	9 a.m. 6:30 p.m.	Inspection by Section Officers. Enemy commences bombardment of MAROEUIL with shells of heavy calibre. This continues intermittently throughout the night.	
MAROEUIL	3	9 a.m. 2 p.m.	Company marches to BRAY. Enemy fires a few shells on MAROEUIL.	
MAROEUIL	4	9 a.m. About noon	Company proceeds by route march to BRAY. Enemy fires a few shells on MAROEUIL.	
MAROEUIL	5	9:15 a.m. 9:45 " 11 a.m.	Inspection. Physical training. C.O's lecture to N.C.O's i/c Gun teams. Gun cleaning, etc.	

T2134. Wt. W708—776. 500000. 4/15. Sir J.C.&B.

WAR DIARY
or
INTELLIGENCE SUMMARY.
(Erase heading not required.)

Army Form C. 2118.

Place	Date	Hour	Summary of Events and Information	Remarks and references to Appendices
MAROEUIL	APRIL 6	9 a.m.	C.O's Inspection.	
		9.15	Physical training	
		10.30	Immediate Action	A.
		11.30	Gun Drill	
MAROEUIL	7	9.30 a.m.	Inspection by Section Officers.	
		10 a.m.	Gun cleaning & packing of limbers	A.
MAROEUIL	8	3 p.m.	Company takes up positions in the line, preparatory to attack.	A.
ROCLINCOURT (CHEMIN CREUX)	9		At 5.30 this morning ten guns of the Company opened fire on barrage lines according to Divisional scheme. During the period 5.30 a.m. to 10.30 a.m., 95,000 rounds were fired. On receipt of information that the Blue Line had been taken, two guns were sent forward to strong posts in A.24.a.10.85 and A.24.a.6.7. Four other guns were also sent forward to consolidate the Blue Line. These guns moved off at 9 a.m. At 12.30 p.m. two more guns were sent forward	A.

WAR DIARY
or
INTELLIGENCE SUMMARY.
(Erase heading not required.)

Army Form C. 2118.

Place	Date	Hour	Summary of Events and Information	Remarks and references to Appendices
ROCLINCOURT (CHEMIN CREUX)	APRIL 9 (con't'd)		to occupy strong post in B.13.c.5.9. in the Blue Line. Enemy retaliation was very feeble, but counter battery work having proved too good for them. During the barrage one complete team & an officer were killed by a direct hit from a 5.9. The mud & earth thrown up by falling shells caused frequent stoppages & put one gun completely out of action till it had been stripped & cleaned.	
Do	10		No targets offered themselves to our guns, as the snow & sleet effectively prevented observation.	
"	9		Casualties in attack of 9.4.17:- Killed 1 Officer 3 O.R. Wounded 50 O.R.	

B.Hughes
O.C. 154 M.G. Co

WAR DIARY
or
INTELLIGENCE SUMMARY.

(Erase heading not required.)

Army Form C. 2118.

Place	Date	Hour	Summary of Events and Information	Remarks and references to Appendices
ROCLINCOURT (CHEMIN CREUX)	11 APRIL		The Company is relieved in the line by the 5th M.G. Coy. and proceeds to "Y" Huts, between MAROEUIL and DUISANS.	
"Y" HUTS. D. between MAROEUIL and DUISANS.	12	9 a.m. 2 p.m. 4 p.m.	Company parades for baths Gun Cleaning Inspection by Section Officers.	
Ditto	13	9.30 a.m. 10 a.m.	Inspection by Section Officers. Cleaning of Clothing & Equipment	
Ditto	14	9.30 a.m. 10 - 11 a.m.	C.O.'s Inspection Company Drill Mechanism.	
Ditto	15	2.50 p.m.	Company proceeds by route march to billets at ST. LAURENT BLANGY.	
ST. LAURENT BLANGY.	16	9.30 a.m. 10 a.m.	Inspection by Section Officers Gun Cleaning	

Army Form C. 2118.

WAR DIARY
or
INTELLIGENCE SUMMARY.
(Erase heading not required.)

Place	Date	Hour	Summary of Events and Information	Remarks and references to Appendices
ST. LAURENT BLANGY.	APRIL 17	9.30 a.m. 10 a.m.	Rifle Inspection. Preparation of Guns.	
Do.	18	9.30 a.m. 10 a.m.	Inspection by Section Officers. Fatigues — Improving dug-outs, etc.	
"	19	9.30 a.m. 10 a.m.	C.O.'s Inspection. Improvement fatigues.	
"	20	9.30 a.m.	Improvement fatigues.	
"	21	9.45 a.m.	"D" Section and 2 teams of "B" proceed to take up positions in the line.	
Do.	22	5 p.m.	Company leaves billets to take up positions in the line.	
SUNKEN ROAD H.24.d.	23		At 4.45 a.m. our bombardment started & eight machine guns of this Company opened fire on a barrage scheme arranged by the Division. The barrage lasted 15 minutes & was directed on the high ground behind the Chemical Works & also on to the outskirts of ROEUX. The object of the barrage was to prevent the enemy bringing	

WAR DIARY
or
INTELLIGENCE SUMMARY.
(Erase heading not required.)

Army Form C. 2118.

Place	Date APRIL	Hour	Summary of Events and Information	Remarks and references to Appendices
SUNKEN ROAD H.24.6.	23		machine guns into shell holes in the open & thus escaping our artillery bombardment which was directed chiefly on to their trenches — 16,000 rounds were fired. Our guns took up their positions the night before the attack — in our front line — two in the Railway embankment & two at the right end of the sunken road which formed the jumping off trench. These guns were placed with the following facts in view:— (1) That there were enemy machine guns situated very close to our lines which undoubtedly had not been knocked out by our artillery & were likely to cause considerable annoyance to our advancing troops — if they opened fire. So counteract this, the four guns of the Company were instructed to open fire at once on any machine gun which opened fire. At zero + 7 minutes an enemy machine gun opened fire along the railway embankment. This gun was promptly engaged by our two guns on the Railway embankment & after two bursts had been fired the enemy gun suddenly ceased fire & was not heard of again. The guns on the right of the sunken road were eng[ag]ed fortunate. Some enemy snipers were dug in behind our line	

Army Form C. 2118.		
WAR DIARY *or* **INTELLIGENCE SUMMARY.** (Erase heading not required)		Remarks and references to Appendices

Place	Date	Hour	Summary of Events and Information	Remarks
SUNKEN ROAD H.24.b.	APRIL 23		and just at zero the officer in charge of these two guns was shot through the head. The Sergeant took charge & was also shot. A Private then took charge & assisted the infantry forward by covering fire on the flank. After hard fighting the infantry pushed forward & these four guns got under cover & awaited the chance of going forward to consolidate the captured line. At 8 a.m. four guns of "A" Section under Lieut. Lawson were sent forward with instructions to go to our front line & feel their way from there to the captured enemy 1st line where they were to take up position & open on previously arranged barrage lines. These guns got into the Black Line at 9.30 a.m. but only took up defensive position as the infantry had not been able to advance as far as had been expected. At 9.30 a.m. two guns pushed forward on the right & took up defensive position in the BLACK LINE at MOUNT PLEASANT WOOD. These guns were to advance to the RED LINE by stages but, as the attack was not progressing as expected,	

WAR DIARY
or
INTELLIGENCE SUMMARY.
(Erase heading not required.)

Army Form C. 2118.

Place	Date	Hour	Summary of Events and Information	Remarks and references to Appendices
SUNKEN ROAD H.24.b.	APRIL 23 (contd)		These guns could not move on. The two guns that were detailed to go forward to the BLUE LINE took up support positions in front of our old front line as the BLUE LINE was not captured. On the night of 23rd it was reported that the enemy had massed behind the cemetery & chemical works for a counter attack. Six guns were turned on to this spot & the counter-attack did not materialise. Casualties during attack of 23/4/17:- Killed 6 Officer 1 O.R. Missing 1 O.R. Wounded 13 O.R.	A
Do.	24		At 4.30 a.m. after a heavy bombardment the enemy again tried to counter attack but were wiped out by the fire of our guns. After this the enemy attempted to dig themselves in about 200 in front of the BLACK LINE but were effectually prevented from doing this. They abandoned the attempt & retired behind the chemical works. An enemy machine gun which had been placed in position to cover digging party was put out of action by our gun. At 6 a.m. when our heavies were bombarding the village of ROEUX parties of the enemy tried to steal away but were all caught by Lieut. Stewart's two guns ("A" Section)	B

Army Form C. 2118.

WAR DIARY
or
INTELLIGENCE SUMMARY.
(Erase heading not required.)

Instructions regarding War Diaries and Intelligence Summaries are contained in F. S. Regs., Part II. and the Staff Manual respectively. Title pages will be prepared in manuscript.

Place	Date	Hour	Summary of Events and Information	Remarks and references to Appendices
SUNKEN ROAD H.24.b.	APRIL 25	6 a.m.	The Company is relieved by the 107th M.G. Company & proceeds to billets at PENIN.	
PENIN	26	2 p.m.	Gun cleaning.	
PENIN	27	9.30 a.m. 10 a.m.	Inspection by Section Officers Kit & Gun Inspection.	
PENIN	28	8.15 a.m. 10.10-10.15 a.m.	Baths Parade	
PENIN	29	9.45 a.m.	Parades for Divine Services.	
PENIN	30	6.30 a.m. - 7.30 - 8.45 9 a.m. to 9.30 9.30 to 10 10 - 11 a.m. 11.15 to 12.15 12.15 to 1 p.m.	New Scheme of Training commences. The day's parades as follows:— Physical Training C.O.'s Inspection. Squad Drill Lecture Drill Musketry Gun Drill Immediate Action.	

B. Hughes /s/
O.C. 154 Machine Gun Coy.

On His Majesty's Service.

154th MACHINE GUN COMPANY

MAY 1917

CONFIDENTIAL

ORIGINAL
WAR DIARY
of
154TH COMPANY MACHINE GUN CORPS

From 1/5/17 to 31/5/17
Vol 17

Army Form C. 2118.

WAR DIARY
or
INTELLIGENCE SUMMARY.
(Erase heading not required.)

Instructions regarding War Diaries and Intelligence Summaries are contained in F. S. Regs., Part II. and the Staff Manual respectively. Title pages will be prepared in manuscript.

Place	Date MAY	Hour	Summary of Events and Information	Remarks and references to Appendices
PENIN	1	6.30 a.m.	Physical Training	
		8.45	C.O's Inspection	
		9 – 10	Company Drill	
		10 – 11	Immediate Action	
		11.15	Gun Drill	
		12.15 to 1 p.m.	Stripping	
PENIN	2	6.30 a.m.	Physical Training	
		8.45	C.O's Inspection	
		9 – 10	Judging Distance & Visual Training	
		10 – 11	Mechanism	
		11.15 to 1 p.m.	Range Practice	
PENIN	3	6.30 a.m.	Physical Training	
		8.45	C.O's Inspection	
		9 – 11	Advanced Gun Drill	
		11.15 to 12.15	Immediate Action	
		12.15 to 1 p.m.	Mechanism	
PENIN	4	6.30 a.m.	Physical Training	
		8.45	C.O's Inspection	
		9 – 10	Rifle Exercises	Continued next sheet.

WAR DIARY
or
INTELLIGENCE SUMMARY.

(Erase heading not required.)

Army Form C. 2118.

Place	Date	Hour	Summary of Events and Information	Remarks and references to Appendices
PENIN	4	10 a.m to 10:30 10:30 to 11 a.m 11:15 to 12:15 12:15 to 1 p.m	Saluting Drill Mechanism Gun Drill Immediate Action	
PENIN	5	6:30 a.m 8:45 9 – 10 10 – 11 11:15 to 1 p.m	Physical Training C.O's Inspection Company Drill Bombing Range Practice	
			Honours & Awards. The undermentioned N.C.O's & Men of the Company have been awarded the Military Medal for gallantry displayed between 9th & 11th April, 1917. 22159 Sgt. GILCHRIST J. Date of award 3.5.17 23049 " PETRIE J. " 29.4.17 23251 A/Cpl MACKENZIE A. " 29.4.17 24486 " JEFFREY R. " 29.4.17 24444 " FENTON S. " 29.4.17 350593 Pte. MUIR W.E. 4th Seaforths. Attd to 154. M.G.C. 29.4.17.	

WAR DIARY
or
INTELLIGENCE SUMMARY.
(Erase heading not required.)

Army Form C. 2118.

Place	Date MAY	Hour	Summary of Events and Information	Remarks and references to Appendices
Penin	6	10 a.m.	Company parades for Divine Service.	
"	7	—	From this date to 11th inst inclusive, the Company being still in the village of Penin continues its training on lines similar to those of the preceding week, parading for various forms of drill & during the earlier hours of the day whilst the later hours are devoted to indoor recreation, sport and work	
"	12	10.15 A.M.	Company parades in marching order for route march to "Huts" (near Etrun) on the ARRAS – ST POL ROAD	
"Y" HUTS ARRAS-ST POL ROAD	13	9.45 A.M.	Divine Services.	
"	14	2.30 P.M.	Company proceeds by route march to ARRAS	
ARRAS	15	9 A.M. 9.30 A.M.	O.C's Inspection of Company. Gun cleaning and belt filling.	

Army Form C. 2118.

WAR DIARY
or
INTELLIGENCE SUMMARY.
(Erase heading not required.)

Instructions regarding War Diaries and Intelligence Summaries are contained in F. S. Regs., Part II. and the Staff Manual respectively. Title pages will be prepared in manuscript.

Place	Date MAY	Hour	Summary of Events and Information	Remarks and references to Appendices
ARRAS ST LAURENT BLANGY	13	10 A.M	Owing to enemy counter attacking in strong force, company proceeds at 10 A.M. from ARRAS to Railway Embankment east of ST LAURENT BLANGY.	
		8 P.M	Company received orders to relieve 152 Bty (MGC) in line. Relief is completed by 2.30 A.M on 14th inst with the exception of two guns in the front line which are unable to be relieved until night of 14th.	
SUNKEN RD H 2.a.b.	14	Day & Evening	Enemy artillery are active all day, especially in CHEMICAL WORKS and ROEUX. His planes also active in the evening.	
		Night	At night we relieve two guns of 152 Coy in the front line, thus completing total relief of that unit.	
"	15	Dawn	Enemy aeroplanes fly over our lines just after dawn. One is engaged by fire of our guns in CORONA TRENCH at height of about 200 feet and is shot crashing to the ground in the left Brigade area.	
		Night	Our machine guns fire short bursts at intervals on trenches round HAUSA and DELBAR WOODS. Enemy artillery inactive.	

Army Form C. 2118.

WAR DIARY
or
INTELLIGENCE SUMMARY.
(Erase heading not required.)

Instructions regarding War Diaries and Intelligence Summaries are contained in F. S. Regs., Part II. and the Staff Manual respectively. Title pages will be prepared in manuscript.

Place	Date	Hour	Summary of Events and Information	Remarks and references to Appendices
SUNKEN RD H.28.b.	MAY 19	mid-night till dawn	Hostile Artillery very active; ROEUX, the area behind (towards the Railway) and the CHEMICAL WORKS are shelled.	
		After noon	Railway cutting at H.23 is shelled, an ammunition dump being blown up.	
		4 p.m. to 7.30 p.m.	A squadron of 14 red "planes is particularly active	
		9-10 p.m.	Enemy put down a heavy barrage on ROEUX-GAVRELLE RD about I.13 central.	

Army Form C. 2118.

WAR DIARY
or
INTELLIGENCE SUMMARY.
(Erase heading not required.)

Instructions regarding War Diaries and Intelligence Summaries are contained in F. S. Regs., Part II. and the Staff Manual respectively. Title pages will be prepared in manuscript.

Place	Date	Hour	Summary of Events and Information	Remarks and references to Appendices
SUNKEN RD H 23 b.	MAY 20.	10AM to 11.30AM.	Our reconnaissance machines fly continuously over our lines. One of our machines is attacked by three hostile Red planes but escapes by skilful manoeuvring. Immediately afterwards one of the German machines plunges down a short distance behind his own lines in direction of GAVRELLE	
"	"	Aftn.	Enemy Artillery keeps up a steady fire on CEYLON and CORONA trenches from 9 p.m. tied 2.15 a.m., 21.5.17	
"	21	Early morn.	From midnight 20/21st enemy artillery continues its fire on CEYLON & CORONA till 2.15 a.m. COLOMBO Trench also is shelled periodically, no direct hits being obtained. The enemy's fire on our front line has become more accurate. Enemy planes cross our lines, several of which are engaged & turn back to their own lines. Enemy dispositions. The ridge in front of COLOMBO trench appears to have been worked on during the night. No hostile patrols do have been an enemy Observation Post in the centre of HAUSA WOOD is unoccupied during the day.	
"	"	5 a.m.	A Vickers' gun, fully loaded & in working order, was dug up from a position about 150 yds. South of CHALK PIT. This is believed to be one of the guns of 165 Company lost on the night of 15/16th 4 of whose fate that was considerable doubt.	

WAR DIARY
or
INTELLIGENCE SUMMARY.
(Erase heading not required.)

Army Form C. 2118.

Place	Date May	Hour	Summary of Events and Information	Remarks and references to Appendices
SUNKEN RD H.2.b.1.	21 (cont'd)		Work done. Two latrines are dug & trench deepened. The trench left of ROEUX emplacement is improved. A new emplacement is made 200 of CARONA trench, whilst the existing ones are improved.	
"	22		Enemy Artillery shells CEYLON trench and ROEUX intermittently throughout the day but is quiet at night. Our machineguns fire 1500 rounds on hostile 'planes throughout the day. Work done. Two emplacements are constructed in CORONA trench. Alternative emplacements are dug in COLOMBO trench. The trench leading to emplacement on left of ROEUX is deepened.	
"	22 (cont'd)		Enemy is very active on our front line system, both with shells & sling bombs	
		4/1 a.m	After 4 a.m. activity dies down somewhat. At this hour an enemy aeroplane, flying low over very extremity of our front line, drops lights in the following order: 2 WHITE, RED, 2 WHITE, WHITE.	
		6.40 a.m	A battery of ours, using a lightshell fuseshort—only fired clearing our front line. Three shells fell behind our front line.	

WAR DIARY
or
INTELLIGENCE SUMMARY.

(Erase heading not required.)

Army Form C. 2118.

Place	Date	Hour	Summary of Events and Information	Remarks and references to Appendices
SUNKEN RD H.23.C.	23	Early Morning	A party of the enemy is seen to leave the SUNKEN ROAD & make for their own lines. Our gun team on the left of CORONA opened fire & two of the party were seen to fall.	
		7 a.m.	There is a fair amount of hostile activity in the air this morning & several machines are engaged. At 7 a.m. one of the machines fired on return.	
		5 p.m.	Between 5 p.m. & 7 p.m. two enemy machines kept circling over our front line system.	
		9 p.m.	From this hour onwards enemy artillery put strong barrage on CEYLON Trench. We also heavily shell CORONA SUPPORT, CRETE & CRUMP trenches at intervals. During the twenty four hours our machine guns fire 1500 rounds.	
-	24		No enemy movements could be observed during the day from our front line guns. Enemy machine guns engaged our aircraft from the North from behind HAUSA WOOD. A few enemy aeroplanes, flying low, cross our lines. Those within range were driven off by our machine gun fire.	

WAR DIARY
or
INTELLIGENCE SUMMARY.

Army Form C. 2118.

Place	Date	Hour	Summary of Events and Information	Remarks and references to Appendices
SUNKEN RD H.23.b.	24 (Cont'd)	8 a.m.	Enemy artillery is very active from 8 a.m. to 11 a.m. on our support & communication trenches.	
		2.30 p.m.	Enemy heavily shells the aforenamed trenches & drops a few shells of heavy calibre at H.9., blowing up a bomb dump.	
	24/25 (thru)	Night	During the night 24/25 one of enemy machine guns in the vicinity of CORONA TRENCH was put out of action by shell fire. No casualties were reported. Work done. French defended area: left gun in CORONA. New gun emplacement made on right of CORONA. Anti-aircraft emplacement completed in I.13.d.9.6. Ammunition expended during the day 300 rounds.	

Army Form C. 2118.

WAR DIARY
or
INTELLIGENCE SUMMARY.
(Erase heading not required.)

Instructions regarding War Diaries and Intelligence Summaries are contained in F. S. Regs., Part II. and the Staff Manual respectively. Title pages will be prepared in manuscript.

Place	Date	Hour	Summary of Events and Information	Remarks and references to Appendices
Sunken Rd H 28 b.	May 25	8 AM	Enemy Artillery shell our support and communication trenches. As many as 32 shells are dropped near CRUMP TRENCH in one minute.	
"	"	1.35 PM to 1.56 PM	Shells (about 20) fall in the same area as above.	
"	"	Night	20 F.C. shells fall in the vicinity of our M G emplacement at I.19 c 5.7. One of our Batteries firing a light shell drops several short of COLOMBO TRENCH (left end)	
"	"	10 pm to 11 pm	Hostile aircraft fly over our lines and a number of lights are dropped. An aeroplane drops three bombs between CORONA TRENCH and ROEUX. All fail to explode.	
"	"		500 rounds are expended against hostile aircraft.	

Army Form C. 2118.

WAR DIARY
or
INTELLIGENCE SUMMARY.
(Erase heading not required.)

Instructions regarding War Diaries and Intelligence Summaries are contained in F. S. Regs., Part II. and the Staff Manual respectively. Title pages will be prepared in manuscript.

Place	Date	Hour	Summary of Events and Information	Remarks and references to Appendices
SUNKEN RD H 29 c.	26	5 A.M. - 6 A.M.	One of our Batteries firing a light shell drops several short of COLOMBO TRENCH (left end).	
"	"	Day & Night	Enemy Artillery active throughout day and night. Between 8 P.M. and 9.30 P.M. the shelling is heaviest on CRUMP TRENCH. At 10 P.M. Gas shells are dropped in the vicinity of CRUMP TRENCH	
"	"	6.15 P.M.	Enemy put up a barrage across the Railway, apparently between CRETE and CRUMP TRENCHES	
"	"		2500 rounds are expended against aircraft.	
"	27	5.15 A.M.	Hostile aircraft are engaged by our machine guns.	
"	"	Day	Enemy Artillery active.	
"	"	Night	Enemy Artillery very quiet	

Army Form C. 2118.

WAR DIARY
or
INTELLIGENCE SUMMARY.
(Erase heading not required.)

Instructions regarding War Diaries and Intelligence Summaries are contained in F.S. Regs., Part II. and the Staff Manual respectively. Title pages will be prepared in manuscript.

Places	Date	Hour	Summary of Events and Information	Remarks and references to Appendices
SUNKEN RD H.29.b.	28	—	Shortly before dawn a strong German working party is seen about I.14.d.2.5 and dispersed by M.G. fire	
		—	A trench appears to have been worked on at approximately I.20.B.1.9	
		Evening	Hostile aircraft fly frequently over our lines.	
		11 P.M.	Behind HAYSA WOOD a flare is observed to commence and burns throughout night. Believed to be a dump on fire.	
	29	10 a.m.	Enemy commence a very lively bombardment on our lines, which lasts in intense form for 4 hours.	
		9 a.m. to 11 a.m.	Enemy open systematic bombardment of our front line system. On our Artillery opening fire at 11am enemy slacken down.	
		1 p.m.	Enemy aeroplane flies very low over our lines. 600 rounds are fired on the plane causing it to withdraw.	
		5 p.m.	One of our planes is observed to fall in flames.	
		9 p.m. to 10 p.m.	Enemy bombard front line fiercely.	

A 5834 Wt. W4973/M687 750,000 8/16 D. D. & L. Ltd. Forms/C.2118/13.

WAR DIARY
or
INTELLIGENCE SUMMARY.
(Erase heading not required.)

Army Form C. 2118.

Place	Date	Hour	Summary of Events and Information	Remarks and references to Appendices
SUNKEN ROAD	MAY 30	4:30 AM	Three enemy planes are fired on by our M.G's, 500 rounds being expended.	
		following	This Company is relieved by 26th M.G Coy and proceeds to billets at ARRAS	
ARRAS	31	2.30	Company proceeds by bus to HOUVELIN.	
HOUVELIN				
			Total Casualties from 16/31st May, 1917 = Officers NIL. OR's 4 killed 4 wounded.	

C.W.Broadman
Officer Commanding
154 Coy. M.G.C

On His Majesty's Service.

154th MACHINE GUN COMPANY

JUNE 1917

CONFIDENTIAL.

ORIGINAL
WAR DIARY
of
154 MACHINE GUN COMPANY
for the month of
JUNE, 1917.

Army Form C. 2118.

WAR DIARY
or
INTELLIGENCE SUMMARY.

(Erase heading not required.)

Place	Date	Hour	Summary of Events and Information	Remarks and references to Appendices
	JUNE		During the past month the Military Medal has been awarded to the undermentioned N.C.O.'s & men of the Company for gallantry displayed between 23rd & 25th April, 1917:— 24516 Pte. Hinton Alexander 15741 L/Cpl. Sutton James (Then Pte.) 35645 " Jones David " 73653 Pte. Enderston Wm. (Formerly 201589 4th Seaforth Highlanders, att'd to 154th M.G. Coy.) Date of Award:— 23.5.17. Authority:— XVIIth Corps No. A.6/46/2. 51st (H) D. No. 317(A).	R.D.

HOUVELIN, PAS-DE-CALAIS	1		Below is shown the State of the Company's personnel on the 1st day of the month:—
			
			            Officers. Other Ranks O.R. attached from Battalions.
			 Strength. 10 166 25
			 Ration Strength. 7 146 24
			
			 Difference between strength & ration strength is as follows:—
			
			 Officers { Courses = 2
			            Rest Camp = 1
			                        = 3
			
			 Other Ranks { F.A. = 5
			 M.G.C. Leave = 4
			          Courses = 4
			          Rest Camp = 3
			          Northampton Hosp = 1
			          Depot Bns = 3
			                    = 20
			
			 Attached. F.A. = 1
				R.D.

Army Form C. 2118.

WAR DIARY
or
INTELLIGENCE SUMMARY.
(Erase heading not required.)

Instructions regarding War Diaries and Intelligence Summaries are contained in F. S. Regs., Part II. and the Staff Manual respectively. Title pages will be prepared in manuscript.

Place	Date JUNE	Hour	Summary of Events and Information	Remarks and references to Appendices
HOUVELIN	1		From this date to 3rd instant the Company is engaged in the usual forms of drill & physical exercise.	RW.
HOUVELIN	4	6a.m.	Company leaves billets to march to others at MONNEVILLE, arriving there at 8.30 a.m.	RW.
MONNEVILLE PAS-DE-CALAIS	5	7.30 a.m.	Company leaves this village & proceeds by route march to VINCLY. The day was very hot & many of the men found the journey a trying one. Distance about 23 kilometres.	RW.
VINCLY PAS-DE-CALAIS	6	8a.m.	The Company's transport leaves to take the two days' journey to LA RECOUSSE	RW.
VINCLY	7	6.30 a.m.	Motor buses take the Company to the village of LA RECOUSSE, arriving 12.30 p.m. The Company's transport arrive later in the afternoon.	RW.
LA RECOUSSE	8		Company strength on this date:— Officers. Other Ranks. 10 194 (including 23 Attached men). Of the above there are:— Officers On Courses = 2 " Rest Camp = 1 —— 3 Other Ranks. F.A. { Leave = 7 (including 3 Attached) Courses = 3 Rest Camp = 3 —— 16 }	RW.

A 5834 Wt. W4973/M687 750,000 8/16 D. D. & L. Ltd. Forms/C.2118/13.

WAR DIARY
or
INTELLIGENCE SUMMARY.

(Erase heading not required.)

Army Form C. 2118.

Place	Date	Hour	Summary of Events and Information	Remarks and references to Appendices
LA RECOUSSE	8 (cont.)	7 a.m. 9 a.m. 9.15 10 a.m.	Route March. C.O's Inspection. Company Drill. "A" Section. — Range Fatigue. Remainder of Company — Gun cleaning & Immediate Action.	
LA RECOUSSE	9	7a.m.to 8a.m. 9 to 10 " " 10 to 11 11 to 12.30 9.15 to 12.30	Reinforcements received = One officer & six O.R. Arrivals from Machine Gun School = One officer & two O.R. " Rest Camp = One " + 3 O.R. Departures: — One O.R. attached from 7th A. & S.H. returned to unit. One O.R. to Hospital, sick. Training:— Route March. C.O's Inspection. Physical training for "A", "C" & "D" Sections. Gun Drill " " " " Immediate Action " " " " "B" Section — Digging on Range.	

WAR DIARY
or
INTELLIGENCE SUMMARY.

Army Form C. 2118.

Place	Date	Hour	Summary of Events and Information	Remarks and references to Appendices
LA RECOUSSE	10		Personnel. Arrival:— One O.R. from leave.	
		7.30am to 10.30	Training:— Baths for whole of Company.	2ℓv.
		2.30pm	Lecture to N.C.O.'s.	
LA RECOUSSE	11		Personnel:— One officer proceeds on leave to U.K. One O.R. struck off Coy. strength. (Sick & evac. from 2nd area)	2ℓv.
		6a.m. to 12.30	Training "A", "C" & "D" Sections:— Field work, i.e. the leading of pack ponies, taking off of guns & getting machine guns mounted & into action on a given target. "B" Section:— Range, firing Part I. Table C.	
		2.30 to 3.15	Gun cleaning	
		2.30pm	Lecture to N.C.O's. Map reading.	

Army Form C. 2118.

WAR DIARY
or
INTELLIGENCE SUMMARY.
(Erase heading not required.)

Place	Date	Hour	Summary of Events and Information	Remarks and references to Appendices
LA RECOUSSE	12		Personnel. Arrivals:— One O.R. from leave. " " " Hospital.	B.W.
			Training.	
			The Brigade practices the attack of the Company takes part in these operations, employing 7 guns at (supposed) enemy strong posts, whilst the remaining 9 are engaged on barrage work in assistance of the Brigade.	
			The chief object of the Machine Gun Company is to afford practice to the infantry in the method of dealing with enemy machine guns, recent operations in the field having shewn the desirability of this.	
			The method employed in dealing with these enemy machine guns is as follows:—	
			When a gun is observed our "Stokes" Gunners & rifle grenade men come into action, either putting the enemy machine gun out of action or compelling its withdrawal.	

Army Form C. 2118.

WAR DIARY
or
INTELLIGENCE SUMMARY.
(Erase heading not required.)

Instructions regarding War Diaries and Intelligence Summaries are contained in F.S. Regs., Part II. and the Staff Manual respectively. Title pages will be prepared in manuscript.

Place	Date	Hour	Summary of Events and Information	Remarks and references to Appendices
LA RECOUSSE	13.		Reinforcement — One Other Rank.	
			Departure — " " " To Hospital sick.	
			Training	
		8 a.m. to 12.30 p.m.	Field work — mounting guns from pack ponies & getting into action. "A" & "B" Sections	
			"C" & "D" Sections — Range Firing.	
		2.30 to 3.15 p.m.	Gun cleaning.	RW.
LA RECOUSSE	14		Personnel. Departures. 2 O.R. to Hosp. sick. 1 O.R. " Leave to U.K. Reinforcement — One O.R.	
			Training	
		7 a.m. to 8 a.m.	Route March	
		9 to 10	C.O's Inspection & Squad Drill.	
		10–11	Physical Training	
		11 to 12.30	Lects on Elementary training (Dickers' Gun)	RW.

WAR DIARY or INTELLIGENCE SUMMARY.

Army Form C. 2118.

Place	Date	Hour	Summary of Events and Information	Remarks and references to Appendices
LA RECOUSSE	15		Company Strength:— Officers. Other Ranks. 11 200 (including 22 Attached). The above figures include :— Officers on Leave = 2, Courses = 1/3. Other Ranks at Field Amb. = 9 (including 3 attached), Leave = 2, Courses = 1/12.	S.D.
		8 a.m. to 12.30 p.m.	Training. Indication & Recognition of Targets. Rapid gun laying at ARDENHAM.	
LA RECOUSSE	16		Personnel. One Officer & One O.R. from Course (Third Army Infantry School)	S.D.

Army Form C. 2118.

WAR DIARY
or
INTELLIGENCE SUMMARY.
(Erase heading not required.)

Instructions regarding War Diaries and Intelligence Summaries are contained in F. S. Regs., Part II. and the Staff Manual respectively. Title pages will be prepared in manuscript.

Place	Date	Hour	Summary of Events and Information	Remarks and references to Appendices
LA RECOUSSE	16	7 a.m. to 8	Route March	Ch.
		9 a.m. 9 to 10	C.O's Inspection Squad Drill	
		10 - 11	Physical Training	
		11.15 to noon	Immediate Action	
		12 to 12.30	Gun Drill.	
LA RECOUSSE	17		Personnel. Arrivals :— 1 O.R. from Hospital ; 1 O.R. from Leave Departures :— 1 O.R. to Hosp. sick ; 1 Officer & 2 O.R. to Antigas Course	Ch.
		5 a.m. to 11 a.m.	Training. Range, Firing Part II, Table C.	
		1.30 p.m. to 4.30 p.m.	Company Parades for Baths.	
LA RECOUSSE	18		Personnel. Arrivals :— 2 O.R. from Hospital.	Ch.

WAR DIARY
or
INTELLIGENCE SUMMARY.
(Erase heading not required.)

Army Form C. 2118.

Place	Date	Hour	Summary of Events and Information	Remarks and references to Appendices
LA RECOUSSE	18 (cont'd)		Training:—	
		7 a.m.	Company Drill	
		8 a.m. to 12.30 p.m.	Recruits:— At Range, firing Part I, Table C.	
		9 a.m.	C.O's Inspection	
		9.15 to 12.30 p.m.	Revolver Practice on Range	
		9 to 9.30	Aiming Instruction (Triangle of Error)	
		9.30 to 10	Musketry (Muscle Exercises)	
		10 to 10.30	Gun Drill	
		10.30 to 11	Rifle Exercises	
		11.30 to 12.30	Immediate Action	
LA RECOUSSE	19		Personnel. Departures:— 1 Officer & 1 O.R. to Hosp. sick.	
			Training	
		8 a.m.	"A" Section:— Stoppages on Range	
		8 to 12.30	"B", "C" & "D":— Fire Orders & Gun Laying, W. Training Area.	
		8 a.m.	Recruits:— Arms Drill, etc.	
		2.15 p.m.	Lecture to Recruits.	

WAR DIARY
or
INTELLIGENCE SUMMARY.
(Erase heading not required.)

Army Form C. 2118.

Instructions regarding War Diaries and Intelligence Summaries are contained in F. S. Regs., Part II. and the Staff Manual respectively. Title pages will be prepared in manuscript.

Place	Date	Hour	Summary of Events and Information	Remarks and references to Appendices
LA RECOUSSE	20		Personnel. Departures. 2 O.R. (Attached) to Hosp., sick.	
			Training.	
		8 to 12.30	"B" Section. — Stoppages on Range	
			"A", "C" & "D" Sections:—	
		8 a.m.	Squad Drill	
		9 "	Rifle & Revolver Exercises	
		9.30	Mechanism	
		10.30	Physical Training	
		11.15	Combined Gun Drill	
		noon to 12.30	Musketry	
		8 a.m.	Recruits. — Squad Drill, etc.	
LA RECOUSSE	21		Personnel. Strength Decrease: — 1 O.R. to Base Depot, 1 O.R. sick evac. from Div. area.	
			Departure: — 1 O.R. (Attached) to Hosp., sick	
			Reversion. — 1 L/Cpl. to Pte. at own request.	

Army Form C. 2118.

WAR DIARY
or
INTELLIGENCE SUMMARY.

(Erase heading not required.)

Instructions regarding War Diaries and Intelligence Summaries are contained in F. S. Regs., Part II. and the Staff Manual respectively. Title pages will be prepared in manuscript.

Place	Date	Hour	Summary of Events and Information	Remarks and references to Appendices
LA RECOUSSE	21 (cont'd)	7 a.m. to 8	Route March	
		8 a.m.	Recruits :- Range	
		9 a.m.	C.O's Inspection	
LA RECOUSSE	22		Personnel.	
			Company Strength :—	
			Officers. Other Ranks.	
			11 300 (including 22 attached)	
			The above figures include :—	
			Officers in Hospital = 1	
			" on Leave = 2	
			" " Course = 1	
			4 Officers.	
			Other Ranks; in Field Amb. = 11 (including 4 attached)	
			" Leave = 1	
			" Courses = 2	
			14 Other Ranks.	

A 5834   Wt. W4973/M687   750,000   8/16   D. D. & L. Ltd.   Forms/C.2118/13.

Army Form C. 2118.

Instructions regarding War Diaries and Intelligence Summaries are contained in F.S. Regs., Part II. and the Staff Manual respectively. Title pages will be prepared in manuscript.

WAR DIARY
or
INTELLIGENCE SUMMARY.
(Erase heading not required.)

Place	Date	Hour	Summary of Events and Information	Remarks and references to Appendices
LA RECOUSSE	22	6.15 a.m.	Company proceed by route march to billets at KINDERBELCK	
KINDERBELCK	23		Personnel. Arrivals:- 1 Officer & 2 O.R. from Anti-gas Course. 1 " from Leave. Departure:- 1 O.R. (attached) to Hosp. sick.	
KINDERBELCK	23 (cont'd)	9.30 a.m. 9.45 to 10.45 10.45 11 to 12.30	Training:- C.O's Inspection Physical Training Gun Cleaning	
KINDERBELCK	24		Personnel. Strength Increase:- 1 O.R. from Base Depot; 1 O.R. from Hosp. Strength Decrease:- 2 O.R. (attached) struck off on evac from Bn area, sick.	

Army Form C. 2118.

WAR DIARY
or
INTELLIGENCE SUMMARY.
(Erase heading not required.)

Instructions regarding War Diaries and Intelligence Summaries are contained in F. S. Regs., Part II. and the Staff Manual respectively. Title pages will be prepared in manuscript.

Place	Date	Hour	Summary of Events and Information	Remarks and references to Appendices
KINDERBECK	24 (Sunday)		The Company parades for Divine Service.	RH
Do.	25		Personnel. Arrival: - 1 O.R. from Hosp. Departures: - 1 O.R. to Hosp, sick. 1 O.R. - Leave 26.6.17 to 26.7.17.	BH
	25	7 a.m. 9 9.15 10.15 11.30 12 to 12.30 12.15 to 3.15	Training. Route March. C.O.'s Inspection. Indication & Recognition of Targets. Overhead fire. Immediate Action. Squad Drill. Lecture — "Characteristics".	
Do.	26		Personnel. Arrival. - 1 O.R. from leave. Departures. - 4 O.R. to Signalling Course at 154th/Bde	RH

Army Form C. 2118.

WAR DIARY
or
INTELLIGENCE SUMMARY.
(Erase heading not required.)

Instructions regarding War Diaries and Intelligence Summaries are contained in F. S. Regs., Part II. and the Staff Manual respectively. Title pages will be prepared in manuscript.

Place	Date	Hour	Summary of Events and Information	Remarks and references to Appendices
KINDERBELCK	26		Training.	
		8 a.m. to 12.30	Field Practice — Machine Guns with Advance Guard.	
		2.15 to 3.15 p.m.	Lecture — Fire Direction.	
Do.	27		Personnel.	
			Arrivals:- 1 O.R. from Hosp.	
			1 O.R. (attached) from Hosp.	
			Departure:- 1 O.R. to Hosp., sick.	
			Strength Decrease. { 1 Officer on evac. from Corps area, sick	
			{ 1 O.R. evac. from Div. area, sick.	
			Training.	
		7 to 8 a.m.	Route March	
		9 a.m.	C.O.'s Inspection	
		9.15 to 11.15	Advanced Gun Drill	
		11.30 to 12.30	Company Drill	
		2 to 3	Lecture — Fire Direction.	

Army Form C. 2118.

WAR DIARY
or
INTELLIGENCE SUMMARY.
(Erase heading not required.)

Instructions regarding War Diaries and Intelligence Summaries are contained in F.S. Regs., Part II. and the Staff Manual respectively. Title pages will be prepared in manuscript.

Place	Date	Hour	Summary of Events and Information	Remarks and references to Appendices
KINDERBECK	28		Personnel. Strength Decrease. 3 O.R. struck off on evac from Bn. on sick 2 O.R. (attached) " " "	18h
		7 to 8	Training. Company Drill	
		9 a.m.	C.O.'s Inspection	
		9.15	Rifle & Revolver Exercises	
		9.45	Mechanism	
		11 a.m. to noon	Lecture — Use of machine guns with outposts.	
Do.	29		Personnel. Company Strength:- (Officers) 10 (Other Ranks) 174 (including 18 attached) The above figures include:- Officers on Leave = 1 Other Ranks, F.A. = 3 " " Course = 1 Leave = 1 2 Officers Courses = 3 / 4 O.R.	18h

WAR DIARY
or
INTELLIGENCE SUMMARY.

(Erase heading not required.)

Army Form C. 2118.

Place	Date	Hour	Summary of Events and Information	Remarks and references to Appendices
KINDERBECK	29		Training.	
		7.68	Route March	
		9.30	C.O's Inspection	
		9.45	Physical Training	
		10.45	Immediate Action	20
		11.45 to 12.30	Lecture — Fire Direction (III)	
		2.30 p.m.	Kit Inspection. Harness & Limber Inspection.	
Do.	30		Personnel. Departure:— 1 O.R. to Veterinary Course.	
		7 a.m.	Route March	
		9 a.m.	Inspection by Section Officers.	20
			The Company Sports, for which all ranks have been training during the past few weeks & which were to have been held to-day, are postponed till the 2nd proximo owing to the unfavourable weather prevailing.	

Army Form C. 2118.

WAR DIARY
or
INTELLIGENCE SUMMARY.
(Erase heading not required.)

Place	Date	Hour	Summary of Events and Information	Remarks and references to Appendices
	June.		<u>Resumé</u>. During the month of June, 1917, the Company, having been out of the line the whole of that period, has spent the time in approved methods of training. One feature has been the practicality of its training. Considerable time having been allotted to practising the attack, in some cases in conjunction with larger units. The machine gun, being the sine qua non of the machine gunner, has been dealt with in all its phases & has received much attention in connection with field operations. The idea under-lying the training programmes has been to specify exercises calculated to result in a maximum of physical fitness & to increase the interest & efficiency of the men in the machine gun. Early in the month all the gunners of the	

Place	Date	Hour	Summary of Events and Information	Remarks and references to Appendices
	June		Company were detailed in practical work on the Range & classified accordingly. For those who did not prove themselves first-class machine gunners a special syllabus has been drawn up to supply the theoretical & practical training requiring perfection & it is anticipated that at the next test a much larger proportion will be shown as 1st Class.

Sustained interest has been taken by all ranks in sport & the postponed Sports of the Company on 2.7.19 bid fair to arouse considerable interest in the various units throughout the Brigade. | |

RMHughes lt
O.C. 154 Machine Gun Coy.

On His Majesty's Service.

154th MACHINE GUN COMPANY

JULY 1917

CONFIDENTIAL.

ORIGINAL WAR DIARY

of

154th Coy., M.G.C.

From 1st July, 1917 To 31st July, 1917.

Vol. XIX

Army Form C. 2118.

WAR DIARY
or
INTELLIGENCE SUMMARY.
(Erase heading not required.)

Instructions regarding War Diaries and Intelligence Summaries are contained in F. S. Regs., Part II. and the Staff Manual respectively. Title pages will be prepared in manuscript.

Place	Date	Hour	Summary of Events and Information	Remarks and references to Appendices

KINDERBELCK	July, 1919 1st.		Personnel. — Strength etc.
			
			 Strength.
			 Officers 10
			 Other Ranks 173
			 Other Ranks — Attached 18
			
			 The above figures include :—
			
			 Officers :— Courses = 3
			 Leave = 1
			       = 4
			
			 Other Ranks :— Hospital = nil
			 Leave = 1
			 Courses = 10
			        = 11	

Army Form C. 2118.

WAR DIARY
or
INTELLIGENCE SUMMARY.
(Erase heading not required.)

Place	Date July	Hour	Summary of Events and Information	Remarks and references to Appendices
KINDERBECK.	1st	a.m.	Company Parades for Divine Services.	Sgd.
Do.	2nd	7a.m to 9a.m. 9.15 to 10 10 to 10.45 11 to 12.30	Route March. C.O's Inspection. Indication & Recognition of Targets. Fire Orders. Gun Drill with Limbers & Pack Animals.	Sgd.
			Personnel. 1 Officer from Leave. 2 O.R. to Hosp., sick (one struck off Coy. strength)	
			1 O.R. to Hosp., sick.	
Do	3	8.30 a.m to 12.30 p.m.	Parades. Company Parades for Baths.	Sgd.
Do	4		Personnel. One Officer & 3 O.R. from Courses 1 O.R. from Hosp. 1 O.R. to "	Sgd.

A 5834 Wt: W4973/M687 750,000 8/16 D. D. & L. Ltd. Forms/C.2118/13

Army Form C. 2118.

WAR DIARY
or
INTELLIGENCE SUMMARY.
(Erase heading not required.)

Instructions regarding War Diaries and Intelligence Summaries are contained in F. S. Regs., Part II. and the Staff Manual respectively. Title pages will be prepared in manuscript.

Place	Date	Hour	Summary of Events and Information	Remarks and references to Appendices
KINDERBECK	4		Parades.	
		9 am	Company Drill	
		8:45	C.O.'s Inspection	
		9 to 12:30	Field Practice — Machine Guns with Outpost	
		2 to 2:45	Lecture — Machine Guns in open warfare.	
Do.	5		Personnel. 2 O.R. to Hosp. sick.	
			Parades.	
		7 to 8	Cleaning gun equipment	
		9 a.m.	C.O.'s Inspection	
		9:15 to 10	Rifle Exercises	
		10 to 12:30	Street fighting	
		2 p.m.	Inspection of gun equipment	
		3 p.m.	Limber & Harness Inspection.	

Army Form C. 2118.

WAR DIARY
or
INTELLIGENCE SUMMARY.
(Erase heading not required.)

Instructions regarding War Diaries and Intelligence Summaries are contained in F. S. Regs., Part II. and the Staff Manual respectively. Title pages will be prepared in manuscript.

Place	Date	Hour	Summary of Events and Information	Remarks and references to Appendices
KINDERBECK	6		Personnel. Strength of Coy. as follows:—	
			Officers 10	
			O.R. 172	
			O.R. – attached ... 18	
			The above figures include:—	
			Officers:– On Courses = 1	
			O.R. Field Amb. = 4	
			Courses = 10	
			Leave = 2	
			Rest Camp = 2	
			Total = 18	

Army Form C. 2118.

WAR DIARY
or
INTELLIGENCE SUMMARY.
(Erase heading not required.)

Place	Date	Hour	Summary of Events and Information	Remarks and references to Appendices
KINDERBECK	JULY 6	6:30 to 7 a.m. 7:50 7:30 to 8:30 9:15 9:45 10:30 noon to 12:30	Parades. "A" & "C" Sections — Packing Limbers Parade ready to move off to ST. MOMELIN training area. " Route March " Physical training " Stable & Feed Gun Drill with Pack Animals } "B" & "D" Sections Rifle & Revolver Exercises.	SCM
KINDERBECK	7	7 a.m. 9 — 11:15 9 a.m. 3 p.m.	Personnel. Arrivals. 1 O.R. from hospital 6 " " courses Departures. 1 O.R. to hospital 7.7.17 1 " " Cadre 4th gun. Parades. Roll Calling General Issuing of Box Respirators Inspection & Overhauling of Gun & Gun Equipment } "B" & "D" Sections Training at ST. MOMELIN — "A" & "C" Sections Lecture "First Aid"	SCM

Army Form C. 2118.

WAR DIARY
or
INTELLIGENCE SUMMARY.
(Erase heading not required.)

Instructions regarding War Diaries and Intelligence Summaries are contained in F. S. Regs., Part II. and the Staff Manual respectively. Title pages will be prepared in manuscript.

Place	Date	Hour	Summary of Events and Information	Remarks and references to Appendices
Kinderbelch	July 8th		Personnel. Lieut R. J. W. Hughes takes over the command of 154/Machine Gun Company from Major G. P. Board (to 47th Division). Strength Serjeants. 1 Officer & 1 O.R. to 47th Div. 1 O.R. to Hospital sick Departure:—	Egypt
Do	8	9 pm	Divine Service	Egypt
Do	9		Personnel. 1 O.R. to Hospital sick gun. Strength/strength 1.55 am. Company leaves billets at KINDERBELCK, marches to ST. OMER & entrains for POPERINGHE. Billets at A.30 Central. "D" Camp arc taken over.	Egypt
"D" Camp A.30 Central	10	9 a.m. 9.15	Inspection by Section Officers Cleaning guns & Bell feeling Personnel. Arrival — 1 O.R. from Hospital	Egypt

WAR DIARY
or
INTELLIGENCE SUMMARY.

Army Form C. 2118.

Place	Date	Hour	Summary of Events and Information	Remarks and references to Appendices
"D" Camp, A.30.central.	July 11	9 a.m.	**Personnel.** One O.R. struck off strength on evac. from Divl. area. Inspection by Section Officers. Company less one section moved to billets to relieve 152nd Company in the front of CANAL BANK.	
Coy Hd C.25.A.8.2.	12	Early morn.	At 2.20 a.m. the Company, having established itself in the battle positions taken over from the 152 M.G. Coy., commenced a harassing scheme with its machine guns on trench junction at CALEDONIA SUPPORT.	
		Early morn.	**Enemy Operations.** The enemy's artillery is very active, especially on FOCH FARM and for half an hour, from 3 a.m., on FUSILIER FARM. Two direct hits are made on BUTT 12 on at one of our machine gun emplacements.	
		10.30 p.m. to m.n.	Enemy artillery is very active also on "X" lines and 3 men of our working party are wounded. One Vickers' gun at STIRLING LANE is damaged by fragments of shell.	
		11 p.m. to m.n.	Our gun teams at C.19.1 and C.19.2 wear their box respirators on account of gas, believed to be enemy gas shells.	

WAR DIARY
or
INTELLIGENCE SUMMARY.
(Erase heading not required.)

Army Form C. 2118.

Place	Date	Hour	Summary of Events and Information	Remarks and references to Appendices
Coy. Hqrs. CANAL BANK C.25.a.8.2.	12		An enemy dump is observed to be on fire in the early hours of the morning. Workdone. Five machine gun emplacements are started in "X" Line.	
Ditto	13	Early morn.	4,000 rounds are fired by two of our machine guns on the enemys reserve lines & tracks. The enemys artillery is active throughout the day & direct hits on	
		5 a.m.	BUTT "42" 400 rounds are fired at a hostile aeroplane which returns to our lines.	
		During afternoon	Enemy operations. On the left sector there is moderate shelling during the afternoon & early evening but little shelling at night.	
			Aircraft. Our planes are very active during the latter part of the day. One is observed to descend about 8pm, apparently damaged.	
		11 p.m.	Two dumps are observed to be on fire. One appears to be an S.A.A. dump about 800 yards West of HIGHLAND FARM. The other is in our area in a S.E. direction.	
			Workdone. The five emplacements begun yesterday are completed and 20 noticeboards in "X" Line.	

Army Form C. 2118.

WAR DIARY
or
INTELLIGENCE SUMMARY.
(Erase heading not required.)

Instructions regarding War Diaries and Intelligence Summaries are contained in F. S. Regs., Part II. and the Staff Manual respectively. Title pages will be prepared in manuscript.

Place	Date	Hour	Summary of Events and Information	Remarks and references to Appendices
Coy. Hqrs. CANAL BANK C.25.a.8.2.	13	noon	**Personnel.** Strength of Company as follows:— Officers .... 9 Other Ranks ... 169 Attached ...... 16 The above figures include:— Other Ranks Field Amb. = 1 Leave = 3 Courses = 2 Rest Camp = 2 ——— 8	
Ditto.	14		**Personnel.** Arrivals — 32 men from the Battalions of the Bde. to be attached to 154 M.g. Coy. for duty.	

WAR DIARY
or
INTELLIGENCE SUMMARY.
(Erase heading not required.)

Army Form C. 2118.

Place	Date	Hour	Summary of Events and Information	Remarks and references to Appendices
Bn. Hqrs. CANAL BANK C.25a.8.2.	14	Early morn	3,000 rounds are expended by our machine guns on indirect fire on FORT CALEDONIA and KEMPTON PARK ROAD. Between midnight & 2 a.m. an enemy machine gun & sniper fire from time to time on "X" Line & junction of JOFFRE TRENCH.	RMah
		4.40 a.m.	On the left sector a German flare is observed flying low over our lines & dropping white lights, which form into streaks of white light. 400 rounds are fired at it by our machine guns, which cause it to withdraw. At Stand-to the enemy puts up a barrage of rifle grenades, sling bombs & light shells on the front line & support fifteen thus lasts half an hour.	
		10.45 a.m.	The enemy is again active, shelling area between HIGHLAND and FUSILIER farms.	
		Early morn	Intelligence. On the right sector an aeroplane with a strong white light, flying very low, pistols "No man's land" for about half an hour after midnight. It is not known whether it is friendly or hostile & is not engaged.	

WAR DIARY
or
INTELLIGENCE SUMMARY.

Army Form C. 2118.

Place	Date	Hour	Summary of Events and Information	Remarks and references to Appendices
Coy. Hqrs. CANAL BANK C.25.a.8.2.	14 (cont.)	4.10 a.m.	Two hostile planes cross our line on the Right Sector. Working. Progress is made in the formation of S.A.A. dumps in "X" Line.	
Ditto	15		During the early hours of the morning the 32nd Machine Gun Coy. took over the battle positions from 28th until the one section left out of the line is now brought in & lent to the 32nd Coy. to man guns with teams are also left in the line.	
Coy. Hqrs. "E" Camp A.30.C.1.10.	16 to 23		During this period the one section lent to of the 32nd Coy. are employed on Machine Gun assistance to 18 guns firing nightly in co-operation with the Artillery on to the German back areas, the object being to harass the enemy & prevent the carrying up of supplies. This section is relieved on night 21/22. A party under Lieut. Clyde constructs 32 machine gun emplacements & kills another working party so engaged in carrying out work for the Royal Engineers & forms the	

Army Form C. 2118.

WAR DIARY
or
INTELLIGENCE SUMMARY.
(Erase heading not required.)

Instructions regarding War Diaries and Intelligence Summaries are contained in F. S. Regs., Part II. and the Staff Manual respectively. Title pages will be prepared in manuscript.

Place	Date	Hour	Summary of Events and Information	Remarks and references to Appendices
Coy. Hqrs "E" Camp. A.30 Central	16 to 23 (cont'd)		Construction of shelters for Machine Gunners. Working parties also forum reserve dumps of S.A.A. in "X" and front lines, for the barrage in pending operations. Fifty men of the Gordon Highlanders are attached for assistance in this work. Casualties (16.7.17 to 23.7.17) 3 Other Ranks killed in action. 1 " " 7 " " Gassed & admitted to dock.	
Ditto.	30		Personnel. Strength of Company as follows:— Officers 10 Other Ranks 165 Other Ranks Attached 48 The above figures include:— Other Ranks { On leave = 2, Courses = 1, Rest Camp = 2 } 5	

WAR DIARY or INTELLIGENCE SUMMARY

Army Form C. 2118.

Place	Date JULY	Hour	Summary of Events and Information	Remarks and references to Appendices
Coy HQrs "E" Camp A.30.Central	24 25 26		The three working parties engaged in (a) the construction of shelters, (b) the making of machine gun emplacements & (c) the forming of ammunition dumps, complete their work on the 24th, 25th & 26th respectively & return to "E" Camp. The Indian Labour Co. carried 18,000 sandbags + 50 rolls of S.W. + 30,000 rounds S.A.A + 130 boxes bombs.	BMA
Do.	27	9 a.m. 9.15 10.15 11.15 12.45 to 1.45 2 to 3.45	The Company, now being at "E" Camp in reserve, awaiting orders, are occupied as follows:- Inspection by Section Officers Physical training Mechanism Immediate Action Gas Drill & in fighting Order Visit to Model trenches by sections	BMA
Do.	27		Personnel. Strength of Company as follows:- Officers .... 10 O.R. .... 175 Attached .... 46 The above figures include:- Other Ranks, Field Amb. 8 (includes 1 attached) Leave 5 Course 1 Rest Camp 2	BMA

Army Form C. 2118.

WAR DIARY
or
INTELLIGENCE SUMMARY.
(Erase heading not required.)

Instructions regarding War Diaries and Intelligence Summaries are contained in F. S. Regs., Part II. and the Staff Manual respectively. Title pages will be prepared in manuscript.

Place	Date	Hour	Summary of Events and Information	Remarks and references to Appendices
"E" Camp A30 Central	28	8.30 a.m. 8.45 9.45 11 a.m. 10.12. 12 M 12.30 11 to 12.30	Inspection by Section Officers Physical training Voluntary Communion Service (C. of E.) Training under Section Officer. Gun cleaning Attached men't — Elementary gun training	
Do.	29	9 a.m. 9.15 to noon	Inspection by Section Officers Pack Saddle Drill	
Do.	30	9 a.m. 9.15.	Inspection by Section Officers. Dress: – Fighting Order. Gun fitting & overhauling. Packing belts, spare parts, etc.	
Do.	31	5 p.m.	The Company awaits orders to move up the line for the attack. Having received orders, the Company proceed to CANAL BANK, C.15.a.8.a.	

WAR DIARY
or
INTELLIGENCE SUMMARY.

Army Form C. 2118.

Place	Date	Hour	Summary of Events and Information	Remarks and references to Appendices
	JULY 1917 31st		Below are figures showing casualties sustained by the Company during the month of July:—	
			Officers Other Ranks. Killed in Action Nil 4 (includes 2 attached) Died of Wounds " 1 Wounded " 5 " (Att'd) Nil 9 (includes 1 att'd) To Hospital, gassed " 2 Accidentally injured Nil	F.H. J.

	31		Strength of Company as follows:—
			          Officers 10
			          Other Ranks 175
			          " (Att'd) 46
			The above figures include:—
			Other Ranks { On leave 2
			                        Courses 1
			                        At Rest Camp 2
			                        Field Amb. 10
				J.H.

			2/Lt Norman 3/scout O for O/C 154 M G Company	

On His Majesty's Service.

154th MACHINE GUN COMPANY

AUGUST 1917

WAR DIARY

OF

154TH M.G. COY.

FOR AUG 1917

Vol 20

VOL. 20

WAR DIARY
or
INTELLIGENCE SUMMARY.

Army Form C. 2118.

CONFIDENTIAL.

ORIGINAL WAR DIARY

of

154th Coy., M.G.C.

For August, 1917.

VOL. 20.

Army Form C. 2118.

WAR DIARY
or
INTELLIGENCE SUMMARY.
(Erase heading not required.)

154th Coy. M.G.C.

Place	Date	Hour	Summary of Events and Information	Remarks and references to Appendices
CANAL BANK C.25.a.8.2.	1917 AUGUST 1		Personnel. Strength of Company as follows:— Officers 10 Other Ranks 169 " Attached #6746 The above figures include:— Other Ranks Field Amb. = 4 Leave = 2 Courses = 2 Rest Camp = 1 / 9	

Army Form C. 2118.

WAR DIARY
or
INTELLIGENCE SUMMARY.

(Erase heading not required.)

Place	Date	Hour	Summary of Events and Information	Remarks and references to Appendices
CANAL BANK C.25a.8.2.	August 1st 1917	5 p.m.	The Company leaves dug-outs on the East Bank of the CANAL DE L'YSER to take over gun positions from the 152nd & 153rd Machine Gun Companies. Headquarters are established at MINTY FARM — Sheet 28 N.W. C.9.d.6.5. at 7 p.m. & the relief is complete by midnight 1–2.8.17.	E.O.M.

Army Form C. 2118.

WAR DIARY
or
INTELLIGENCE SUMMARY.
(Erase heading not required.)

Instructions regarding War Diaries and Intelligence Summaries are contained in F. S. Regs., Part II. and the Staff Manual respectively. Title pages will be prepared in manuscript.

Place	Date	Hour	Summary of Events and Information	Remarks and references to Appendices
Hqts. MINTY FARM Sheet 28 N.W. C.9.d.6.5.	1917 August 2	9.30 p.m.	Our artillery is very active, particularly in the evening. S.O.S. signals sent up on the left & Our artillery & machine guns reply. The machine guns of this Company at FRANCOIS FARM fire 2,000 rounds. Our guns in the front positions fire 500 rounds in reply to S.O.S. No attack on our immediate front is observed. The remainder of the night is very quiet. Hostile artillery is very active. VON VERDER HOUSE KITCHENER'S WOOD, MINTY FARM & BLACK LINE receive especial attention from the enemy's heavies. Work done. M.G. emplacements improved.	BM.
Do.	3	4 p.m.	MINTY FARM is shelled by the enemy with 8" howitzers, a direct hit being obtained on a small demolished building on the North side. Work done. Machine gun emplacements improved & revetted.	BM.

WAR DIARY
or
INTELLIGENCE SUMMARY.
(Erase heading not required.)

Army Form C. 2118.

Place	Date	Hour	Summary of Events and Information	Remarks and references to Appendices
Hqrs. MINTY FARM Sheet 28 N.W. C.9.d.6.5.	August 1917 4	8.45 a.m.	The machine guns of this Company at FRANCOIS FARM fire 2,000 rounds in response to S.O.S. sent up on the left.	
			The enemy puts down a barrage on our front & support lines which lasts half an hour.	Enid.
		6.00 a.m.	An aeroplane flies low over our lines. Owing to low visibility, sentries could not state whether it was ours or the enemy's.	
		11.30 a.m.	An enemy aeroplane, which had streamers attached to lower planes, flies over our lines.	
		1.30 p.m.	Enemy puts down a very heavy barrage on our front line. Two enemy aeroplanes fire on Battalion relief coming in between RUDOLF & FRANCOIS FARMS & in the vicinity of MINTY FARM.	
Do.	5	3.30 a.m.	The M. guns of this Company are relieved in the right sector by 8 guns of the 232nd Machine Gun Company.	Enid.
		9.30 p.m.	Enemy shells our lines, many gas shells being used. Enemy appears to be very active on the right sector. He sends	

WAR DIARY or INTELLIGENCE SUMMARY

Army Form C. 2118.

Place	Date	Hour	Summary of Events and Information	Remarks and references to Appendices
Hqrs. MINTY FARM Sheet 28 N.W. C.9.d.6.5.	August 1917 5 (con't)		A golden rain rockets + our S.O.S. goes up on the right also. Our sector was quiet throughout the night. Work done. Emplacements repaired + dug-outs drained.	EMA
Do.	6		Enemy artillery + our own are normal throughout the day. There are several aerial combats, no results being observed. One section is relieved.	EMA
Do.	7	MORN.	The remaining 8 guns of the Company are relieved on the left by 33rd Machine Gun Company. Four of these guns, with teams, remain at CANAL BANK + rejoin the Company at ST JANSTER BIEZEN on the 8th inst.	EMA
			Casualties of 154 M.G. Coy. between 1.8.17 + 7.8.17:— Killed in action = 1 O.R. Wounded " " = 5 O.R.	EMA

Army Form C. 2118.

WAR DIARY
or
INTELLIGENCE SUMMARY.

(Erase heading not required.)

Instructions regarding War Diaries and Intelligence Summaries are contained in F. S. Regs., Part II. and the Staff Manual respectively. Title pages will be prepared in manuscript.

Place	Date 1917	Hour	Summary of Events and Information	Remarks and references to Appendices
"D" Camp, A.30 Central.	August 8	5.30 a.m.	Company proceeds by route march to "N" Camp, ST. JANSTER BIEZEN.	
"N" Camp, ST. JANSTER BIEZEN.	9	9 a.m. 9.15	Inspection by Section Officers. Kit Inspection. Gun Cleaning. Inspection of gun equipment.	
Do	10	7 a.m. 9 a.m. 1.40 p.m.	Fatigues – loading motor lorry, etc. Physical training. Company parade & march to PROVEN, entraining there for WATTEN. The remainder of the journey to billets at HELLEBROUCQ is made by route march. Personnel Officers = 10 O.R. = 184 " attached = 45 On leave 2 Bn Hoth, 1 Leave, 1 Course 2 " " 2 "	
HELLEBROUCQ	11	1.30 a.m.	Company arrive in billets at HELLEBROUCQ.	
Do	12		Sunday – Company parade for Divine Services.	

WAR DIARY or INTELLIGENCE SUMMARY.

(Erase heading not required.)

Army Form C. 2118.

Place	Date	Hour	Summary of Events and Information	Remarks and references to Appendices
HELLEBROUCQ	13	8.45 a.m.	C.O's Inspection	
		9 to 10	Physical Training	
		10 - 12	Repairing & Refilling Belts	
		12 to 12.45	Gun Cleaning	
		2.15 to 3 p.m.	Lecture — Firing on enemy aircraft.	
Do.	14	8.45 a.m.	Inspection by Section Officers	
		9 to 10	Physical Training	
		10 to 12.45	Cleaning limbers, etc.	
		10 to 11	Mechanism ⎫	
		11 - 12	Immediate action ⎬ Attached men only.	
		12 to 12.45	Gun Drill (elementary). ⎭	
Do.	15	7 a.m.	The Company moves off to take part in Brigade operations. Four of our guns, with teams, go with each of the Battalions of the Brigade for consolidation purposes.	

Army Form C. 2118.

WAR DIARY
or
INTELLIGENCE SUMMARY.
(Erase heading not required.)

Instructions regarding War Diaries and Intelligence Summaries are contained in F. S. Regs., Part II. and the Staff Manual respectively. Title pages will be prepared in manuscript.

Place	Date	Hour	Summary of Events and Information	Remarks and references to Appendices
HELLEBROUCQ	August 1914. 16	8·45 a.m. 9 to 10 10-11 11-12 12-12·45 2·15 to 3	Inspection by Section Officers. Physical Training Light setting & practice in firing on enemy aircraft. Immediate Action Gun cleaning Lecture — Consolidation, strong points & protection of flanks.	[signature]
Do.	17	8·45 a.m. 9 to 10 10-12 12 to 12·45 2·15 to 3	C.O's Inspection Physical Training Gun Drill including use of YUKON packs. Cleaning guns Lecture — First Aid	[signature] Strength of Company Officers = 10 Other Ranks = 144 These figures include:— Officers on loan = 1 Other Ranks F.A. = 2 " " = 3 [illegible]
Do.	18	8·45 a.m. 9 to 10 10-11 11-12 12-12·45 2·15-3	C.O's Inspection Physical Training Immediate Action Gun Drill with Box Respirators on. Gun cleaning Lecture — Characteristics.	[signature]

Army Form C. 2118.

WAR DIARY
or
INTELLIGENCE SUMMARY.
(Erase heading not required.)

Instructions regarding War Diaries and Intelligence Summaries are contained in F.S. Regs., Part II. and the Staff Manual respectively. Title pages will be prepared in manuscript.

Place	Date August 1917.	Hour	Summary of Events and Information	Remarks and references to Appendices
HELLEBROUCK	19	10 a.m. / 11.15	Sunday — Divine Services.	[sgd]
Do.	20	8.45 a.m. / 9 to 10 / 10–11 / 11.15 to 12 / 12 to 12.45 / 8.45 a.m.	C.O.'s Inspection / Squad Drill / Gun Drill / Arms Drill / Gun cleaning / Rec'd Drafts & Attached men — Firing on Range.	[sgd]
Do	21	8.45 a.m. / 9 to 10 / 10.15 to 12 / 12 to 12.45 / 2.15 to 3.30 / 8.45 a.m.	C.O.'s Inspection / Route March / Barrage Drill / Demonstration etc — Defence without arms / Lecture — Indirect Fire. / Firing on Range — Same party as yesterday	[sgd]

WAR DIARY
or
INTELLIGENCE SUMMARY.

(Erase heading not required.)

Army Form C. 2118.

Place	Date	Hour	Summary of Events and Information	Remarks and references to Appendices
HELLEBROUCQ	1917 August 22	8.45 a.m. 9 to 10 10 " 11 11 " 12	Inspection in full marching order by C.O. Physical Training Lecture – Indirect Fire Arms Drill	
Do.	23	8.45 a.m. 9 to 10 10 " 11 5 p.m.	Inspection by Section Officers Physical Training Rifle Exercises Company leaves billets at HELLEBROUCQ, entrains at WATTEN for ABEELE whence a route march is made to "N" Camp, ST. JANSTER BIEZEN.	

"N" Camp
ST. JANSTER BIEZEN.
	24	4 a.m.	Company arrives in tents at "N" Camp, ST. JANSTER BIEZEN.
			
			Personnel. Strength of Company as follows:—
			    Officers 10
			    Other Ranks 196
			    " Attached 43
			
			The above figures include:—
			  Officers on Leave = 1
			    " Field Amb. = 5
			  Other Ranks Leave = 4 including 1 Attached (4th Gordons)
			    " Courses = 1	

WAR DIARY
or
INTELLIGENCE SUMMARY.
(Erase heading not required.)

Army Form C. 2118.

Place	Date	Hour	Summary of Events and Information	Remarks and references to Appendices
"N" Camp ST. JANSTER BIEZEN	1917 August 25	8.45 a.m.	C.O.'s Inspection	
		9 to 10	Physical Training	
		10–11	Company Drill	Attached men on Gun.
		11–12	Gun Drill	
		12.12.45	Gun cleaning	
		2.30 p.m.	Baths	
Do.	26	7.15 & 10.15 a.m.	Divine Services.	
		2.30 p.m.	Inspection of Equipment, etc.	
Do.	27	6.45 a.m.	C.O.'s Inspection	
		11.15	Inspection by G.O.C. 51st Highland Division	
Do.	28	8.30 a.m.	C.O.'s Inspection	
		9 to 10	Physical Training	

Army Form C. 2118.

WAR DIARY
or
INTELLIGENCE SUMMARY.
(Erase heading not required.)

Instructions regarding War Diaries and Intelligence Summaries are contained in F. S. Regs., Part II. and the Staff Manual respectively. Title pages will be prepared in manuscript.

Place	Date 1917	Hour	Summary of Events and Information	Remarks and references to Appendices
ST. JANSTER	August 29	5 am	Company proceeds by route march to MURAT CAMP.	Appx
BIEZEN				
MURAT CAMP B.30.6.5.5. (Sheet 28 N.W.)	30	9 am	Instruction by Section Officers	Appx
		9.15	Reconstruction of dug-outs & bivouacs	
Do	31	9 am	Instruction by Section Officers	Appx
		9.15	Physical training	
			gun cleaning	
		10.11		
		11.12	Bed-filling	
			Personnel Strength of Company as follows:-	
			Officers 10	
			Other Ranks 173	
			attached 43	
			The above figures include Other Ranks {Hosp. = 2, Leave = 6, Course = 1, Rest Camp = 1} Attached Hosp. = 1, O.R.	

Army Form C. 2118.

WAR DIARY
or
INTELLIGENCE SUMMARY.
(Erase heading not required.)

Instructions regarding War Diaries and Intelligence Summaries are contained in F. S. Regs., Part II. and the Staff Manual respectively. Title pages will be prepared in manuscript.

Place	Date	Hour	Summary of Events and Information	Remarks and references to Appendices
	August 1917 31		Aggregate casualties during the month of August 1917:— Officers .... Nil Other Ranks ... { One killed in action { Five wounded " "	[signature]

[signature] Capt.
Officer commanding
154 Machine Gun Coy

On His Majesty's Service.

154th MACHINE GUN COMPANY

SEPTEMBER 1917

CONFIDENTIAL.

ORIGINAL WAR DIARY of

154th Coy., MACHINE GUN CORPS

MONTH of SEPTEMBER, 1917.

VOL. 21.

Army Form C. 2118.

WAR DIARY
or
INTELLIGENCE SUMMARY.
(Erase heading not required.)

Place	Date	Hour	Summary of Events and Information	Remarks and references to Appendices
MURAT CAMP B.30.c.5.5. (Sheet 28 N.W)	1.9.17		Personnel. Strength of Company as follows:— Officers = 10 Other Ranks = 172 O.R. (Attached) = 43 The above figures include:— Hospital = 2 Leave = 6 } Other Ranks Courses = 1 Rest Camp = 1 Hospital = 1 } O.R. Attached.	

Army Form C. 2118.

WAR DIARY
or
INTELLIGENCE SUMMARY.
(Erase heading not required.)

Instructions regarding War Diaries and Intelligence Summaries are contained in F. S. Regs., Part II. and the Staff Manual respectively. Title pages will be prepared in manuscript.

Place	Date	Hour	Summary of Events and Information	Remarks and references to Appendices
MURAT CAMP B.30.c.5.5 (Sheet 28.N.W.)	1.9.17	9 a.m.	Parades. C.O's Inspection	MK
		9.15 to 10	Physical Training	
		10.15 to 11.15	Gun Drill	
		11.30-12.30	Mechanism. Immediate Action	
Do.	1917		Our machine guns on anti-aircraft work. Immediately on arrival at MURAT CAMP on the 29th ultimo emplacements were made for machine guns to be utilised against enemy aircraft.	
Do.		1.15 a.m.	About 1.15 a.m. the sound of machine gun fire in the vicinity of CANAL BANK is heard. Presently an aeroplane, travelling westward at no great speed, at a height of approximately 600 ft., is recognised in the moonlight, by our gunners as a German reconnoitring machine & when at 400 yards range two of our guns open fire. Simultaneously the	

Army Form C. 2118.

WAR DIARY
or
INTELLIGENCE SUMMARY.
(Erase heading not required.)

Instructions regarding War Diaries and Intelligence Summaries are contained in F. S. Regs., Part II. and the Staff Manual respectively. Title pages will be prepared in manuscript.

Place	Date	Hour	Summary of Events and Information	Remarks and references to Appendices
MURAT CAMP J.B.20.6.5.5 (Sh. et 28 N.W.)	1.9.17		Boche is fired upon by the Lewis guns of the 9th Gordon Highlanders on our right & those of the 9th Royal Scots on the left. Two belts (500 rounds) are expended by our gunners. The attack is too much for the Boche, who loosing the machine down to his own lines. The engines stop & the 'plane' is ridded with bullet crashes to earth on the West bank of the CANAL DE L'YSER, about a mile N.E. of this camp.	
Do.	2.9.17	9.45am	Presbyterians parade for Divine Service.	
		10am	C of E. " "	
		noon	Inspection of Iron Rations.	
			Enemy Operations. During the afternoon 7 enemy hostile German 'planes are observed reconnoitering over our back areas at a great height. After dark a number of enemy aeroplanes carry out a bombing raid on the back areas. Simultaneously MURAT CAMP	

Army Form C. 2118.

WAR DIARY
or
INTELLIGENCE SUMMARY.

(Erase heading not required.)

Instructions regarding War Diaries and Intelligence Summaries are contained in F. S. Regs., Part II. and the Staff Manual respectively. Title pages will be prepared in manuscript.

Place	Date	Hour	Summary of Events and Information	Remarks and references to Appendices
MURAT CAMP B.30.8.5.5 (Sheet 28 N.W.)	M.N. 2-9-17		is shelled, a direct hit being obtained on a tent on an immediate right occupied by eighteen of the 8th Gordon Highlanders. The hostile machines carrying out the raid were at once engaged by the machine guns of this Company & by others throughout the neighbourhood but no result is ascertained.	
Do.	3.9.17	9a.m. to 12.30 p.m. 9 a.m. to 10 a.m. 10 to 11 11.15 to 11.45 11.45 to 12.30 2 p.m. to 3	"A" Section — Range Physical Training Immediate Action Gas Drill Musketry Gun cleaning	M.K.
Do.	4.9.17	8.30 a.m.	The Company, having received orders to move owing to hostile shelling of MURAT CAMP, proceeds by route march to billets at "D" Camp, A.30 Central.	M.K.

WAR DIARY
INTELLIGENCE SUMMARY.
(Erase heading not required.)

Army Form C. 2118.

Place	Date	Hour	Summary of Events and Information	Remarks and references to Appendices
"D" Camp, A.30 Central	5.9.17	8.45 a.m.	Inspection by Section Officers	
		9 to 10	Physical Training	
		10.15 to 11	Saluting Drill	
		11.15 to 12.30	Overhauling guns.	N.K.
Do	Do		Intelligence. During the night of 4-5th enemy aircraft fly over the vicinity of the camp at A.30 Central between the hours of 10 p.m. & 3 a.m. Our machine guns fire 1,000 rounds, & two aeroplanes are forced to land — one East, & the other West, of the camp.	
Do	Do	Night	Intelligence. Enemy aeroplanes are observed to pass over the camp flying in the direction of POPERINGHE about 11 p.m., returning about 11.30 p.m.	

Army Form C. 2118.

WAR DIARY
or
INTELLIGENCE SUMMARY.
(Erase heading not required.)

Instructions regarding War Diaries and Intelligence Summaries are contained in F. S. Regs., Part II. and the Staff Manual respectively. Title pages will be prepared in manuscript.

Place	Date	Hour	Summary of Events and Information	Remarks and references to Appendices
"D" Camp. A.30.Central	6.9.17	2:30 p.m. -3:30 p.m.	Company leaves "D" Camp & proceeds by Sections to Canal Bank – Gordon Terrace.	M.M.
	7 "	11 p.m.	The Company takes over the line from 152nd Coy. Machine Gun Corps.	
Coy. Hqrs. CANE TRENCH.	7.9.17		Personnel. Strength of the Company as follows:—	M.M.
			Officers ——— 10	
			Other Ranks ——— 174	
			" Attached — 42.	
			These figures include:— Officers:— 1 On Leave.	
			Other Ranks { 10 " Leave 1 " Courses 1 " Rest Camp	
			✱ Includes one man attached from 4th Gordon Highlanders.	

WAR DIARY
or
INTELLIGENCE SUMMARY.
(Erase heading not required.)

Army Form C. 2118.

Place	Date	Hour	Summary of Events and Information	Remarks and references to Appendices
Coy Hq. CANE TRENCH.	7	From 2a.m. to 3 a.m.	4,000 rounds are fired by our machine guns in barrage scheme on valley of STROOMBEEK.	
			Hostile aerial activity is normal. Our artillery is active throughout the day whilst that of the enemy is but normal. Work done Dug-outs cleaned. Fresh machine gun emplacements made for night firing.	MR
		Aft.	Clouds of smoke are seen to rise from behind enemy lines slightly to the right of POELCAPELLE, apparently from enemy dumps. Casualties Two O.R. slightly wounded.	
Do	8	Early morn.	Our machine guns open fire at intervals in the early morning on the LEKKERBOTERBEEK, 4,000 rounds being expended. There is much activity on the part of the enemy's artillery till 4.30 a.m., gas shells being used. FERDINAND FARM is shelled rather heavily between the hours of midnight & 3 a.m. Dug-out at COCKCROFT FARM receives a direct hit.	MR

Army Form C. 2118.

WAR DIARY
or
INTELLIGENCE SUMMARY.
(Erase heading not required.)

Instructions regarding War Diaries and Intelligence Summaries are contained in F. S. Regs., Part II. and the Staff Manual respectively. Title pages will be prepared in manuscript.

Place	Date	Hour	Summary of Events and Information	Remarks and references to Appendices
Coy Hqrs CANE TRENCH	Sept 8 1917 (cont)		Withdrew. One emplacement at FERDINAND FARM employed, also trenches leading to the gun positions. Dug-outs cleaned.	M.R.
		10pm	We open an intense bombardment on the right enemy pts by opening up on his usual barrage lines, also using his machine gun on our line. During this bombardment the enemy sent up the following lights:– 2 greens, 2 reds (separately) received good return.	
Do.	9	10am	Four enemy aeroplanes cross our lines, apparently observing their artillery fire. During the night our machine gun fire 3,500 rounds at targets of roads behind enemy lines.	M.R.
		5pm	Four direct hits by small shells are observed on a concrete strong point in the vicinity of PHEASANT FARM. A direct hit by a heavy shell is then observed & the strong point is apparently destroyed.	
		6.30pm	50 rounds are fired by our machine guns at enemy formation of A'plane	

Army Form C. 2118.

WAR DIARY
or
INTELLIGENCE SUMMARY.
(Erase heading not required.)

Instructions regarding War Diaries and Intelligence Summaries are contained in F. S. Regs., Part II. and the Staff Manual respectively. Title pages will be prepared in manuscript.

Place	Date	Hour	Summary of Events and Information	Remarks and references to Appendices
Coy Hqrs. CANE TRENCH	1917 Sept 9		The sector is quiet, also FERDINAND FARM, is heavily shelled by the enemy. Dirk done. Cleaning & disinfecting dug-outs & surrounding ground. Salvage collected & deposited at GROUNIER DUMP. Work started on emplacements.	NV
Do.		10 Early morn.	During the night & early morning our machine guns fire 4,000 rounds at targets behind enemy lines. The firing after do not stop the enemy, as after every burst, he immediately brings his searchlights into play as if the mistakes the sound for the guns of our aeroplanes.	NV
		aft.	Enemy aeroplanes are active during the afternoon, one of which is engaged by our Lickers guns at 5 p.m.	
		5 p.m.	A brightly coloured plane flies fairly low over MILITARY ROAD area.	
			Work done. Dug-outs improved & disinfected. Protection for doors	

Army Form C. 2118.

WAR DIARY
or
INTELLIGENCE SUMMARY.
(Erase heading not required.)

Instructions regarding War Diaries and Intelligence Summaries are contained in F. S. Regs., Part II. and the Staff Manual respectively. Title pages will be prepared in manuscript.

Place	Date	Hour	Summary of Events and Information	Remarks and references to Appendices
Coy. Hq.rs CANE TRENCH	10 (contd)		of trench erected. Salvage collected.	
Do	11		4,000 rounds are fired by our machine guns during the night in the vicinity of ROSE HOUSE in accordance with instructions from 15th Inf. Bde. Aircraft very active. Two of our aeroplanes are observed to come down on East side of the STEENBEEK — one in flames & the other under control. From dusk onwards enemy aircraft patrolled STEEN-BEEK area, searching roads etc, with his machine gun. Work done. Clearing & disinfecting dug-outs including COCKCROFT. Emplacements completed. Direction boards made.	
Do	12	1 a.m.	Enemy shells railway & track from FERDINAND FARM to HURST PARK between 1 a.m. & 2 a.m. & again between 3 a.m. 9 a.m.	
		3 to 3.30 a.m.	The COCKCROFT and FERDINAND FARM are shelled with gas shells.	

WAR DIARY
or
INTELLIGENCE SUMMARY.
(Erase heading not required.)

Army Form C. 2118.

Place	Date 1917	Hour	Summary of Events and Information	Remarks and references to Appendices
Coy H.Q.rs CANE TRENCH (contd)	Sept. 12	9 p.m.	The Company is relieved in the line by 153rd Machine Gun Coy. & Proceeds to tents at SIEGE CAMP.	M.R.
SIEGE CAMP	13	noon	Inspection by Section Officers.	M.R.
Do.	14		Personnel. Strength of Company as follows:— Officers = 10 Other Ranks = 192 " Attached = 41 The above figures include:— One officer on leave 12 O.R. " " " 1 " " Courses 1 " " at Rest Camp. including 3 attached.	M.R.

Army Form C. 2118.

WAR DIARY
or
INTELLIGENCE SUMMARY.
(Erase heading not required.)

Instructions regarding War Diaries and Intelligence Summaries are contained in F. S. Regs., Part II. and the Staff Manual respectively. Title pages will be prepared in manuscript.

Place	Date	Hour	Summary of Events and Information	Remarks and references to Appendices
SIEGE CAMP	14	8.45 a.m.	C.O.'s Inspection Kit Inspection	
		9 a.m.	Gun cleaning; checking spare parts, etc.	
Do.	15	8.45 a.m.	C.O.'s Inspection	
		9 a.m.	Field Practice.	
Do.	16	9.15 a.m.	Divine Service.	
Do.	17	9.45 a.m.	Field Practice, with guns, in conjunction with other units of the Brigade.	
Do.	18	3.50 a.m.	Company move off to take part in Brigade Operations, i.e. practising the attack.	
Do.	19		Company leaves SIEGE CAMP to take up positions in the line preparatory to the attack.	

WAR DIARY
or
INTELLIGENCE SUMMARY.
(Erase heading not required.)

Army Form C. 2118.

Place	Date	Hour	Summary of Events and Information	Remarks and references to Appendices
Coy. Hqrs. FERDINAND FARM.	1917. Sept. 20, 21st 22nd		An account of the attack & operations of 20th & 21st Sept., under the heading "Action of Machine Guns" is attached hereto. The punishment inflicted on the enemy unfortunately was attended with considerable cost in personnel, the following being a list of casualties for the three days named :— Officers :— { Two killed in action (Capt. E.J. Hughes, Commanding Officer) { (2/Lt. W.F. Wortman) { One missing Other Ranks :— Killed in action = 9 Died of wounds = 1 Missing = 5 Wounded = 30 (one of whom remained at duty)	W.R.
SIEGE CAMP	23	9.45 a.m.	Divine Services.	W.R.
Do	24	9 a.m. 9.15 10.30 a.m. 4 p.m.	C.O's Inspection Kit Inspection Physical Training Company proceeds by route march to billets at POPERINGHE.	W.R.

Army Form C. 2118.

WAR DIARY
or
INTELLIGENCE SUMMARY.
(Erase heading not required.)

Instructions regarding War Diaries and Intelligence Summaries are contained in F. S. Regs., Part II. and the Staff Manual respectively. Title pages will be prepared in manuscript.

Place	Date	Hour	Summary of Events and Information	Remarks and references to Appendices
108 RUE DE YPRES POPERINGHE	25.9.17	9 a.m. 9.15	Inspection by Section Officers Gun cleaning at Transport Lines. Reinforcements - arrival of 15 O.R.	N.N.
Do	26	9 a.m. 9.15	Inspection by Section Officers Parades under Section Officers.	N.N.
Do	27	9 a.m. 9.15	Inspection by Section Officers Gun cleaning at Transport Lines. Reinforcements - arrival of 16 O.R.	N.N.
Do	28	4.45 p.m.	Company marches to HOPOUTRE SIDING, POPERINGHE, & entrains there for BAPAUME.	
Do	28		Personnel. Strength of Company as follows:- Officers ------- 7 Other Ranks ------- 164 (Attached) 31 The above figures include:- Officers Hospital = 1 Leave = 13 (including 2 overstayed Pass + 2 O.R. attached) Other Ranks { Courses = 1 W.R.R.T.O. = 1	N.N.

WAR DIARY
or
INTELLIGENCE SUMMARY.

(Erase heading not required.)

Army Form C. 2118.

Place	Date	Hour	Summary of Events and Information	Remarks and references to Appendices
COURCELLES	29.9.17	4.45 a.m.	The Company detrains at BAPAUME & marches to camp at COURCELLES.	
Do	Do		Personnel. Three officers (2nd Lieuts) arrive as reinforcements to replace casualties of 20th & 21st.	
Do	30.9.17	10.30 a.m.	Divine Service (Voluntary)	
		9.30 a.m.	Gun cleaning & re-packing of limbers.	

W. F. Rawson
Lt.
O.C. 154th Coy., Machine Gun Corps.

154th Coy., Machine Gun Corps

Action of Machine Guns.
20.9.17.

At Zero two guns at VIEILLES MAISONS opened fire on Block Houses at C.6.b.7.5. Four guns under 2/Lt. A.T. STEWART advanced after Blue Dotted Line had been captured & got into positions at PHEASANT FARM CEMETERY ⸺ two on right & two on left. These guns engaged the enemy retiring & from 12.30 p.m. till about 5 p.m. kept firing at enemy advancing from vicinity of RETOUR Cross Roads.

Two guns under 2/Lt. E.G. de W. Holding advanced to V.25.C.1.2. & took up positions.

Four guns under 2/Lt. W.B. PARKER advanced after Blue Line had been reached by infantry & two of these guns came into action at MALTA HOUSE & one at ROSE HOUSE ⸺ one gun was put out of action on way to ROSE HOUSE.

Four guns under 2/Lt. L.F. NORMAN advanced after capture of BLUE LINE & took up positions as follows:⸺

2.

Action of Machine Guns 20.9.17 (cont'd).

two at BAVAROISE HOUSE & two 100 yds. in front of FLORA COTT., as this was the best position obtainable to cover ground in front of QUEBEC FARM.

During the counter-attack on 20th the gun at ROSE HOUSE was in action till team was all wounded & the last man put gun out of action.

The guns at PHEASANT FARM fired until enemy outflanked them. One gun kept in action until team were wiped out (The N.C.O. in charge kept the gun firing although twice wounded — before leaving he put his gun out of action by destroying it.) One man managed to get his gun back. The other two guns retired to PHEASANT TRENCH, where they took up positions & held up the enemy.

The guns at MALTA HOUSE were in action & the officer (2/Lt. W.B. PARKER) and teams are missing with the exception of one N.C.O. & man who brought their gun back but, owing to enemy pressure, had to put it out of action.

The BAVAROISE HOUSE guns were in action & stopped enemy assembling.

The FLORA COTT. guns engaged enemy at different times firing direct overhead

3.

Action of Machine Guns, 20.9.17. (cont'd).

fire in the vicinity of QUEBEC FARM. These guns were again in action during the 21st instant.

W.E. Rawson
Lt.

O.C. 154th Coy., Machine Gun Corps.

23.9.17.

On His Majesty's Service.

154th MACHINE GUN COMPANY

OCTOBER 1917

WAR DIARY or INTELLIGENCE SUMMARY.

Army Form C. 2118.

Place	Date	Hour	Summary of Events and Information	Remarks and references to Appendices
COURCELLES -LE-COMTE	1-10-17		**PERSONNEL.** The strength of the Company is as follows:— Officers = 10 Other Ranks = 166 O.R. attached = 31* The above figures include:— (Other Ranks) { In Hospital .... 1 On leave to U.K. ...... 12 (Includes 2 men attached from 2nd Seaforths) Courses of instruction ... 1 With R.T.O. as reinforcement guide 1 *ATTACHED made up as follows:— 9th Royal Scots = 8 2nd Seaforth High^{rs} = 11 4th Gordon " = 2 7th A. & S. H. = 10 — 31	

Army Form C. 2118.

WAR DIARY
or
INTELLIGENCE SUMMARY
(Erase heading not required.)

154 Coy. M.G. Corps.

Instructions regarding War Diaries and Intelligence Summaries are contained in F.S. Regs., Part II. and the Staff Manual respectively. Title pages will be prepared in manuscript.

Place	Date	Hour	Summary of Events and Information	Remarks and references to Appendices
COURCELLES -LE-COMTE	1917 OCT. 1		General Training.	
	2		General Training.	A.C.I.
	2		Capt. H.G. HARCOURT reported from 21/9 Coy., to assume command of 154 vice Capt. E.J.W. HUGHES. K. in A. 20.9.17. In accordance with orders four officers reconnoitered the line in the VIS-EN-ARTOIS sector preparatory to relieving 150 M.G. Coy., on 5th instal.	A.C.II.
	3/4		General Training and Preparation for relief.	A.C.I
	5th	8.30 a.m.	Coy. struck at COURCELLES - Coy. (less Transport) entrained and proceeded to CARLISLE LINES (M17a 2.7) Transport followed by road.	A.C.II.
CARLISLE LINES.		5 p.m.	Section moved off to relieve 150 Coy. re APPENDIX I.	
			Relief completed 10.30 p.m. Distribution of Company as follows:- Coy. H.Q. & 1 subsection N16a 1.8. 10 Guns VIS-EN-ARTOIS SECTOR. MAP "A" APP. 2. One section, awheels and transport CARLISLE LINES (M17a 2.7.)	APP. 2.
VIS-EN-ARTOIS SECTOR.				
Ref. MAP. SHEET 51B. 1:40,000.				

Army Form C. 2118.

WAR DIARY
or
INTELLIGENCE SUMMARY.

(Erase heading not required.)

154 Coy, M.G.Corps.

Instructions regarding War Diaries and Intelligence Summaries are contained in F.S. Regs., Part II. and the Staff Manual respectively. Title pages will be prepared in manuscript.

Place	Date 1917	Hour	Summary of Events and Information	Remarks and references to Appendices
VIS-EN-ARTOIS SECTOR. L.BDE. SECTOR.	OCT. 6.		Defence scheme for the line and S.O.S. line for guns checked. Position in forwards of repair – works programme commenced. No work of importance occurred – line extremely quiet. A reorganisation of gun teamworks was proposed allowing performance.	H.C.J.
" "	7		Situation Quiet – very slight shelling on support line on regimental sector, Co. 5/6 yards in IBIS slightly knocked about. The enemy shows himself a good deal. Work on position carried on.	H.C.J.
" "	8		Quiet – Improvements carried on – D.A.G.O. visited line in reference to redistribution. Four guns of 232 M.G. Coy. in RAKE TRENCH, LEFT SUB-SECTOR visited. Training that carried out on St. ROHART'S FACTORY by and from SUNKEN RD. 019.a.15.60. also on DEVON BANK. Four of two guns from HOE SUPPORT (LEFT S.S.) in conjunction with Lethal Gas Bombardment. 3000 rds.	H.C.J.
VIS-EN-ARTOIS TRENCH MAP SHEET 51BSW2. 1:10,000	9		Quiet – Indirect fire from 019.a.15.60 on bombs running and from RAKE TR. on to SUNKEN RD. 0154.80.15. 2000 rounds.	H.C.J.

WAR DIARY or INTELLIGENCE SUMMARY

Army Form C. 2118.

154 Coy. M.G. Corps

Place	Date	Hour	Summary of Events and Information	Remarks and references to Appendices
VIS-EN-ARTOIS SECTOR 10. L.BDE., SECTOR	1917 OCT. 10.		Quiet – but our artillery more active. Interchange of comic on – all positions now in good repair with alternative emplacements. Ammunition reserves commenced. Indirect fire as follows:– 2 guns HOE SUPPORT (LEFT.S.S) on HILL TOP WORK O.21.c.7.7.; One gun from O.19.a.15.60 on to area about HILL SIDE WORK O.21.a.6.7.: 2500 rds.	A.C.I.
	11		Quiet – Artillery on both sides more active than activity during day one night of 10/11th. Our own reviewed to cover a large area by groups of 12 Division on our left with an airplane barrage – 8 guns were used. Position for above arranged by BISON RES., & 2 in RAKE TRENCH (LEFT. S.S). Looking for enemy gun emplacements for above done during night of 18/11/2. Indirect fire as for 10th. One M.G. gun on HOE SUPT opening fire as an enemy gun revealed its position – fire was repeatedly brought to bear on any flashes or on suspected enemy emplacements.	A.C.I.
VIS-EN-ARTOIS TRENCH MAP. SHEET 51BSW2. 1:10000.				

Army Form C. 2118.

154 C.V. M.G.Corps.

WAR DIARY
INTELLIGENCE SUMMARY

Place	Date	Hour	Summary of Events and Information	Remarks and references to Appendices
VIS-EN-ARTOIS SECTOR	1917 OCT. 11 (contd)		Position of hostile gun - after three bursts it ceased fire. Indiscriminate fire continued. 2750 rounds fired.	A.C.B.
L. Bde. Sector	12.	Early A.M.	The enemy attempted a raid on one of our posts N. of the new Coyeul. He was driven off leaving one wounded prisoner of 162 I.R. in our hands. Enemy strength about forty. Several of our own wounded. Work on position continued. Enemy carried out enemy ops. Prisoner captured states that the enemy were expected to relieve during night 12/13 as I have seventy-five rounds continuously covered and on all known places of assembly and lines of approach, generally if observing extent our fire was held during daylight - our posts received orders to be known only if enemy were out. 6000 rds expended. An enemy aeroplane flew low down over our lines. Indirect fire carried over on enemy approach & communication.	A.C.B.
VIS-EN-ARTOIS TRENCH MAP SHEET 51B S.W.2 1:10000.	13.			A.C.B.
			7000 rds expended.	

Army Form C. 2118.

WAR DIARY
or
INTELLIGENCE SUMMARY.
(Erase heading not required.)

Instructions regarding War Diaries and Intelligence Summaries are contained in F. S. Regs., Part II. and the Staff Manual respectively. Title pages will be prepared in manuscript.

154 Coy. M.G. Corps

Place	Date 1917	Hour	Summary of Events and Information	Remarks and references to Appendices
VIS-EN-ARTOIS SECTOR, L. BDE.	OCT. 14.	FORE NOON	Our artillery very active on once to be reason – Artillery busy also on enemy lines opposite our own front. Enemy artillery quiet.	
		2.4. p.m.	Our artillery bombardment greatly increased – enemy making weak reply.	
		4.45.	All our guns ready to fire barrage – artillery barrage commenced immediately. Guns are ready to fire. Enemy infantry. The artillery open up barrage. nothing unknown anywhere to remember.	Att.
		4.55 p.m.	ZERO Hour – infantry advance barrage lift on enemy barrage put down. Smoke barrage also that widely scattered and varied ones. The enemy artillery opened up rapidly invisible fired all over the front. It immediately commenced on various area about 5.10 p.m. with the exception of 4.2" which apparently reached Lawrence APE SUPPORT guns funny is	
VIS-EN-ARTOIS TRENCH MAP SHEET 51b SW.2. 1:10000.				

WAR DIARY
INTELLIGENCE SUMMARY

Army Form C. 2118.

152 Coy M.G.C.

Place	Date 1917 OCT.	Hour	Summary of Events and Information	Remarks and references to Appendices
VIS-EN-ARTOIS SECTOR. L. BDE.	14	5 p.m. 5.20.	The enemy appeared to think Vickers guns were firing from APES on who outpost was known to occupy the left of our line at 5.20 p.m. he opened on BISON - this shooting was very erratic - if anyone had been hit on the trench but none never shot & do so a gun. Rate of fire for enfilade barrage:- ZERO to Z+10 — 125 rds per gun per minute. Z+10 to Z+30 — 75 " " Z+30 to Z+55 — 125 " " Z+55 until artillery ceased 50 " "	T.O.T.
		5.42.	6 cases June were fired at 5.42 p.m. Ammunition expended about 35,000 rds. Casualties nil. The raid seemed to be quite successful - enemy barrage even rockets exploded heavy, neither did he appear to have many machine guns. Reports from 12 Div. state 200 enemy killed, 2 off. 6 2 O.R. captured with 2 M.G.S.	
VIS-EN-ARTOIS TR MAP 51B S.W.2. 10.000.			Further details covering the night on ST. ROHARTS QUARRY	

Army Form C. 2118.

154 Coy. M.G.C.

WAR DIARY
or
INTELLIGENCE SUMMARY.

(Erase heading not required.)

Instructions regarding War Diaries and Intelligence
Summaries are contained in F. S. Regs., Part II.
and the Staff Manual respectively. Title pages
will be prepared in manuscript.

Place	Date 1917	Hour	Summary of Events and Information	Remarks and references to Appendices
VIS-EN-ARTOIS SECTOR L. BDE.	OCT. 14.	7pm 10pm	As it was thought that the enemy might reorganise in that vicinity, long run from SUNKEN RD O.19.a. was fired for 4 hrs.	A.G.H.
	15.		Uneventful. – no special enemy activity on night to be reported. Artillery active every day in enemy work – recent CERISY – No shell gun fire kept attempts enemy night to detail working parties repairing damage. 12,000 rounds expended.	A.G.H.
	16.		Uneventful – not activity – Enemy fire carried out on ourselves trying to arrange enemy in line. (5000 rds) Hoped to make two extra fourteen in SUNKEN RD O.19.a. for B. GSA GUN. to enable who lake	A.G.H.
VIS-EN-ARTOIS & CERISY TR., MAPS, SHEET 51B SW2 1:10000			control the COJEUL VALLEY. Position commence commenced for above purpose.	

154 CRY MGC

WAR DIARY or INTELLIGENCE SUMMARY

Army Form C. 2118.

Instructions regarding War Diaries and Intelligence Summaries are contained in F.S. Regs., Part II. and the Staff Manual respectively. Title pages will be prepared in manuscript.

(Erase heading not required.)

Place	Date 1917	Hour	Summary of Events and Information	Remarks and references to Appendices
VIS-EN-ARTOIS SECTOR, L. BDE.	OCT. 17		Normal activity by artillery on both sides. Enemy MG's swept outposts a few times — fired — carried out on front taken over — 1000 rounds expended.	H.A.I.
	18		Situation Quiet — little activity — 10,000 rounds fired on dumps about VIS-EN-ARTOIS, during the night. ← NIGHT LINE	H.A.I.
	19		Situation Quiet — 6" Lens, now Lt. ps — evening were opposite Bde., left Boundary. Three of our planes — throughout the evening night — by Germans from KESTREL & TRIANGLE WOOD September AVENUE. Active areas near TRIANGLE WOOD — truncated fire — 4,000 rds, expended.	H.A.I.
	20		Issue activity on either side — usual shelling by a few okay — heavy Inter action relief carried out. Knell. owing of signal fire on area about ST, RAMARTS QUARRY. 1,500 rds.	H.A.I.
VIS-EN-ARTOIS TR. MAP, 51.B. SW. 2. 1:10000.	21.		E. enemy artillery more active than usual — noticeably on LEFT Bn. frontbetween 7p.m. – 6 a.m. – on a Pt. during early morning, 1975 (hostile) active during the day.	H.A.I.

WAR DIARY
or
INTELLIGENCE SUMMARY

Army Form C. 2118.

54 Coy. M.G.C.

Place	Date	Hour	Summary of Events and Information	Remarks and references to Appendices
VIS-EN-ARTOIS. L.BDE., SECTOR 2	1917 OCT 21 CONT'D		Indirect work and mounted was observed at a hole, in bank about 020.865. Also ripening the infantry 1000 yds over front at the target. No more S. was seen. The front was too dark during the night for activity. The S.O.S. signal was observed on the enemy's flare over my R.P. No 58 #(1) coming up forty the active front line. No one to kill - no visible active flashes – gun missed. Ceased fire after 10 minutes. Good marks were found on parts of activity where every line - Sts Rohart's F.T.V. Every round opened at addition. A few gun shells were usually by the enemy in our battery M.P. - no uneasy shells were found.	HCJ
	22		Some artillery shelling by both sides – known M.G. offensive to be nearby for SUNKEN RD. relief 5pm + 8pm. – one gun on target from attack from were not further movement. 6,500 rounds fired on selected points and areas during the day and early morning.	HCJ
VIS-EN-ARTOIS TR. MAP. 51.B.SW.2. 1:10,000	23		Hostile activity normal – our artillery bombarded on this area during the night. 12,000 rounds went from H to enemy working parties	HCJ

154 Coy. M.G.C.

Army Form C. 2118.

Instructions regarding War Diaries and Intelligence Summaries are contained in F.S. Regs., Part II. and the Staff Manual respectively. Title pages will be prepared in manuscript.

WAR DIARY
or
INTELLIGENCE SUMMARY
(Erase heading not required.)

Place	Date	Hour	Summary of Events and Information	Remarks and references to Appendices
VIS-EN-ARTOIS L.BDE. SECTOR	1917 OCT. 24.		Situation normal, — damage caused to parapets on HILLTOP WORK seem not to be repaired — Indirect fire last night appeared very effective. 5,500 rounds fired on selected targets threatening rear refier conservation — HILLTOP WORK.	A.C.I.
	25		Trench activity on both sides — 6,300 rounds fired on points of activity on enemy lines, between the bank at map ref. O.19.b.98.65 & gun firing on	A.C.I.
	26		Divisional front — an artillery action in vicinity of our front line top 8 ring O.9.c. noted — clearly only a bow for fresh on KESTREL AVENUE — clearly only a bow for fresh on area S. of 150 x wide. 12,500 rounds fired on area S. of CHERISY after artillery bombardment. The 16th D.V. on our right (10th & Sam) Wing the bomber who turned the enemy to fallen to firing into an appeal from front to rear. 2 RED VEREY LGTS, 2 GREEN do, and one GOLDEN RAIN rocket.	A.C.I.
VIS-EN-ARTOIS TR. MAP 51.B.S.W.2. 1:10000			Red Verey Lights were observed during the night over F.8. ARTS. FTY. at 20 minute intervals — no visible action followed	

WAR DIARY

Army Form C. 2118.

154 Coy M.G.C.

Instructions regarding War Diaries and Intelligence Summaries are contained in F.S. Regs., Part II. and the Staff Manual respectively. Title pages will be prepared in manuscript.

Place	Date	Hour	Summary of Events and Information	Remarks and references to Appendices
VIS-EN-ARTOIS. L.Bde, SECTOR.	1917 OCT. 27	2	Normal – Enemy MGs a bit more active than usual at 5.00 a.m. about 6 enemy MGs encountered for one minute on BISON RESERVE – Frontal fire Barrel 1 round. This was repeated at 6 a.m. The reason for this was not apparent. No inspection to inspect fire broken came in either. This must mean the barrage/shoots to 1st lines. Infantry working parties to shelters still heard about time 1.7. Firing very 1 of 26 Lt. but no one was fired at the about time. 5,500 rounds fired. Received Trench information from a youngster in front of BUCK RES. – Direct frontal fire was used. The enemy indicated to the outer towers of GRANATEN-WERFER – on [?] was manned and harassed. A copy of following a likely concealed corner of Trk. are at Jnr. alone at the gun, to blow the round of the gun in a different direction, was used. Ideas ??? It appeared to be effective as the installation was quite near [??] enroyed by every ??? thrown like fancy ???	STROHART HILL
VIS-EN-ARTOIS. TR. MAP 51 B.SW.2. 1:10,000				

Army Form C. 2118.

WAR DIARY
or
INTELLIGENCE SUMMARY.
(Erase heading not required.)

Place	Date	Hour	Summary of Events and Information	Remarks and references to Appendices
VIS-EN-ARTOIS SECTOR, LEFT BDE.	1917 OCT 28		Situation normal — unusual artillery activity — T.M's (Stokes) especially active to STOKES bombarded enemy post in some movement along the post few cop near ST. ROHART'S FACTORY. The line on Jonders of ground by 12 or and a few new trite position to the left on 1 port, near the sun feet ground moving rifle no.1. Dummac was believed some named from unbroken days to 5500 wards. The approach Tarroneayment of 7 mine the even rained from Devacoon F.O. Stigun are distributed as apart to a preliminary are the S.O.S damage is considerably stronger. The infantry bombardment of the Boyal were relieved by the evening of the 18 of the 18th BDE, 4th DIV. — relief carried out owning a system The F.O. Battery are ourselves stay in the line under orders of it of Bon.	#1

VIS-EN-ARTOIS TRENCH MAP 51 B S.W. 2
1:10000

/54 COY MGC

WAR DIARY
or
INTELLIGENCE SUMMARY
(Erase heading not required.)

Army Form C. 2118.

Place	Date	Hour	Summary of Events and Information	Remarks and references to Appendices
VIS-EN-ARTOIS L.BDE. SECTOR	1917 OCT. 29		Shiskow Lind – Ordinary shelling – T.M. activity on battalion. Indirect fire about 4000 r.p.m.	H.Q.J
	30		Shiskow Lind – little activity. Orders received that we were to be relieved on 1st by 102 Bde. M.G. Coy – O.C. 102 M.G. Coy visited the line during the afternoon. Only 8 gunners were to be taken over. 559 + 60(1) being worked out. The scheme for near general of guns was explained – no action taken by us till guns in the line were left for 102 company out after day. In interference in relation to its 5000 rds, 8 guns firing on St ROHART's during the night remained to the enemy (observation) every day.	H.Q.J
VIS-EN-ARTOIS TR.MAP. 51B.S.W.R. 1:10000.	31.		Very little activity – general artillery work on our front. Relieved formally by 102 Coy.	H.Q.J

Army Form C. 2118.

154 Coy M.G.C.

Instructions regarding War Diaries and Intelligence Summaries are contained in F. S. Regs., Part II. and the Staff Manual respectively. Title pages will be prepared in manuscript.

WAR DIARY
or
~~INTELLIGENCE SUMMARY.~~
(Erase heading not required.)

Place	Date	Hour	Summary of Events ~~and Information~~	Remarks and references to Appendices
VIS-EN-ARTOIS L.BDE., SECTOR —	31		The whole period was one of intense grind for men. The enemy was bombard -ed and so far as visible by shelling status and L.G.'s — forward area. 16,000 rounds were fired on various HQ and selected points behind the enemy line. No casualties were suffered and general conditions were quite good.	
VIS-EN-ARTOIS TR. MAP. 51B.S.W.2. 1:10,000				

H. Harcourt Butler
Cam ag 154 Coy. M.G.C.

WAR DIARY
or
INTELLIGENCE SUMMARY.
(Erase heading not required.)

Army Form C. 2118.

Place	Date	Hour	Summary of Events and Information	Remarks and references to Appendices
VIS-EN-ARTOIS L. Bde. Sector	Oct 31, 1917		The strength of the Company is as follows:— Officers　10 Other Ranks (M.G.C.) 180 " Attached 30 The above figures include:— Officers. Leave = 1 Other Ranks (M.G.C.) Hosp. = 4 Leave = 8 Courses = 1 With R.T.O. = 1 Rest Camp = 1 —— 15 O.R. Attached. Leave = 3 Rest Camp = 1 —— 4	

H. Townsend　CAPT.,
COMDG. 154th COY, M.G. CORPS.

SECRET

Copy No. 10.
3rd Oct 1917

154 COY., MACHINE GUN CORPS
OPERATION ORDER No. 4

APPENDIX NO. I
to WAR DIARY
5·10·17.

REF. MAP SHEET 51B 1:40,000
51 B S.W. 2 1:10,000

1. **RELIEF.** The Company will relieve No. 150 M.G. Coy in the sector on the night of 5/6th October.

2. **SECTION RELIEFS** will be as follows:-
   (a) "A" Section to relieve No. 1 Section of 150 M.G. Coy — 4 guns in positions :-
   No. 59 BUCK RESERVE (one gun) approx. O.19.d.6.9
   No. 60 (3 guns) approx. O.19.b.6.4
   Section H.Q. in BUCK RES at approx. O.19.b.8.2.

   (b) "B" Section to relieve No. 2 Section with two guns in positions:-
   No. 55A (one gun) approx. O.19.a.2.3.
   No. 60A (one gun) approx. O.19.a.4.7
   Section H.Q. in SUNKEN ROAD approx. O.19.a.2.6.
   No. 4 sub-section will be at Company H.Q., N.14.b.

   (c) "D" Section to relieve No. 4 Section with 4 guns in positions:-
   No. 56 (1 gun) in IBIS TRENCH approx. O.26.a.3.7.
   No. 57 (1 gun) off KESTREL AVENUE approx. O.19.d.2.1.
   No. 58 (2 guns) off BISSEN TRENCH at approx. O.20.c.3.2.

   (d) "C" Section will be in rest at   (to be notified later)

3. The Company (less Transport) will proceed at 8.30 AM on 5th by bus to Cross Roads at N.20.b.7.8. and from there march to Company H.Q. at N.14.b central. A distance of 200 yards between Sections will be maintained.

4. Sections going into the line will meet guides and Section Transport at Cross-roads N.22.b.3.9 at 4.15 p.m. These guides will take each Section and Transport to Dumps as follows, where guides for each gun position will be picked up :-
   "A" and "D" Sections to LION DUMP O.19.c.8.8.
   "B" Section to Section H.Q. at O.19.a.2.6.
   The relief will then proceed as usual.

5. LIEUT. FLETCHER will arrange to have the necessary Section Transport at above Cross-roads by 4.15 PM.
   On Sections moving off the Transport will return to Transport lines at M.17.c.5.9

6. The defence scheme for the line will be taken over and clearly explained to all gun teams at the earliest opportunity.

2.

6. Handing over Receipts will be given and kept respectively
(Con) for Maps Defence Scheme and Trench Stores taken over.
A separate copy of each, signed by both Officers concerned, will be sent to Company H.Q. with relief complete certificate.

7. CODE WORD for completion of relief "HANDSOME" - to be sent to Company H.Q. by runner.

8. Nos. 1 and 2 of each team of 150th Company will remain in the line for 24 hours after relief. These men will then proceed in accordance with Orders given them by 150th Coy.

9. All S.O.S. lines, gun positions, and bearings must be most carefully checked and corrections, if any, reported to Company H.Q. Nil returns required.

10. DRESS. Fighting Order plus great-coat and one pair of socks.
Rations up to midnight 6/7th will be taken in.

11. RATION DUMPS will be as in para 4 above. Rations will arrive at these Dumps by 8.30 o'clock each evening where ration parties will meet them.
Water supply is at or near gun positions.

12. MEDICAL ARRANGEMENTS
Regimental Aid Posts
Right Battalion N 24 d. 9. 9.
Left Battalion O 13 b. 2. 5.
Advance Dressing Station N 14 d. 3. 2. MARLIERE CAVES

13. ACKNOWLEDGE

H.C. Honeoured
Capt.
O.C. 154 Coy. M.G. Corps.

Issued at:-
Copies Nos 1 & 2   H.Q.
          3   O.C. "A" Sect
          4   " B " "
          5   " C " "
          6   " D "
          7   Transport Officer
          8   O.C. 156 M.G. Coy
          9   51 D.M.G.O.
    10/11   WAR DIARY

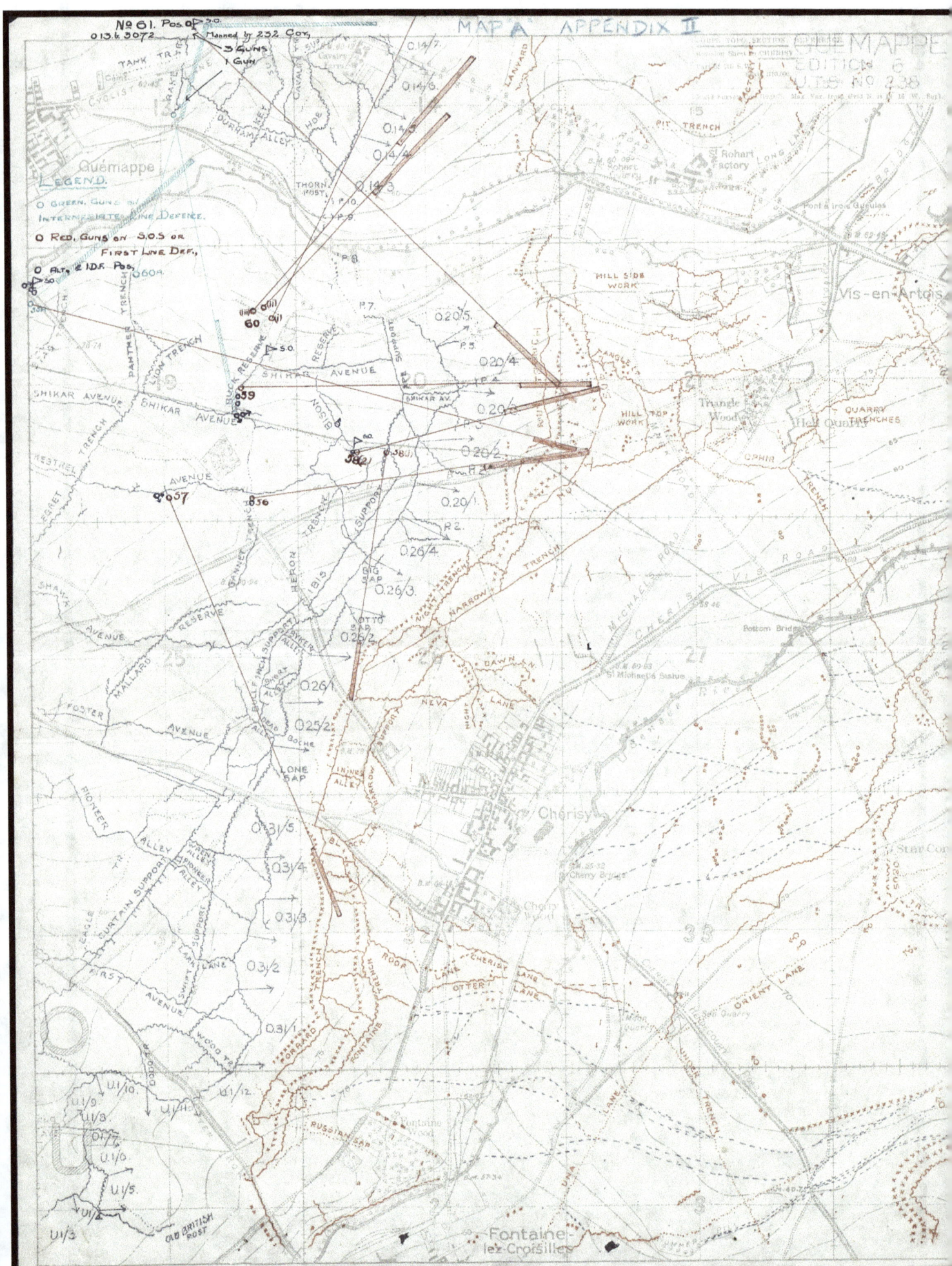

154th Brigade.
51st Division.

154th MACHINE GUN COMPANY - NOVEMBER 1917.

Attached:-

Report on Operations Cambrai

CONFIDENTIAL.
No 71 (A)
HIGHLAND DIVISION.

Vol 23

24

Confidential

ORIGINAL

WAR DIARY

154 Coy.   M.G. Corps.

From 1st to 31st November - 1917.

Volume - - -

WAR DIARY or INTELLIGENCE SUMMARY

Army Form C. 2118.

154 Coy. M.G.C.

Place	Date	Hour	Summary of Events and Information	Remarks and references to Appendices
VIS-EN-ARTOIS, L. Bde., Sector.	Nov. 1917 1st		The day was one of the usual quietness. Very well. The transport moved during the day to QUESNES-le-COMTE to the place to which the coy was long fol- -lowed.	A.C.I.
	2nd	5pm	Relief commenced with 102 Coy. - carried through without any great inconvenience - complete by 10pm.	
		11pm	The gun teams from the line marched to MERCATEL where lorries conveyed them to QUESNES-le-COMTE. Brewis went about 1 am.	
			Carried out of all stores, guns, equipment exhibit - Cleaned up - carried out. All billets fairly comfortable.	
	3rd		General Parades & Training Programme commenced. Lectures and Records given by Officers and then	
VIS-EN-ARTOIS, TR. MAP. 51B.S.W.8. 1:10,000		Sheet 51c 1:40000	for the company during the operation at YPRES on 20th and 21st September were published as follows	

Army Form C. 2118.

WAR DIARY
or
INTELLIGENCE SUMMARY
(Erase heading not required.)

Instructions regarding War Diaries and Intelligence Summaries are contained in F. S. Regs., Part II. and the Staff Manual respectively. Title pages will be prepared in manuscript.

154 Coy, M.G.Corps,

Place	Date	Hour	Summary of Events and Information	Remarks and references to Appendices
OVESNES LE-COMTE	1917 Nov. 3		Bar to M.C. Temp/2Lt. Q.T. Stewart M.C.	
			AUTHORITY:- XVIII Corps' Wire G.488, 51(H) Div. 355/Ad 16.10.17.	
			D.C.M. 248878 Pte. P. Phillips (Y.A.S.H. attd 154 Coy, M.G.C.)	
			73665 L/Cpl. Donaldson R.C. 154 Coy M.G.C.	
			AUT, XVIII Corps Wire G.508, 51(H) Div. 355/Ad 16.10.17	
			Military Medal.	
			23256 Cpl. D. McIntosh. 154 Coy. M.G.C.	
			3892 Pte. W.G. Perrin " " "	
			86451 " J. Ayre " " "	
			48644 " F. McGill " " "	
			97738 " J.D. Pardington " " "	
			246812 " J.L. Kennedy Y.A.S.H. attd,	
			9.4TH, XVIII Corps. D.1/314, of 51st(H) Div, 3539 d.21.10.17	

154 Coy. M.G.Corps.

Army Form C. 2118.

WAR DIARY
INTELLIGENCE SUMMARY
(Erase heading not required.)

Place	Date	Hour	Summary of Events and Information	Remarks and references to Appendices
YVESNES LE-COMTE.	5th to 16th		The period between these dates was employed in General Tactics and Company Training. Elementary work was re-thought and more advanced instruction was carried out. In spite of bad weather work was carried on and the efficiency considerably improved. Afternoons were all devoted to Recreational training. Football tournaments every evening were the favourite events, the latter found exceptional favour among all ranks. The 13th being the anniversary of the Divisions very successful action at BEAUMONT-HAMEL was in case a General Holiday. The company had an excellent dinner in the evening, a York Lunch, all the expenses for this was paid by Divis. Canteen Fund.	HQ

Sheet 51c.
1:40,000

154 Coy. M.G.C.

Army Form C. 2118.

WAR DIARY
or
INTELLIGENCE SUMMARY
(Erase heading not required.)

Place	Date	Hour	Summary of Events and Information	Remarks and references to Appendices
AVESNES LE-COMTE.			Period 5th – 16th. Instructions that the Brigade would move to take part in certain operations on the IV Corps front were received on the 10th. Conferences were held on several dates with respect to these operations. The operation in question consisted of an attack by the 3rd Army on a two Corps front from the CANAL-DU-NORD (W. of HAVRINCOURT) – southwards. The 51st (H) Division which was to be right division of the IV Corps was to attack with 152nd Brigade on the right – 153rd Brigade on the left – 154th Brigade (ourselves) in Reserve. The attack was to be a complete surprise to the enemy + with this idea in view no preliminary bombardment was to take place. Tanks reinforced by a field artillery barrage would assist the attacking battalions of the two forward Brigades in mounting the front + support lines, there were the HINDENBURGH LINE and HINDENBURGH SUPPORT with the village of FLESQUIERES. The 151st + 153rd Brigades were then to push on over RIDGE + consolidate on a line in front	
Sheet 51.c. 1:40000.				

154th Coy M.G. Corps.

WAR DIARY
or
INTELLIGENCE SUMMARY
(Erase heading not required.)

Army Form C. 2118.

Place	Date	Hour	Summary of Events and Information	Remarks and references to Appendices
	5-16" cont		of the ridge. Up to this stage of the advance 154th Brigade would be following in reserve, but on the forward Brigades reaching the above line the 154th Brigade would "leap-frog" them & move forward to the answer & capture of FONTAINE-NOTRE-DAME, taking CANTAING on the right & ANNEUX on the left if necessary. On FONTAINE-NOTRE-DAME being taken the Brigade would consolidate in front & await orders. The 1st G.H. & 4th A & S.H. were detailed as forward battalions of the Brigade with the 9th R.S. & 7th A.S.H. in support respectfully. Two machine guns were to accompany each forward battalion, the remainder of the company would move in reserve with the support Battalions.	

151st COY M.G.CORPS.

Army Form C. 2118.

WAR DIARY
or
INTELLIGENCE SUMMARY.
(Erase heading not required.)

Instructions regarding War Diaries and Intelligence Summaries are contained in F. S. Regs., Part II. and the Staff Manual respectively. Title pages will be prepared in manuscript.

Place	Date 1917	Hour	Summary of Events and Information	Remarks and references to Appendices
AVESNES LE-COMTE	Nov 16th		Orders were received for move to BAPAUME on 14th to concentrate for the attack. Own transport, which moved to-day by road to MOYENVILLE en route for BAPAUME.	H.C.I.
	14th	1-45 P.M.	Company marched to Station at BEGUMETZ, entrained + proceeded to BAPAUME, arriving there about 11-30 P.M. Accommodated in huts just outside town. Transport marched quite near on rejoining	H.C.I.
BAPAUME			Orders were received for march to YTRES – LECHELLE area on night of 18th + from there to METZ on night of 19th/20th.	H.C.I.
	18th	4 P.M.	Moved off for YTRES – LECHELLE area; arrived about 10-0 P.M. Billeted in huts at LECHELLE.	H.C.I.
LECHELLE	19th		Final conference at Brigade Headquarters. Packs + blankets stored – Company to move off in fighting order to-morrow.	H.C.I.
		4-0 P.M.	Transport moved off to hand with Brigade transport in front of NEUVILLE.	H.C.I.
METZ Sheet 57c. 1:40000	20th	2-0 A.M.	Company marched off to proceed to METZ – halt called at transport-lines near NEUVILLE to prepare the pack animals for the	H.C.I.

151st Coy M.G. Corps

Army Form C. 2118.

WAR DIARY
or
INTELLIGENCE SUMMARY.
(Erase heading not required.)

Place	Date 1917	Hour	Summary of Events and Information	Remarks and references to Appendices
METZ	20th cont		Occurrence. Reviewed METZ 5.30 A.M. Final arrangements made & instructions given.	
		6-20 A.M.	ZERO hour received. = 6-20 A.M.	
		6.20 A.M.	The forward battalions assembled in front of METZ. 2Lt PAINTER with 2 guns reported to Lt G.H. & 2Lt WHEATLEY with 2 guns to Lt A+S.H.	
		10.30 A.M.	Forward battalions moved off. Support battalions assembled at this time. Reserve guns assembled in their places. Behind support battalions. The forward battalions reached the old British front line but were unable to advance further owing to the attacking Brigades being held up in front of FLESQUIERES.	JCI
	4.0 P.M.		Orders received for Brigade to sent but to be ready to move forward again at a moment notice.	
21st	10 A.M.		Orders received to move forward to old British front line at 6.15 A.M. Instructions were given for 2 guns to be attached to each of the support	

Sheet 57c
1:40000

Army Form C. 2118.

WAR DIARY
or
INTELLIGENCE SUMMARY.

(Erase heading not required.)

15th COY. M.G. CORPS

Instructions regarding War Diaries and Intelligence Summaries are contained in F. S. Regs., Part II. and the Staff Manual respectively. Title pages will be prepared in manuscript.

Place	Date 1917	Hour	Summary of Events and Information	Remarks and references to Appendices
	21st Oct		battalion.	
	21st	3.A.M.	Reserve guns at METZ marched off to proceed to TRESCAULT, on arrival 2/Lt STEWART M.C. reported at S.H. & 2/Lt MILLER reported to 9th R.S., the remainder of the guns (8) joined at Brigade Headquarters Q.M.D.S.S. under Lieut CLYDE. Pack animals were with all gun teams at a scale of one p[er] gun & tripod, one for ammunition, four reserve ammunition animals were with reserve guns.	F.B.T.
		6.15	ZERO hour: Support guns moved forward. After this time forward & support guns moved forward by bounds as the situation permitted.	
		10.A.M.	Brigade Headquarters established at FLESQUIERES & Company Headquarters established in sunken road about L.94.d.62.s.0.	
		11.30 A.M.	The 11th G.H. attacked CANTAING & at	
Sheet 57c SE 1:20000		12.30 P.M.	held the village & the 2 guns with this battalion were placed in position on the N.E. edge at F.28.D.25.85. During the	
LIERGNIES Tr. Map 1:20000			evening the 9th R.S. relieved the 4th G.H. but the guns placed in the	

WAR DIARY
OR
INTELLIGENCE SUMMARY

15th Coy M.G Corps

Army Form C. 2118.

Place	Date	Hour	Summary of Events and Information	Remarks and references to Appendices
METZ	1917 27		Above positions did not move, the guns attacked to attk R.S. forth up positions about.	
			The 1st A+S.H. on left moved forward to LA JUSTICE followed by the 11th S.H.	
		5.30 p.m.	The left forward & support battalions proceeded to assault FONTAINE-NOTRE-DAME (the Brigade's final objective) which they held by 6 p.m. + had an outpost line on NORTH side.	
FLESQUIERES.			The guns with the 2 left Battalions were placed on the W. & South on being the most dangerous, owing to BOURLON WOOD still remaining in enemy hands. There 4 guns had positions on a line from F.21.A.3.4. to F.15.E.2.5.70.	
		8.0 p.m.	Orders were received to send 2 more guns to 4th S.H. in FONTAINE-NOTRE-DAME, this was done and on arrival 2.Lt STEWART he placed one gun at F.16.C.95.80. and one at F.9.2. A.1.4. (in local alarm) All the line was visited during this night, the situation was extremely quiet. All teams dug open emplacements + consolidated their positions.	
MERGNIES TriMap 1:20000				

Army Form C. 2118.

15th Coy MG Corps

Instructions regarding War Diaries and Intelligence Summaries are contained in F.S. Regs., Part II. and the Staff Manual respectively. Title pages will be prepared in manuscript.

WAR DIARY
or
INTELLIGENCE SUMMARY.

(Erase heading not required.)

Place	Date	Hour	Summary of Events and Information.	Remarks and references to Appendices
FLESQUIERES	1917 Nov 23rd		During the forenoon CANTAING was shelled fairly heavily by 5.9 & 4.2 H.E. Little damage. FONTAINE was also heavily shelled + at 12 noon the enemy launched a counterattack against our position there, the infantry withdrew to a line on the ridge in front of LA JUSTICE. The six guns in position here resisted the enemy counter-attack to their utmost + caused heavy losses to the advancing waves. The guns on the WEST remained in action until they were surrounded by the enemy + their teams had either become casualties or were made prisoners. 2/Lt WHEATLEY was captured at this point with his two guns. One gun of the original four fell back a short distance in an attempt to cover the retirement of the other three guns but the attempt was unsuccessful, this one gun only with three of its team remaining escaped.	A.C.I
MERGNIES 1:20000			The guns in local reserve at F.22 A.1.7 came into action at	

15th COY M.G. Corps

WAR DIARY
or
INTELLIGENCE SUMMARY.

Army Form C. 2118.

Place	Date 1917 Nov.	Hour	Summary of Events and Information	Remarks and references to Appendices
FLESQUIERES	22nd contd		that point against the enemy advancing from the East + then when the infantry were clear, moved west to a position in the SUNKEN ROAD F.29.c.05.30. The gun which was in position at F.16.c.95.80. was seen later in the attack surrounded by the enemy but still in action. The sergeant at this position (when he saw escape impossible) ordered 4 of his team to go back, he + his No 1 remained + were either killed or captured, only two of the four ordered back reached our lines. The guns around the village kept up a sturdy resistence + fought until the last; their lor can be explained by the failure of other troops to hold their ground + the levels of evening fire when their withdrawal could have been effected. The situation in CANTAING was quite quiet except for slight shelling	H.C.H.
MAP: HERMIES 1:20000		At 12 NOON	orders were received to send four guns from	

Army Form C. 2118.

WAR DIARY
or
INTELLIGENCE SUMMARY.

15th COY M.G Corps

Instructions regarding War Diaries and Intelligence Summaries are contained in F. S. Regs., Part II. and the Staff Manual respectively. Title pages will be prepared in manuscript.

(Erase heading not required.)

Place	Date	Hour	Summary of Events and Information	Remarks and references to Appendices
FLESQUIERES	22nd contd		moved to the 9 at S.H at LA JUSTICE, to help to consolidate the line to which the infantry had retired.	
		2.0 P.M.	Lieut CLYDE took there gun forward & after reporting proceeded to place them in positions at F21 C 30.35. F20.C.05.10. F26.A.9.2. F26 D20.85. to cover the line held by the infantry & the valley south of FONTAINE-NOTRE-DAME. The one gun of the original 4 on the west of the valley joined LIEUT CLYDE about 8.0 P.M.	H.C.J
		5.0 P.M.	An a counter attack on CANTAING seemed probable the remaining 2 guns in reserve were sent to 9 at R.S., these guns were placed in positions at L3 C 90.85. L3 D 1.7. South of the village to cover the ground in L.4. forward	
			No enemy infantry action took place on this front	
MAP	10-12 p.m.		The 7th R.H. (152 Inf Bde.) relieved the 7 A+S.H. on the	
MERGNIES 1/20,000			left sector covering the right outgoing div at day-break their positions	

WAR DIARY or INTELLIGENCE SUMMARY

(Erase heading not required.)

154 Coy, M.G.C.

Army Form C. 2118.

Place	Date	Hour	Summary of Events and Information	Remarks and references to Appendices
FLESQUIERES	1917 Nov. 23		During the forenoon the 152 Inf Bde. carried out an attack on FONTAINE. The attack was unsuccessful, although the extreme left, where a portion of BOURLON WOOD was taken and held by troops of the Brigade. Enemy shelling was reasonably in active during the day.	
		8.15 pm	Orders for a relief by a company of the Cheshire Division were received. O.C.s 152 & 232 Coys. were met, and arrangements were made by which the positions held by three companies were to be relieved. Orders were sent to all sections to be ready for relief.	HQ 1
	24th 2.0 am		No sign of relieving company.	
MAP MERGNIES 1:20000		2.30 am	Orders were received from 13.C.L. 152 Inf Bde. to withdraw the company from the line	HQ 2

154 Coy M.G.C.

Army Form C. 2118.

WAR DIARY
or
INTELLIGENCE SUMMARY.
(Erase heading not required.)

Place	Date	Hour	Summary of Events and Information	Remarks and references to Appendices
FLESQUIERES	24th Month	5.30 am	Company Killergow and collected at FLESQUIERES from which proceeded to METZ by train	
METZ		11.0.	Arrived METZ - orders received famous to YTRES to entrain for journey to DERRANCOURT area.	
Map 57.C 1:40000		10 pm	March to YTRES railhead - entrained after 3 p.m. Were awaiting the recovery the remainder of the day the room.	
TREUX	25	9.0 am	Arrived EDGEHILL station (DERRANCOURT AREA) and marched to billets in TREUX - Company comfortably settled down - Overhaul of stores + equipment commenced	A.C.H.
Map France			The transport which came by road from lines near NEUVILLE, arrived before the above, arrived about	
AMIENS 17		4 pm	4 pm - Good lines	

Army Form C. 2118.

154 Coy M.G.C

Instructions regarding War Diaries and Intelligence Summaries are contained in F.S. Regs., Part II. and the Staff Manual respectively. Title pages will be prepared in manuscript.

WAR DIARY
or
INTELLIGENCE SUMMARY
(Erase heading not required.)

Place	Date	Hour	Summary of Events and Information	Remarks and references to Appendices
TREUX	1917 NOV 26	30	Enroll Survey carried out. Electors very few.	
MAP (Amiens 17)			notes of deficiencies made up.	ACI
	30.	2pm	Orders received from Brigade to move at once to	
			ALBERT and to entrain there for BAPAUME.	
		3.30	Company moved to move off.	
			Orders now received that entraining would cease	
			to take place at EDGE HILL station at 5.30 p.m –	ACI
			further – on arriving at BAPAUME to march to billets	
			at ROCQUIGNY.	
		5.30 p	Entrained.	
		10.30 pm	Arrived at BAPAUME and proceeded to march to	
ROCQUIGNY		1.35am	ROCQUIGNY – arriving there about 1.35 am on 1.	
MAP SHEET 57c			December.	
1:40000			The strength at the end of the month stood at	
			9. OFF. 184 O.R.S – the months casualties were	
			Rec. hoss – 1 Officer (2/Lt Wheatly) 22 O.R.S	

J.C Turncourt Capt.
O.C 154 Coy M.G.C

154TH COMPANY,
MACHINE GUN
CORPS.

Report of Operations of
154 Coy. M.G. Corps
during period Nov 21st to 24th.

REF. MAPS   BEAUCHAMP   1:10000
            NIERGNIES   1:20000

Tuesday 20th
ZERO + 2 hours
8.20 a.m.
FORWARD BNS.

On the two attacking bns. of the Brigade assembling, 4 GORDONS about Q.20.b.3.4, and 7th A.&S.H. about Q.20.b.2.4, 2nd Lieuts Painter and Wheatley assembled with these bns, respectively, with two guns each.

10.30 a.m

These bns moved to the old British Front Line when they were held up by situation in front. These bns. stayed here until early morning of the 21st.

12.30 NOON.

SUPPORT BNS.
10.30 a.m.

The 9th R.S. & 4th S.H. moved out to the above assembly points on attacking bns. moving off. The remaining guns of the company assembled behind these two support bns.

4.p.m.

The support bns. and reserve guns received orders to return to billets in METZ, but to be ready to move at a moments notice. A move was made at 4 a.m. on 21st.

Wednesday 21st
6.15.a.m

The guns with attacking bns. followed them forward into the German Front System.

On the support bns. being moved forward to the Old British Front Line orders were received to attach two guns to each. Lieut Stewart M.C and 2nd Lieut Miller reported to Commanding Officers of 4th Seaforths

(2)

and 9th R.S. respectively.

6.15. a.m. The reserve guns were moved into position at Q 4. d. 5. 5.

The attacking bns. moved forward by stages through FLESQUIERES and halted in the SUNKEN RD. between LA JUSTICE and K 8. b. Central.

10.30 a.m ~~Support bns. followed them through at~~ ~~an~~ th interval.

RIGHT FRONT BN.

The 4 GORDONS on right from here attacked CANTAING which was in our hands by about 12. NOON.

12.30. Two guns with 4 G.H. took up positions on N.E of CANTAING, about F 28 d. 25. 85. and F 28 d 80. 60 (this latter gun was later moved to a position at L 28 d. 30. 35)

These two guns engaged numerous parties of the enemy in and about LA FOLIE WOOD and on the ground in K 22 b & d. also E. of FONTAINE.

RIGHT SUPPORT BN.

This bn. followed the RT. FORWARD BN. and eventually relieved it in CANTAING. The two guns attached, were placed in position about L 3 d. 6. 4 and L 3. b. 1. 1. for defence of the flanks of the village.

LEFT FORWARD BN.

10.30. a.m. The guns moved forward to LA JUSTICE but were not incorporated with any action until they were taken over by Lieut STEWART attached to 4th Seaforths in operations CANTAING MILL.

see Notes re L. S. BN.

LEFT SUPPORT BN.

9.45
11.0. a.m
11.45. a.m.

The LEFT SUPPORT BN. moved forward from K. 23. C to LA JUSTICE and from there towards FONTAIN-NOTRE-DAME via CANTAING MILL.

3.30 p.m. The guns with this bn. took up positions in front of the mill in F. 24. C. ~~when the mill was taken.~~

(3)

3.30 p   Lieut. Stewart M.C. returned to LA JUSTICE and brought the guns attached to 7th A & S.H. forward to this point.

The four guns then advanced on FONTAINE and as this village had been occupied by 4th Seaforths and some companies of the 7 A & S.H., positions were taken up, after consultation with C.O's Battalions,

6.5.p.m.   on a line from K.21.a.3.4. to K.15.C.25.40. to protect the left of village from BOURLON WOOD.

8.0 to 8.30 p.m.   Orders were received from Bde. H.Q's. to send two guns forward to 4th Seaforths. — this was done one gun being placed at K.16.C.75.80. and the other in reserve about K.22 a.1.4

THURSDAY
22nd
           The position on the front during early morning seemed quiet.

1.0 - 5.30 a.m   Gun teams all dug open emplacements and ammunition expended had been made up, with a small reserve.

11.15. a.m.   Orders were received from Bde. to send four guns to LA JUSTICE at once. These were moved off under Lieut. CLYDE and were placed in positions about F.21.C.30.35. – F.20.C.05.10. – F.26.a.9.2. – F.26.d.20.85. to cover the valley on the S of FONTAINE and the W., approaches.

COUNTER ATTACK.

12.30 p.m.   During the counter attack the 6 guns around FONTAINE fought a delaying action the whole time. Considerable losses were inflicted upon the enemy but 4 guns were captured in the enemy advance. One at F.16.C.75.80, which was seen to be firing until the enemy were all around it, and three at the W. of the village.

The four guns on the West made an attempt to cover each others withdrawal, after the Infantry were clear, but, as they had covered this latter movement for so long, their own was cut off, except for one gun which reached the sunken road at F.21.a.y.1. and came into action there. This gun later came under orders of Lieut. CLYDE who had 4 guns just in rear of this position.

All the teams around FONTAINE showed great devotion to duty during the attack, and were the sole cause of the battalions being able to get clear to the extent they did. These guns fought without any support from either flank during the attack, except for that from one gun in CANTAING. (below)

One of the CANTAING defence guns at F.28.d.55.85 engaged several targets on the E. of FONTAINE and several small parties in LA FOLIE WOOD. The fire of this gun was effective although at rather a long range.

5.0.p.m.
The position in the line was still uncertain and as CANTAING was open to counter attack, and in a salient, the two remaining guns were sent up to strengthen the defence.

They were placed in positions on the S. to cover the ground in L.4. - from positions about L.3.c 90.85 and L.3.d.1.y.

The gun which was at K.22.a.1.y. was now in position about K.22.c.0.4. where it remained until the company withdrew from the line

(5)

10-12 p.m.   The 4th R.H. (152 Bde) relieved the 4th A.& S.H. in the left sector during the night. Our guns here did not change their positions.

THURSDAY 23rd

During the forenoon the 152 Inf. Bde carried out an attack through our line on FONTAINE but were unsuccessful. At nightfall the line remained as before on our front except for the S.E corner of BOURLON WOOD being held by a small force. Nothing of importance happened in the CANTAING sector.

8.15.p.m.   Orders for a relief by a Company of the Guards Division were received.

Arrangements were made with O.C's 152 and 232. Coys, who also had guns in the line, as to which guns were to be relieved.

2.a.m.   Up to 2 a.m. no sign of relieving company was seen when orders were received from B.G. Comdg. 152 Bde. to withdraw the Company from the line.

5.30.a.m   All teams were out, and moved to FLESQUIERES.

The Company then marched to METZ during forenoon.

H.G. _____
CAPT.,
COMDG. 154th COY., M. G. CORPS.

On His Majesty's Service.

154th MACHINE GUN COMPANY

DECEMBER 1917

CONFIDENTIAL

ORIGINAL

M 24

WAR DIARY

154 Company, M.G. Corps.

Period: December 1st to 31st 1917.

Volume 24.

Army Form C. 2118.

154 Coy M.G.C.

Instructions regarding War Diaries and Intelligence Summaries are contained in F. S. Regs., Part II, and the Staff Manual respectively. Title pages will be prepared in manuscript.

WAR DIARY
~~INTELLIGENCE SUMMARY~~
(Erase heading not required.)

Place	Date 1917	Hour	Summary of Events and Information	Remarks and references to Appendices
ROCQUIGNY.	Dec. 1	1.30am.	The company arrived by rail from BARAUME – having started by rail from TREUX. Billeted in huts.	
		3am	Orders received from Bde., to be in readiness at ½ hours notice – Transportation from TREUX by rail.	
		8.20am.	Brave received for move to BERTINCOURT, with Eschelon B. All troops to please Lighting Kitchen on arrival.	
		10.15	Marched off to proceed to BERTINCOURT arriving Bar. on 1 hour notice.	A.C.I.
BERTINCOURT.		2.5pm	Orders received at 2.5pm for move of two Bdes and the company to BEUGNY. Marched off at 5pm	
		5pm		
BEUGNY.		7pm	On arriving at BEUGNY about 7pm – no billets at all except the shelter of a railway embankment. After "diplomatic" enquiries a workshop billet was found in the village. Company marched in to billets at 11 pm.	
		11pm.		

154 Coy M.G.C.

WAR DIARY or INTELLIGENCE SUMMARY

Army Form C. 2118.

Place	Date 1917	Hour	Summary of Events and Information	Remarks and references to Appendices
BEUGNY.	DEC. 2	2 a.m.	Orders received to move forward at 1.25 p.m. to H.Q. of 169 Coy (36 Div) with 16 guns to relieve this company. Reconnaissance of line carried out during morning by officers of the position — general scheme taken over from O.C. 169 Coy.	
DOIGNIES.		4.30 p.m.	The company moved off by road during the afternoon arriving at H.Q. near DOIGNIES about 4.30 p.m. Guns were put into positions. Four covered from Louville shell fire on the way to H.Q.	A.G.I.
		10 p.m.	Relief completed. All positions — an excellently successful and easy relief under the circumstances. Disposition of Company as follows: Coy. H.Q. J 10 a 6.1. 5 guns on E. OLD GERMAN OUTPOST LINE at, (4) E 25 & 7.4. and (1) E 25 a 9.5 under 2/Lieut STEWART	

Ref. Maps
Sheet 57c 1:40,000
57cNE 1:20,000
MOEUVRES Special Sheet 1:20000

Army Form C. 2118.

154 Coy M.G.C.

WAR DIARY
or
INTELLIGENCE SUMMARY.
(Erase heading not required.)

Instructions regarding War Diaries and Intelligence Summaries are contained in F. S. Regs., Part II. and the Staff Manual respectively. Title pages will be prepared in manuscript.

Place	Date	Hour	Summary of Events and Information	Remarks and references to Appendices
DOIGNIES Coy. HQ. J10 a 6.1	1917 DEC. 2	10 A.M.	1 gun manned 2/Lt HOLDING in OLD GERMAN OUTPOST LINE (O.G.O.L.) at approx. D24 6.8.4.	
			6 guns under 2/Lt MILLER in the OLD BRITISH LINE (O.B.L.) at approx. J5 b 1. 9/J6 b 15.75. - J5 b 8.4. - J5 b 9055 - J5 b 2.1. & J6 8.4.1.	
			4 guns under Lt CLYDE in the INTERMEDIATE LINE at approx. J17 b 6.7 - J10 a 5.1. - J10 c 9.5. & J10 a 0.6.	M.G.1
			The guns in the O.G.O.L. were all in close defence fire for the protection of that line un-once the HINDENBURG LINE which was in rear being in our front was broken.	
			Lines of fire for the protection of the forward line were given to all of these guns.	
			The remaining guns in the O.B.L. are the INTERMEDIATE LINE were all in positions for the defence of tactical features. Comparatively good lay - intermittent shelling of front near Stafford line. (HINDENBURG - O.G.O.L.)	M.G.1

MOEUVRES 1:20000 Special Sheet.

154 Coy M.G.C.

Army Form C. 2118.

WAR DIARY
INTELLIGENCE SUMMARY

Place	Date	Hour	Summary of Events and Information	Remarks and references to Appendices
DOIGNIES Coy.H.Q. J.10.a.6.1.	1917 Dec.	3	Permission was obtained from Bde H.Q. to move the guns in position about D.24.d.8.4. to about E.19.c.3.9. These guns were also to send an extra gun each to reinforce the defence of the O.G.O.1. - one of the guns in the O.B.1. at J.6.b.2.1. moved forward for this purpose and took up position about E.19.c.3.6. The lines of fire of all 7 guns on the O.G.O.1. were rearranged - the taking of A-1 at E.25 & 7.4 of lock on S.O.S. barrage gave to the extreme front line on the right. Two out in E.19.c. completed the S.O.S. barrage on the right. The area between the two outer guns enemy from MOEUVRES through E.25.a.9.5. broken after by the guns at E.25.a.9.5. A complete belt of fire could be placed by these guns on the whole front. - The positions were excellent and the ground lends itself to good M.G. work.	H.1
MOEUVRES Special Sheet 1:20000				

WAR DIARY
~~INTELLIGENCE~~ SUMMARY

Army Form C. 2118.

154 Coy. M.G.C.

Instructions regarding War Diaries and Intelligence Summaries are contained in F. S. Regs, Part II, and the Staff Manual respectively. Title pages will be prepared in manuscript.

(Erase heading not required.)

Place	Date	Hour	Summary of Events and Information	Remarks and references to Appendices
DOIGNIES	1917 Dec. 4	8pm	Nothing of great interest occurred during the day. Enemy artillery was more active on our front & support line.	
Coy. HQ J10a.6.1.		2pm	Orders were received that the line at present held would be withdrawn on night of 4/5. The Boyau was to be used to effect withdrawal-132 Brigade taking over the O.B.L. before our withdrawal commences. All surplus stores and equipment removed from the forward positions & more after dark as possible.	Stat.
		11pm	The withdrawal on the forward area commenced. Their movements to the rear - leaving behind posts on our front line and on our flanks - and the support of these the former were to close in the support. Of these the former were to go back at 5am on 5th and the latter at 7.45am on 5th	
MOEUVRES Special Sheet 1:20,000				

WAR DIARY or INTELLIGENCE SUMMARY

154 Coy. M.G.C.

Army Form C. 2118.

Instructions regarding War Diaries and Intelligence Summaries are contained in F. S. Regs., Part II. and the Staff Manual respectively. Title pages will be prepared in manuscript.

(Erase heading not required.)

Place	Date	Hour	Summary of Events and Information	Remarks and references to Appendices
DOIGNIES A Coy H.Q.	1917 Dec 3		As far as could be ascertained generally, the action was as follows.	
J.10.d.6.1.		10 pm	The four guns in O.B.L. were relieved by 6 guns of 152 Coy – relieved teams proceeded to billets in BEUGNY.	
		11 pm	On the main bodies of the battalions moving out [illegible] 4 guns also withdrew, leaving one gun withdrawn platoon in all, to the support line. These guns were taken down at 1.45 am with the lead of infantry. The line was quiet owing mostly of the enemy and the front line of our withdrawal was carried out successfully. Total 3 guns.	A.C.I.
MOEUVRES 1:20,000	5	4.45 am	Previous through the O.B.L. to Hellwig Beugny. – So mishaps at all throughout the movement.	A.C.I.

Army Form C. 2118.

WAR DIARY
or
INTELLIGENCE SUMMARY
(Erase heading not required.)

/54 Coy, M.G.C.

Instructions regarding War Diaries and Intelligence Summaries are contained in F. S. Regs., Part II. and the Staff Manual respectively. Title pages will be prepared in manuscript.

Place	Date 1917 DEC.	Hour	Summary of Events and Information	Remarks and references to Appendices
DOIGNIES	5 conts		Disposition of company as now —	
Coy.H.Q.		6.30 a.m.	Coy. H.Q. J.10 a 6.1.	
J.10 a 6.1.			4 Guns in same positions on INTERMEDIATE LINE.	
			These guns remained in positions for several days.	A.1
			Reserve Line guns.	
			12 Guns in billets at BEUGNY.	
		1 a.m.	Coy. HQ moved about 1 a.m. to BEUGNY leaving the above 4 guns in position under 2nd Lieut. CLYDE.	
MOEUVRES 1:20000.			These guns were subsequently under the orders of O.C. 152 Coy.	
BEUGNY.			Company marched – billets fair.	
			Enemy aircraft active during evening.	
	6		Overhead of guns stores and general strong	M.A.1
			up.	
Sheet 57c 1:40000	7		General Inventory. Inspection Progr. Protection against Air Bomb fragments put around all billets.	Hat

Army Form C. 2118.

154 Coy. M.G.C.

Instructions regarding War Diaries and Intelligence Summaries are contained in F. S. Regs., Part II. and the Staff Manual respectively. Title pages will be prepared in manuscript.

WAR DIARY
or
INTELLIGENCE SUMMARY
(Erase heading not required.)

Place	Date	Hour	Summary of Events and Information	Remarks and references to Appendices
BEUGNY	1917 DEC 8/9		General Parados and Enemy Rhoda front system cable being in fair of importance forward Enemy artillery active	
	10		Personell of coy. moved from billets in the village to huts at Sugar Transport Lines	H.L.
	11		Enemy thoroughly cleared - cleaned and kept in repair as far as possible.	H.Q.
	12		One gun from the line was ordered to advance to coy. HQrs Gravina on Parcus. Orders were received from the relief of the runners 3 guns in the line by 152 coy on the right of 18th Bal. during the during of 12. The mining teams from 152 turned up tomorrow. The relief was carried out 2nd Bat. H.Q. and teams reporting on being relieved.	H.Q.

Sheet 57c.
1:40000.

WAR DIARY
or
~~INTELLIGENCE SUMMARY~~

(Erase heading not required.)

Army Form C. 2118.

154 Coy. M.G.C.

Instructions regarding War Diaries and Intelligence Summaries are contained in F. S. Regs., Part II. and the Staff Manual respectively. Title pages will be prepared in manuscript.

Place	Date 1917	Hour	Summary of Events and Information	Remarks and references to Appendices
BEUGNY	DEC 13		The whole company concentrated. Europe S.C. Lewis revived. The various sub-sections opened one extra casserole and were able to refresh one another — recall however no man on the command.	A.C.A.
	14.		Course training. Billets improved.	A.C.A.
	15.		Training carried on. Orders received for Coy to relieve 153 M.G.Coy on night 16/17. Reconnaissance – 16 guns to take up position	A.C.A.
	16		Preparation for relief carried out. Relief named APPENDIX No.1 as per O.O. No. 5.	APPENDIX No.1 A.C.A.
LINE Coy HQ J.2.b.central	17		Disposition of Company as in APPENDIX No. above. A successful relief from M.G. shelling by enemy.	A.C.A.
MOEUVRES 1:20000	18.		was quite uneventful and heavy. Sixteen Lewis Guns Zero Yimberly coming to	A.C.A.

154 Coy MGC

WAR DIARY
or
INTELLIGENCE SUMMARY.

Army Form C. 2118.

Place	Date	Hour	Summary of Events and Information	Remarks and references to Appendices
LINE.	DEC 1917			
H.Q. J2 B cent. d	17		Enemy fly. Enemy artillery active during night moderate	Map
	18.		shooting.	
			Visibility still poor — Very cold — Snow fell heavily during the day — Lessed fairly	
			Enemy artillery active away the day — Our guns active at intervals during the night.	
			Enemy signals with a fresh lamp were seen from our front line — apparently signalling from he Rd to	Map
			Lateau. Reported to Infantry observers.	
			M.G.s not very active	
	19		Normal — not necessarily a victory or extreme — visibility still very bad. What enemy artillery fire there was shewed much greater accuracy than on preceding days — shooting on STRAND particularly that	
			good. Enemy Lewis BARBICAN during the day, be appeared to select that one particular line.	
MOEUVRES				
1:20,000				

Army Form C. 2118.

WAR DIARY
or
INTELLIGENCE SUMMARY.

(Erase heading not required.)

Place	Date	Hour	Summary of Events and Information	Remarks and references to Appendices
LINE, H.Q. J & C. central	1917 DEC 20		Very cold – heavy frost and poor visibility. Enemy carried out raids on and near enemy lines by 5" gun – about 4000 to be expected. While M.G.A was firing in approximation with S.A., the enemy appeared along the front line near the position to be on the position – moved 8 yards – the two guns appeared to annoy him considerably. Usual activity on both sides.	HQA
	21.		Poor visibility – usual artillery activity – may still fire on and about our J.T.B. – a large number of the usual "duds" – strafing, however still exceeds. Nothing of unusual importance.	
			Orders received for relief by 152 M.G. Coy – arrangements made with O.C. 152.	HQA
MOEUVRES 1:20000			Instructions received that Div. Soton had been issued to 2 Bat. Light that 153 recruits would be on a post.	

154 Coy M.G.C.

WAR DIARY or INTELLIGENCE SUMMARY

Army Form C. 2118.

Place	Date	Hour	Summary of Events and Information	Remarks and references to Appendices
LINE	DEC. 1917			
H.Q.J.26.central	21 contd.		2 Lewis from Lofft Battery to about D29.a.2.4.	
	22		Relief of our guns slightly carried out. O.C. 153 Coy met and arrangements made for the relief of fourteen M.G. 5, 6, 7, 54, 5. B.M.2.5.1. Position at R.5. to be taken over by D.M. Coy. (282) and all other positions on right of Canal by 152 Coy.	A.C.1.
MOEUVRES 1:20000		9/m	Relief carried out - as O.O. no. 6. attention to detail. Relief complete - most satisfactory - no casualties. Company moves back to former Camp at 12.8.b. (57c)	APPENDIX 2
Nr. BEUGNY	23.		Rest and cleaning up.	A.C.1.
12.8.b.8.2.4.	24.		Overhaul of all Stores, Guns etc. Cleaning up.	A.C.1.
	25.		Christmas Day. – Rest.	A.C.1.
	26		Owing to enemy Air Raids being frequent, our trenches were dug near each Hut. Company cold. Each hut I known by all ranks.	A.C.1.
Sheet 57c 1:40000				

Army Form C. 2118.

WAR DIARY
or
INTELLIGENCE SUMMARY.
(Erase heading not required.)

Instructions regarding War Diaries and Intelligence Summaries are contained in F. S. Regs., Part II. and the Staff Manual respectively. Title pages will be prepared in manuscript.

Place	Date	Hour	Summary of Events and Information	Remarks and references to Appendices
BEUGNY 1.28.B.8.9.	1917 Dec. 26		The bathing of the Division thoroughly overcome	A.C.I.
	27			
	28		General Entrenchment the army carries division being	
Sheet 57c.I. 1:40000	29		Orders received for relief of 152 Company in the Right Division line was reorganised and arrangements	A.C.I.
	30		were for relief night 30/31st. Preparation for relief received 11.9 orders. Relief moves out at O.O. b.2.4.	A.C.I. APPENDIX 5.
LINE. Coy H.Q. 21 J 10d 6.1.	31	8.20 p.m.	Relief complete - disposition of Company on OO above. Laid right on a day - small amount of enemy air own shelling. Lashing of importance to note. Line extremely quiet.	A.C.I.
MOEUVRES 1:20000			The general condition throughout the month has been good, held on and out of the line, albb'10 a few the cases has been rather severe. On the	

154 Coy. M.G.C.

Army Form C. 2118.

WAR DIARY or INTELLIGENCE SUMMARY

(Erase heading not required.)

Place	Date	Hour	Summary of Events and Information	Remarks and references to Appendices
LINE.	1917 DEC. 31.		whilst the sickness of my service period was little, and that among the weaker men who were not above the freezing snow. Morale of men excellent.	
COY H.Q.			During the month 18 OR. Reinforcements were taken on strength from Base Depot.	
J.10.d.6.1.		1.0↑	2nd Lieuts E.G. at W. HOLDING + SIDDAL were invalided sick	H.A.T
			Lieut W.T. CLYDE proceeded to Ceylon for transfer to the Indian Army.	
			The following awards were made to the company during the month for gallantry near Le Cambrai operations 20-29 November.	H.A.T

M. MEDAL.

No. 20061 A/Cpl. HAROLD SMITH.
No. 85964 Pte. CYRIL CHARLES BARTON.

MOEUVRES				
1:20000			Auth, IV Corps No. I. 51/56 to 69	
			51 (H) Div No. 366.(A)	

Army Form C. 2118.

WAR DIARY
or
INTELLIGENCE SUMMARY.
(Erase heading not required.)

154 Coy M.G.C.

Instructions regarding War Diaries and Intelligence Summaries are contained in F. S. Regs., Part II, and the Staff Manual respectively. Title pages will be prepared in manuscript.

Place	Date	Hour	Summary of Events and Information	Remarks and references to Appendices
LINE	1917 DEC. 31.		Strength of Company at end of month as follows	
Coy. HQ.				
J.10.a.6.1			OFFICERS 7. O.R.s 192.	
			INCREASE during month 1.Off. 18 O.R. DECREASE during month. 3 Off. 11 O.R.	
			consisting of 2 Kd. 2 Wd. 7. evacuated sick or from other causes	
			2 Lt. H.G.Berrett joined the company on 3rd.	H.C.L
			H.C. Harcourt Cotton	
MOEUVRES			Comdg. 154 Coy. M.G. Corps	
1:20,000				
			B.G.L.	
			31.12.17.	

SECRET   COPY NO. 10.

                                              APPENDIX 11/4

154 MACHINE GUN COMPANY

OPERATION ORDER NO. 5.

REF. MAPS   54C. 1:40,000 and MOUVRES 1:20,000.

1.   The Company will relieve 153 Coy. on the Divisional Front on night of 16/17 Dec.

2.   The line will be held with

        4 Guns in FRONT LINE
        5 do. in SUPPORT do.
        4 do. in RESERVE POSITIONS

3. DISPOSITION

(a) Coy. H.Q will be at CROSS ROADS J.2.b. central.

(b) B.SECTION 2nd LT. MILLER and 1 TEAM D.SECTION will take over LEFT GROUP in the following positions.

    M.G. 7. approx   D.22.c.2.4 ⎫
    M.G. 6.   "   D.22.c.5.4 ⎬ FRONT LINE
    M.G. 5.   "   D.22.d.5.2 ⎭
    S.4   "   D.24.d.25.45 ⎫ SUPPORT LINE
    S.5   "   D.24.d.15.50 ⎭

SECTION H.Q. J.3.a.65.35.

(c) D.SECTION less 1 gun 2nd LT. STEWART will take over CENTRE GROUP at following positions.

    M.G. 4. approx   J.5.b.10.85 ⎫ FRONT LINE
    M.G. 3.   "   J.5.b.8.3   ⎭
    S.3   "   D.29.c.20.35 SUPPORT LINE

SECTION H.Q J.5.b.1.4.

(d) A.SECTION 2nd LT. PAINTER will take over RIGHT GROUP at following positions.

    M.G.1. approx. J.6.d.44   ⎫ FRONT LINE
    ?   "   K.4.a.4.4   ⎭
    S.1   "   J.12.a.40.85 ⎫ SUPPORT LINE.
    S.1A   "   K.4.a.0.5   ⎭

SECTION H.Q. J.6.d.50.35.

(e) C.SECTION under Sgt. TRAIN will take over REAR GROUP of guns at following positions:—

    R.5.   approx   J.9.b.45.40   RESERVE LINE
    B.M.2.   "   J.8.a.35.45 ⎫
    B.M.3.   "   J.8.a.8.4   ⎬ BEAUMETZ LINE
    B.M.4.   "   J.8.c.1.9   ⎭

SECTION H.Q. J.4.b.85.10.

NOTE. Special orders for an early relief may be issued to Sgt. TRAIN during morning of 16th.

4. GUIDES

(a) One guide per position will be picked up at the group dumps

II

stated in para 5. at 5.30 p.m. 16th inst.

Section Officers will detail teams to definite positions before proceeding to the line therefore a quick start to be made after arrival at the dump.

Each team N.C.O. will know by this which guide to ask for.

(b) In the event of the light holding out on the 16th, Section Officers will not pass CROSS ROADS J.8.c.y.3. before dusk.

5. The following dumps will be used for all supply purposes.

COMPANY H.Q. and LEFT GROUP at J.2.b. central (Coy. H.Q.)

CENTRAL and RIGHT GROUPS :- Near entrance of FISH ALLEY J.5.c.35.60

REAR GROUP. CROSS ROADS J.8.c.20.15.

RATIONS each night at 6 p.m. except REAR GROUP which will be at 5.15 p.m.

6. TAKING OVER

All teams except the 4 Rear ones (C. SECTION) will take over Tripods – 10 Belts and usual TRENCH STORES (each team will take 2 belts extra into the line.)

C SECTION. will move in complete with all usual trench equipment (8 belts per gun)

S.O.S. lines and defence schemes must be carefully checked by all section officers and gun team commanders.

A full description of the position, its vicinity and all concerning it is to be obtained from outgoing teams, 1 man per position from 153 Coy. will stay in for 24 hours after relief.

Mutual receipts to be given for all positions and stores taken over.

7. WATER

There is no water supply in line. All water will be sent up with rations. Water tins will be taken over.

8. REPORTS

DAILY INTELLIGENCE REPORT to reach Coy. H.Q. by 8 a.m. each morning for period 7. a.m. to 7. a.m., pro forma attached.

There are several positions from which excellent observation of enemies lines can be obtained – a GOOD look out must be kept in these positions – all sentries should keep a log.

9. DISCIPLINE

Good Trench Discipline must be maintained – all ranks must be as clean as circumstances permit.

Sentries must keep a rigid and sharp outlook during hours of darkness as the enemy is in the habit of patrolling close to our lines.

10. RELIEF COMPLETE will be reported to Coy H.Q. by code word

"FANNY ADAMS"

One signaller per section will go forward with each section officer. On relief being complete this signaller will come to Coy. H.Q. with the outgoing section officer or runner as the case may be.

The section runner will bring the DAILY REPORT on the following morning, 14th.

11. S.O.S. From noon on 14th December the S.O.S signal will be two GREEN and 2 WHITE Very Lights or Rifle Grenades.

These will be issued.

12. ACKNOWLEDGE.

Issued at

15.12.14.

Copy No 1   Coy. H.Q
        2   O.C. A. SECTION
        3   "   B   "
        4   "   D   "
        5   T.O.
        6   O.C. 153. Coy. M.G.C.
        7   C.S.M.
        8   C.Q.S.M.
        9   Sgt. TRAIN C. SECTION
    10-11   WAR DIARY.
      12   File.

H.N.G.C.

French Clones

To be handed over
to relieving Section
Officer

WAR DIARY.
Feb. 1918
APPENDIX I
154 M.G.COY

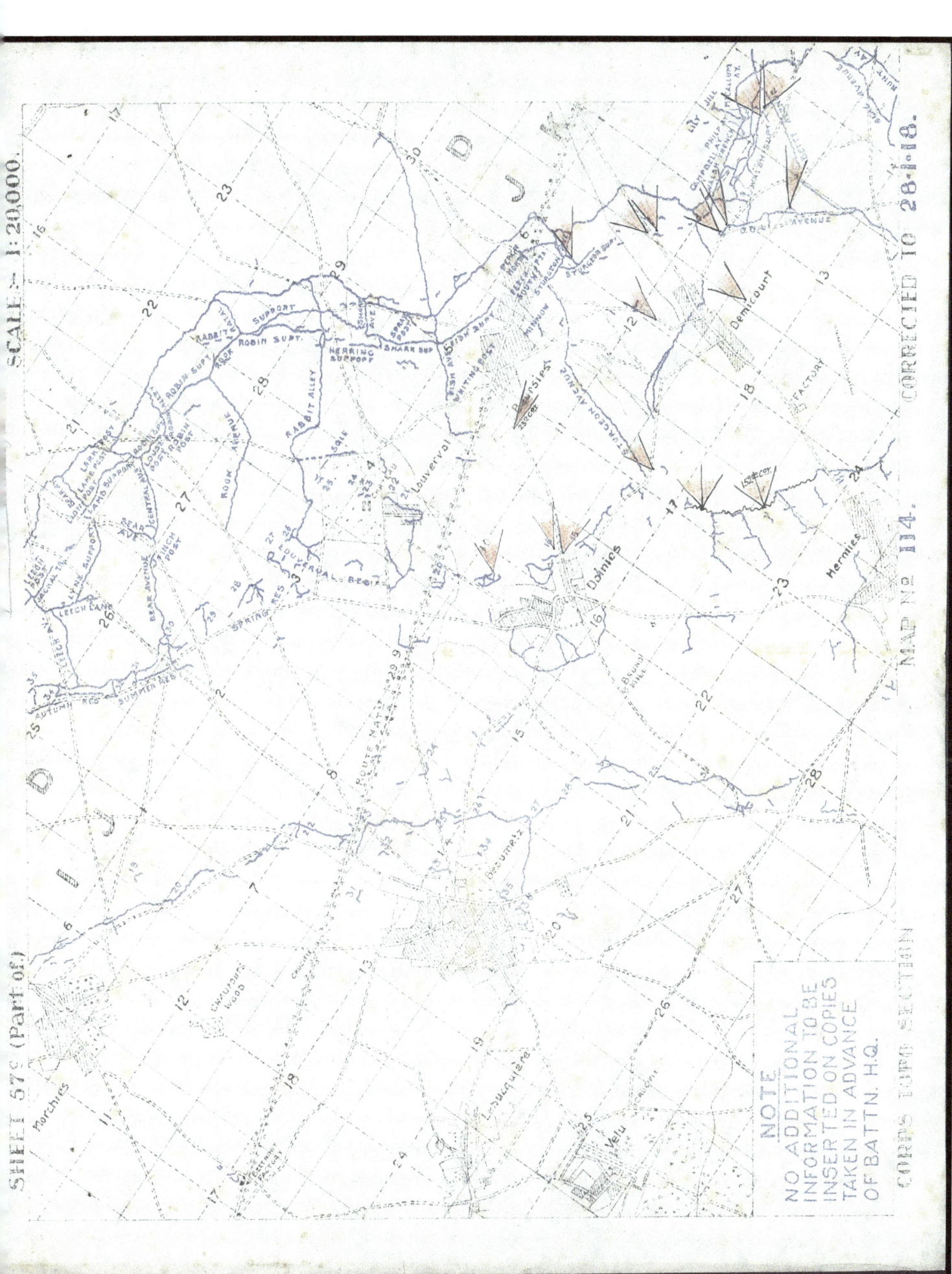

SECRET   COPY No. 9

154 MACHINE GUN COMPANY   APP. No. 2
OPERATION ORDER No. 6

REF. MAPS. $5y^C$ 1:40,000 and MOEUVRES 1:20,000

1. **RELIEF**   The company will be relieved on night of 22/23 by 152 and 153 M.G. Coy.

2. **SECTION RELIEFS**

   RIGHT GROUP (A. SECTION) will be relieved by B. SECTION 152 with 4 guns.

   CENTRE GROUP (D. SECTION) by C. SECTION 152 with 3 guns.

   LEFT GROUP (B. SECTION) by ~~D. SECTION~~ 5 guns 153.

   C. SECTION will be relieved by 4 guns 153 at 2.30 p.m.

3. **GUIDES**

   (a) **RIGHT, CENTRE AND LEFT GROUPS** GUIDES will be at Group Dump at 5.30 p.m.

   C. SECTION GUIDES will be at SECTION dump J.8.C.3.2 by 2.30 p.m.

   One guide from each position.

4. **HANDING OVER**

   Tripods - 12 belt boxes and the usual trench stores will be handed over.
   C. SECTION will take out all equipment.
   Mutual receipts to be obtained.
   Dug-outs and emplacements will be cleaned and in correct order.
   All Maps, plans and any instructions referring to positions or trenches to be handed over and carefully explained.
   No Gum Boots will be handed over, - all are to be brought out.

5. **TRANSPORT**

   RIGHT CENTRE AND LEFT GROUPS

   Two half limbers will be at FISH dump for A and D. SECTIONS at 9.30.p.m.

   Two limbers at H.Q dump at 9.30 p.m.

   Transport Officer will send one limber, to bring out C. SECTION guns and equipment, to REAR dump by 3.p.m.

6. **RELIEF COMPLETE** to be reported to Coy. H.Q Code word "LOOK IN".

   To expedite relief complete of A and D. SECTIONS reaching Coy. H.Q., a relay post consisting of Cpl. YULE and 1 signaller will be established at FISH dump.

   O/c A and D. SECTIONS will hand their relief complete report to Cpl. YULE, together with a copy from the 152 officer.

   The reports will then be brought to Coy. H.Q by cyclist.

   On completion of relief sections will march to the billets previously occupied.

7. **ACKNOWLEDGE.**

   ISSUED AT 11. A.M.

   22.12.17.

   COMDG. 154th COY. M.G. CORPS

   COPY No. 1.   H.Q
           2   O.C. 152 M G COY.
           3   O.C. A SECTION
           4   O.C. B "
           5   O.C. D "
           6   T.O.
           7   C.Q.M.S.
           8   Sgt. TRAIN (i/c C. SECTION)
           9-10 WAR DIARY
           ~~11   FILE.~~

ADDENDA. NO. 1. TO OPERATION ORDER NO. 6.

(1) RELIEF OF R.9 and R.5. POSITIONS.

Para 2. OPERATION ORDER NO 6. as far as it refers to C. SECTION will be cancelled.

B.M. 2, 3, and 4 Positions will be relieved by 153 Coy.

R.5. Position will be relieved by a team of 232 Coy. at point in position R.9., after this team's relief by a team of 153 Coy.

A Guide from R.5. is to report to Coy. H.Q at 4. p.m for the purpose of guiding 232 Coy. team from R.9 to R.5.

ISSUED AT 11 A.M.

22.12.17

Copies to all concerned

H. C. Lancaster, CAPT.
COMDG. 154th COY. M.G. CORPS.

SECRET   COPY NO 9.

154 COMPANY MACHINE GUN CORPS

OPERATION ORDER NO. 4.

App. No. 3

REF. MAP.   MOEUVRES 1:20,000

1. RELIEF

The Company will relieve 152 M.G. Coy in the Right Divisional Sector on night of 30/31st with 11 guns.

2. SECTION RELIEFS

Company H.Q will be at J.10.d.60.15

A. SECTION (2nd Lieut Painter) 4 guns will relieve 4 guns 152 Coy ~~2nd Lieut Potter~~ in RIGHT GROUP (positions formerly held by this section)

Group Dump as now at S.1. POSITION

B. SECTION (2nd Lieut Miller) 4 guns will relieve 4 guns 152 Coy in RESERVE POSITIONS R.1, R.2, R.3, R.4,

SECTION H.Q and DUMP at Coy. H.Q

C. SECTION less 1 gun (2nd Lieut Benett) will relieve 3 guns 152 Coy ~~at~~ in LEFT GROUP at positions -

         M.G.3 - J.5.b. 85.45.
         M.G.4 - J.5.b. 10.90.
         S.3   - D.29.c 20.40.

SECTION H.Q J.5.b. 10.85 (near M.G.4)

GROUP DUMP. END OF FISH TRENCH J.5c. 30.60.

D. SECTION ± 1 Gun C. SECTION will remain at Transport Lines under 2nd Lieut Stewart. Work Programme for period will be given to 2nd Lieut Stewart.

3. GUIDES

Guides (1 per position) will be at Group Dumps by 5. p.m.

4. TAKING OVER. Tripods, Belt Boxes, S.O.S.

II

Fire Schemes and usual Trench Stores will be taken over.

Care is to be taken in checking and obtaining all information in regard to S.O.S. lines, fire schemes, and the sector.

Mutual Receipts to be given and taken. One copy to be forwarded to Coy. H.Q. by first T.P.R. runner after relief.

5. <u>RELIEF COMPLETE</u> will be reported by Section Runners to Coy. H.Q. by code words;

"THIRD WORD SEWING"

6. <u>REPORTS</u>

T.P. REPORT is to reach Coy. H.Q. by 8 a.m. each morning on usual pro forma.

A Special report re any occurrence will be sent when necessary.

7. <u>ACKNOWLEDGE</u>.

Issued at 9 pm
29.12.17.

Copy No 1. Coy H.Q.
      2. O.C. A Section
      3. O.C. B.
      4. O.C. C.
      5. O.C. 153. M.G. Coy for information
      6. O.C. D Section
      7. T.O.
      8. C.S.M. & pass to C.Q.M.S.
      9-10. WAR DIARY.

H.C. Lancent
CAPT.

CONFIDENTIAL

ORIGINAL

WAR DIARY.

154 Coy. M.G. Corps.

Period January 1st to 31st 1918.

Volume 25

Army Form C. 2118.

WAR DIARY
or
INTELLIGENCE SUMMARY
(Erase heading not required.)

154 Co MGC

Instructions regarding War Diaries and Intelligence Summaries are contained in F. S. Regs., Part II. and the Staff Manual respectively. Title pages will be prepared in manuscript.

Place	Date	Hour	Summary of Events and Information	Remarks and references to Appendices
LINE. 5½ St MOEUVRES. Coy HQ J10a 6.1	1918 Jan 1		The hostile artillery was quiet - no enemy infantry occurred. Trench lines were normal and quiet during the night. Verlies targets in the enemy's lines, 2500 rounds fired.	A.1
	2.		Enemy aircraft slightly active about midday, 5 machines flew over our lines for about an hour.	
	3.		Enemy artillery was active. Louverval was shelled throughout the day. R5 Pavilion was at one time engaged by 4.2 flieuven. Enemy lines every R1 Pavilion area were patrolled successfully and several lines were sent from the machine to our positions. A measure was sent a question - side the enemy line.	A.1
			2900 rounds expended and harassing fire throughout the night. An enemy M.G. which was in the house of occupying the centre sector of the front sector.	
MOEUVRES 1.20000			Silenced by fire from over the CAMBRAI ROAD. C.good	

Army Form C. 2118.

WAR DIARY
or
INTELLIGENCE SUMMARY.
(Erase heading not required.)

154 Coy MGC

Instructions regarding War Diaries and Intelligence Summaries are contained in F. S. Regs., Part II. and the Staff Manual respectively. Title pages will be prepared in manuscript.

Place	Date	Hour	Summary of Events and Information	Remarks and references to Appendices
LITTLE 2 Wet MOEUVRES Cor HQ Fied	1918 Sept 2(&c. &c.)		each of the 4 guns was sited on the ground right and opening fire on the enemy troops of was advance until expose fire — the powder pumps sought to be about K.16.81 — after too heavy bursts no more were experienced from that gun. Situation normal — no just activity or otherwise except for digging, and of guns under 3500 on our front on which hope on experience that. The enemy were very quiet throughout the night.	Sgt. Sgt. Sgt.
	3		Situation on our front — normal. Enemy artillery and rifle were active then our guns on from his artillery nothing at all.	
	4		The morning 6.15 am very heavy artillery fire was heard on the left. The enemy was feeling very slightly much inclined to live on the night — he appeared to have	Sgt. I.
MOEUVRES 1:20000				

Army Form C. 2118.

WAR DIARY
or
INTELLIGENCE SUMMARY.
(Erase heading not required.)

154 M.G.Coy.

Instructions regarding War Diaries and Intelligence Summaries are contained in F. S. Regs., Part II. and the Staff Manual respectively. Title pages will be prepared in manuscript.

Place	Date	Hour	Summary of Events and Information	Remarks and references to Appendices
LINE. S.W. of MOEUVRES	Jan 1918 4th		Yesta in BARBICAN. 3730 rounds were fired from position along all the sector during the night. Patrolling became fiere on the left a little.	AZ1
	5.		Line Quiet — — a few enemy seen near to enemy wire are active placing his outpost line Figs a. F9 a. a. b — extreme forward an easterly of the line from position M.G. 3,4 or 5.5 fires on Leo Sentier.	AZ2
	6		300 rounds harassing fire during the night. Lines throughout Day — not unusual activity on enemy side. Two guns from the a.m. Section at K.4.c.2020 were moved about 2 a.m. to a position at J.18.d.2580 near DEMICOURT. This alteration was made necessary though a "eastery" of 6 guns of the 2nd Div, being moved from	AZ3

MOEUVRES
1:20000.

Army Form C. 2118.

WAR DIARY
or
INTELLIGENCE SUMMARY.
(Erase heading not required.)

54 MGC

Instructions regarding War Diaries and Intelligence Summaries are contained in F. S. Regs., Part II. and the Staff Manual respectively. Title pages will be prepared in manuscript.

Place	Date	Hour	Summary of Events and Information	Remarks and references to Appendices
LINE	1918 Jan 6		D Section at J.24.B.6.9. are engaged by	
SW of MOEUVRES			enemy with no serious injury.	
H.Q. J.10.d.			Lines of fire of the two enemy guns were at K.7 & 8.b.40 approx. Shots to five on our own front. 2000 Rounds fired on enemy barrage during enemy attack	
	7.		Situation Quiet. — no minnen activity. 152 Bde relieved 154 during the 24 hrs. by relief complete by about 10 pm.	
MOEUVRES 1:20000 BEUGNY. 1.28.B.92.	8.		Rev a Cheque below.	
	9 - 14th		During this period we supplied working parties and supplies nightly to digging cable trenches on the forward zone. Lewis were machine gun Course Lorry.	
	15		The Company relieved 152 by. in the line with 7 guns & 232 Coy with 7 guns. the arrangement following full in all former provisions for	
5/c. 1:40000				

Army Form C. 2118.

WAR DIARY
or
INTELLIGENCE SUMMARY.
(Erase heading not required.)

1/54/19. G. Coy

Instructions regarding War Diaries and Intelligence Summaries are contained in F. S. Regs., Part II. and the Staff Manual respectively. Title pages will be prepared in manuscript.

Place	Date	Hour	Summary of Events and Information	Remarks and references to Appendices
LINE.	Jan 1918			
Sw. of Moeuvres	15.		Enemy carried on preparations to strengthen his winter position.	
HQ. J28.b.6.1.	16.		Enemy the stores etc after heavy frosts made the working very uncomfortable, carrying supplies a little vexed. Listening posts covered the line and were reinforced by an officer of receiving companies by 6th Dth.	H.C.I.
	17.		Visibility low, owing to fog, a slightly heavy afternoon. Relief was ordered to be commenced about 9.30 pm — completed by 6.30 pm quite quick in view of the wet heavy going. Company marched back to billets at J.28.b.8.2. near BEUGNY.	
Mrs MOEUVRES L. 20000				
BEUGNY J28.b.8.2				
COURCELLES/8	9.0am		Company paraded by coy. to COURCELLES-le-COMTE. marched via road about 12.30. Billets fair.	H.C.I.
Le COMTE.				
Map 57c 1/40000				

WAR DIARY
or
INTELLIGENCE SUMMARY.
(Erase heading not required.)

Army Form C. 2118.

151 N.G.C.

Instructions regarding War Diaries and Intelligence Summaries are contained in F. S. Regs., Part II. and the Staff Manual respectively. Title pages will be prepared in manuscript.

Place	Date	Hour	Summary of Events and Information	Remarks and references to Appendices
COURCELLES le COMTE	Jan 1918 19		Cleaning up before leaving for area on 20th	HQ
	20.	9.0 am	Leaving by train to POMMIER — marching from railway station to our billets	HQ
POMMIER		9.30		
		about 2.30 pm	Moved to final billets for rest at BASSEUX.	
BASSEUX	21.	10.00	Billets made good, all comfortable.	HQ
	22.		Cleaning up, overhaul of billets, overcoats & ablution sheds fixed up.	
	23–31		During this period the coys carried out much movement & drill of squads. A good field firing and use of cover range giving of the majority of gunners good familiarity on Lewis Gun[?]. A Draft of 9 men joined the company under Lieut Tyres	

M.P.A.
L.M.3.14
1,050,000

(A/83S) D. D. & L., London, E.C. Wt W.S./M1672 350,000 4/17 Sch 58a Forms/C/2118/14

Army Form C. 2118.

154 M.G. Coy

WAR DIARY
or
INTELLIGENCE SUMMARY.
(Erase heading not required.)

Place	Date	Hour	Summary of Events and Information	Remarks and references to Appendices
BASSEUX	Jan 1917		Lt J.E. CHARLTON, 18th London Regt. joined the company on the 1st - 2 Lt. A.T. STEWART, M.G.C. proceeded to UK on exchange on the 24th	321
			The strength of the company stood at 8 Officers 180 O.R. & 21 attached from Infantry. Total drafts received on month 1 Officer 19 men Evacuations 1 Officer, 8 other ranks + 2 atta. men	
Lens II 1:100000			A.C. Stewart Lt Col Comdg 154 Coy M.G. Corps.	
			13 8 J 2.2.18	

M 26

CONFIDENTIAL

ORIGINAL

WAR DIARY

154 Coy. MACHINE GUN CORPS.

From 1st February 1918 to 28th February 1918

VOLUME 26.

Army Form C. 2118.

154 M.G.Coy.

WAR DIARY
or
INTELLIGENCE SUMMARY.
(Erase heading not required.)

Instructions regarding War Diaries and Intelligence Summaries are contained in F. S. Regs., Part II. and the Staff Manual respectively. Title pages will be prepared in manuscript.

Place	Date 1918	Hour	Summary of Events and Information	Remarks and references to Appendices
BASSEUX	Feb 1		Orders received that Company would proceed to LOGEAST WOOD area on the 2nd.	W.H.
			Cleaning up and preparing for the move.	
M.4.P.57.C G.14.0000 G.14.69.8	2	9.15am	Marched to LOGEAST WOOD area. Roads fair, marching good.	W.H.
		1.30pm	Arrived at BUCHANAN CAMP (sheet 57C G.14.69.8). Erected Cook House and placed stores in huts. Camp not completed.	W.H.
	3		Dug in Latrines and improving Camp.	W.H.
	4		16 A.A. Emplacements dug. M. Guns mounted for defence against Enemy Aircraft.	W.H.
	5		Work in new Stables commenced. Work on new frozen huts for instruction sqd. and Enemy Aircraft. 2nd Lt. H.S. Bisset proceeded to IV Corps G.A.S. School.	W.H.
	6		Range Practice - 100 yards firing - stoppages. Musketry. Grouping and sighting application.	W.H.
	7		Practice Attack in village. B Section, to the rest to Lt Gordons	W.H.

(A-283) D.D. & L., London, E.C. (4283) Wt W8591/M1672 250,000 4/17 Sch 52a Forms/C/2118/14

154 M.G.C.

WAR DIARY
or
INTELLIGENCE SUMMARY.
(Erase heading not required.)

Army Form C. 2118.

Place	Date 1918	Hour	Summary of Events and Information	Remarks and references to Appendices
MAP 57C 1/40,000 Q4, Q8 BUCHANAN CAMP	Feb 7		"A" and "C" Section moved to Lesforts. Preparations for inspection by G.O.C. Division.	M.R.
	8	10am	Company inspected by G.O.C. Division.	M.R.
	9		"A" Section inspected by G.O.C. Division in coming into action from pack ponies. Targets 12½ & 3¾ angles pposed range about 600yds. 50% of targets hit. "B" "C" & "D" Sections Range Leads firing. Battalion R.G. Horsent practical in care. 2nd Lt G.M.C. Gardner reported.	M.R.
	10		Church Parade.	
	11		G.O.C. Division witnessed practice attacks in ACHIET LE GRANDE by 17th Loforts the 11th C section attached, and in ABLAINZEVILLE by the 9th Bn. H. with D section attached.	M.R.
FREMICOURT	12 Feb	11.45am	Company marched to LINDOP CAMP, FREMICOURT. Arrived in FREMICOURT and came under temporary command of 6th Division till 13th inst.	M.R.

WAR DIARY

154 M.G. COY.

Army Form C. 2118.

Place	Date	Hour	Summary of Events and Information	Remarks and references to Appendices
FREMICOURT	1918 Feb 13) 14) 15)		Company at two hours notice to move into line if required.	M.R.
			All guns mounted for A.A. defence. Improvement of Camp. Protection of huts from aircraft.	W.R.
	16		General training. Between 7 p.m. & 9 p.m. guns engaged Enemy Aircraft.	W.R.
	17.		Between 7.30 p.m. & 9.30 p.m. guns engaged Enemy Aircraft.	W.R.
	18.		Enemy Aircraft in several times between 7 p.m. & 11 p.m.	W.R.
	19	10 a.m.	Company inspected by Medical Officer. General training carried out during forenoon of 17.18.19.	M.R.
	20		Preparation for relief. North 16 guns of this Coy. 2 guns of 152 Coy and 2 guns of 232 Coy.	M.R.
MAPS:- MOEUVRES 1/20000 SHEET 57C 1/40000 LINE COY H.Q. J10d 6.1.	21.	8.30 p.m.	Relief complete - Dispositions as per appendix I. Quiet night and day, no activity on either side.	M.R.
	22		Enemy very active. His artillery stained sheet lits on SUNKEN ROAD at J18d. Working party on Intermediate line, J17a.d & J23d was dispersed.	M.R.

Army Form C. 2118.

WAR DIARY
or
INTELLIGENCE SUMMARY.
(Erase heading not required.)

157 M.G.Coy

Instructions regarding War Diaries and Intelligence Summaries are contained in F.S. Regs., Part II. and the Staff Manual respectively. Title pages will be prepared in manuscript.

Place	Date	Hour	Summary of Events and Information	Remarks and references to Appendices
LINE Coy. H.Q. J10d 6.1	1918 Feb 22		Enemy M.Gs very active against our aircraft and a SUNKEN ROAD in K7c.	M.R.
	23		1500 rounds expended in harrassing fire during the night.	M.R.
			Quiet during night and day. The fired 2000 rounds during the night. Enemy M.Gs fired intermittant bursts during night.	
	24		Enemy artillery active during the day on BOURSES and DEMICOURT. We fired 2000 rounds in harrassing fire and on enemy machine guns at E.25.c & 65.c.35.	M.R.
	25		Artillery active on both sides. Enemy shelled DEMICOURT and SUNKEN ROAD in K7c with 5.9's. DOIGNIES and BEAUMETZ were shelled at intervals and the road between these villages received several direct hits. Our aircraft very active. We fired 5,000 rounds in harrassing fire on tracks and places where much movement had been observed.	M.R.
	26		Little activity. BOURSES and DEMICOURT were shelled occasionally. We fired 2000 rounds during night on X roads at E.26.d.35.15 which appears to be an Assembly point for working parties.	M.R.
	27		Very quiet except for aircraft. As many as 10 E.A being over at times at once between 11am and 11.30 am. Bombs being dropped on the CAMBRAI ROAD	M.R.

154 M.G. Coy.

WAR DIARY
INTELLIGENCE SUMMARY
(Erase heading not required.)

Army Form C. 2118.

Place	Date	Hour	Summary of Events and Information	Remarks and references to Appendices
LINE Coy H.Q. J.16 a.6.1	1918 Feb 27		Enemy Aeroplanes were up during the forenoon, neglected bullet line & drifted over our line. Our aeroplanes attacked and set men free and caused another to take her down. 1500 rounds were fired between 6pm and 4am in the vicinity of E.27.c central where much movement had been observed.	Nil.
	28		Enemy Artillery shelled BEAUMETZ - DOIGNIES ROAD and the railway track near HERMIES. Little firing was done by us machine guns owing to working parties and patrols only 750 rounds being expended in X road at 26d.35.15. During the month Lt. F.W. STRAPP and 2nd Lt. G.M.C. TURNER joined the Company. 28351 Cpl. Conroy H. was sent in place of 23052 Cpl. Bethune W. sent home on six months in exchange. 5 O.R. were attached from the Battalion. The following award was made to the Company during the month. BELGIAN CROIX DE GUERRE No.46647 L/Cpl. WILLIAM BARRATT.	Nil.

Cer. to V Corps V.A. 287 of 2.2.18
5-1st (H) Div. No. 370/A.

154 M.G. Coy.

WAR DIARY
or
INTELLIGENCE SUMMARY.
(Erase heading not required.)

Army Form C. 2118.

Instructions regarding War Diaries and Intelligence Summaries are contained in F. S. Regs., Part II. and the Staff Manual respectively. Title pages will be prepared in manuscript.

Place	Date	Hour	Summary of Events and Information	Remarks and references to Appendices
LINE Coy. H.Q. J.10.d.6.1	1918 Feb 28		The strength of the Company at the end of the month stood as follows:— OFFICERS 9. O.R's 166. O.R's att. 21. Total drafts during month 3 Officers and 5 attached men. Evacuations 1 Officer, 14 other ranks and 5 attached men. Note:- 2Lt. C.M. WIGGIN taken on strength on reaching DIV. WING. He was evacuated from DIV WING and struck off company strength. Auth. D.A.G's List No 1045 dtd 19.2.18. B.E.F. 1.3.18	W.S. W.T. Raeven Lt. Commanding 154 Coy M.G.C.